Sonia Fischer

FOUNDATION DAMS
OF THE AMERICAN QUARTER HORSE

D0144111

PUBLISHED BY THE UNIVERSITY OF OKLAHOMA PRESS
IN COOPERATION WITH
THE AMERICAN QUARTER HORSE ASSOCIATION

Foundation Dams of the
American Quarter Horse

by
Robert M. Denhardt

A Digest of Known Information About the Distaff Side
of Horses Whose Descendants Appear in the Early Volumes
of the *Official Stud Book and Registry of the
American Quarter Horse Association,*
Together with a Brief Account of Recent Changes
in the Breed

By Robert Moorman Denhardt

The Quarter Horse (3 volumes, Amarillo, 1941-50)
The Horse of the Americas (Norman, 1947, 1975)
Horses of the Conquest (editor), by R. B. Cunninghame Graham (Norman, 1949)
Quarter Horses: A Story of Two Centuries (Norman, 1967)
The King Ranch Quarter Horses: And Something of the Ranch and the Men That Bred Them (Norman, 1970)
Foundation Sires of the American Quarter Horse (Norman, 1976)
The Quarter Running Horse: America's Oldest Breed (Norman, 1979)
Foundation Dams of the American Quarter Horse (Norman, 1982)

The illustration facing the title page is adapted from an illustration in W. H. Herbert, *Frank Forester's Horse and Horsemanship of the United States,* 1857.

Library of Congress Cataloging in Publication Data

Denhardt, Robert Moorman, 1912–
  Foundation dams of the American quarter horse.

  Companion volume to Foundation sires of the American quarter horse.
  Bibliography: p. 223
  Includes index.
  1. Quarter horse. 2. Horses—Stud-books. 3. Mares. I. Title.
SF293.Q3D367 1982   636.1'33   82–40323
ISBN: 0–8061–2748–1 (paper)

Copyright © 1982 by the University of Oklahoma Press, Norman, Publishing Division of the University. All rights reserved. Manufactured in the U.S.A. First edition, 1982. First paperback printing, 1995.

4   5   6   7   8   9   10   11

This book is dedicated to
The female offspring of the immortal *Janus

. . . darkness was upon the face of the deep.
And the spirit of God moved upon the waters.
And God said, Let there be light:
And there was light.

Short racing was never to be the same again.
Now it took sheer blinding speed.
In truth, after *Janus his descendants had to race each other.
They had no peers.

Contents

FOUNDATION DAMS
OF THE AMERICAN QUARTER HORSE

I

Introduction

If, in years past, you asked a Quarter Horse man why he preferred to match short races, you might receive the laconic reply, "I enjoy them more." That would have ended the discussion as far as he was concerned. The Arabs used to have a saying, according to R. B. Cunninghame Graham: "My donkey's left forefoot is right over the center of the earth. If you don't think so, go measure for yourself." The American short-horse man's answer and the Arab saying have an attribute in common: neither encourages much further discussion. Indeed, to understand fully the appeal of short racing, you just have to "measure it yourself."

The Lure of Short Racing

Love of short racing does not seem to be an inherited trait; you have to acquire it. Once you have the appetite for it, however, the hunger lingers on and on. Any number of men from colonial days have lived out their lives in the sole pursuit of match racing, and who can say that they were not as happy as, or happier than, their soil-tilling brethren?

Perhaps one factor that makes short racing such an intriguing sport is the special challenge created by all the variables inherent in it. The idea is to do a better job of assembling the critical elements than your neighbor or friend does and so win the race, or the wager, and the right to crow. Today horse racing at recognized tracks is under the supervision of state governments, who see it as their duty to present to the public all the facts about the horses, the jockeys, and the conditions of the race and track. These variables are not

3

immediately apparent at a match race. To make a valid match for your horse (or a sensible wager on such a race), all above factors, and more, have to be determined. Since facts may be scarce, a good deal of gossip and rumor must be evaluated before a judgment can be reached. Often intuition is as valuable as knowledge, and the successful match-race devotee cannot always say where one ends and the other begins.

One of the first lessons to learn is not to be gullible. It is necessary to accept all statements about the match with a grain of salt. You can believe only what you personally know to be true. After a few races most of those who lay a dollar on their favorite have become adept, as well as dedicated. One can tell also the fan who has paid his dues by the way he accepts the outcome of the race. The knowledgeable zealot always accepts it as something ordained, as though a superior being has determined the outcome. The verdict is no more to be questioned than the wind or the rain.

When one tears himself away from the thrill and tension of a well-run match between two good Quarter Horses, it is nothing less than captivating to watch the true devotees gather in small groups, where each explains how he knew who the winner was going to be (even when he had bet on the other horse). The discussion also covers in minutest detail just where the trainer or jockey made the big mistake. These men are as serious in demeanor as any ambassador to the United Nations and, it could be added, probably have equal comprehension of the topic under discussion.

There is another group of short-race enthusiasts: those who bet little or not at all on the outcome of a match. For them the simple pleasure of watching two horses thundering down the raceway and flashing over the finish line at almost the same moment is reward enough. Many Quarter Horse breeders belong to this group. Their reward comes in raising a faster horse than their neighbor's. Two common human traits are the desire to compete and the desire to excel.

4

Raising and racing Quarter Horses meet both desires admirably.

There is still another factor, one that was more common in the days before trucks, trains, and airplanes began shuffling horses from one racing establishment to another. That was the bond of affection that arose between the owner and his racehorse. On today's circular tracks the closest approximation to that relationship is the fondness that may develop between the trainer or stableman and his charge. During the first three-quarters of the nineteenth century the owner traveled with his horse from town to town, state to state, matching races as he could. They got to know each other well. Possibly the feeling they shared has been expressed best by Sam Hildreth. Writing about his early career with Quarter Horses, he tells how he and his father (the whole family, in fact) took Red Morocco from Missouri all the way to Texas to match a race with Sheriff Jim Brown. When they returned home to Missouri, the Hildreths were distraught because they had lost the race and had had to leave their beloved Red Morocco with the sheriff.

Some of the lure of short racing has been sketched above, but the only true way to understand it is to expose yourself to a match race—if you can find one. Pari-mutuels and state racing commissions are rapidly making the old two-horse match an endangered species. The reason is obvious (but nonetheless regrettable): there cannot be successful pari-mutuels when half or more of the people are betting on one horse. The only places where match racing has a home today are the few states that have local tracks and no pari-mutuels. Attend one. You'll like it.

Recent Changes in the Quarter Horse[1]

The first, and the greatest, sire of Quarter Horses was an imported English stallion named *Janus. The descriptions of

---

[1] Portions of this chapter originally appeared in *Chronicle of the Horse* (Middlebury, Va.), February 9, 1976.

*Janus indicate that he stood a little over 14 hands, had great bone with tremendous muscles, and was compactly built. For two hundred years his conformation was considered to be the ideal. When the American Quarter Horse Association was formed in 1940, he was still considered the model Quarter Horse. His conformation was adopted as typical for the breed. By 1940 three exceptional twentieth-century Quarter Horse sires had been identified that were built along the general lines of *Janus: Joe Bailey, Joe Moore, and Red Dog.

Dan D. Casement, writing in the introduction to the first edition of the American Quarter Horse Association *Stud Book* (1940), described the ideal Quarter Horse as follows:

There is the small, sensitive, alert ear, his wise bright eye, the amazing bulk and bulge of his jaw which seems to betoken his bulldog tenacity and resolution. There is his short back, deep middle and long belly, his low-slung center of gravity, and the astonishing expanse of his britches, seen from the rear, surpassing the width at the croup.

In the same article Casement quoted William Anson, the famous turn-of-the-century Texas Quarter Horse breeder, as saying that the immense breast and chest; the enormous forearm, loin, and thigh; and the heavy layers of muscle were not to be found in like proportions in any other breed in the world. Casement ended his article with the warning that only negative and harmful purposes would be served by any attempt to refashion the shape of the Quarter Horse in imitation of any other breed. He was, of course, referring to the Thoroughbred.

It is doubtful that Johnny Ferguson with his Thoroughbred Top Deck ever worried about early descriptions of the Quarter Horse. Top Deck, Three Bars, Depth Charge, and other great Thoroughbred sires of the modern Quarter Horses produced too many horses with blazing speed. Their get are the ones who win the futurities and stake races and whose sons are syndicated for large sums of money. Their owners are not concerned that they have seven-eighths or more Thoroughbred blood and that they are at least a full hand taller than the ideal Quarter Horse of 1940.

Dan D. Casement was not the only early official of the American Quarter Horse Association who wanted a bulldog, not a greyhound. Of the first officers of the fledgling organization—Bill Warren, president; Jack Hutchins and Lee Underwood, vice-presidents; Jim Hall, treasurer; and Bob Denhardt, secretary—one, Jack Hutchins, was a race-horse man. He kept his running horses—most of them sired by a son of the Thoroughbred Chicaro—separated from his Quarter Horses and did not try to register any of them. His principal Quarter Horse stallions were Lobo and Billy. Both of them were bulldogs. Bill Warren's principal stallion was Pancho, a heavyset 14-2-hand grandson of Little Joe. Lee Underwood had two principal stallions, Chief and Dexter, and neither was a greyhound. My Del Rio Joe was also of the bulldog type.

Jim Hall did not own any Quarter Horses himself, but his wife, Anne Burnett Hall, had a great many. Jim was interested in running horses. In 1941 he started the Quarter Stud Horse Cavaliers of America, a short-lived but spirited organization of Quarter Horse breeders. It organized the Quarter Horse Race Meeting Association of America, with Jim as president; George Clegg and Raymond Dickson, vice-presidents; Helen Michaelis, secretary; and Jess York, treasurer. It held only one race meet, at Eagle Pass, Texas, and then bowed out in favor of an older and better-run organization in Tucson, Arizona.

Hall's association put out a newsletter entitled *Voice of the Quarter Horse Race Meeting Association.* In the March, 1942, issue the following appeared:

Weights and Two-Year-Olds

We have repeatedly pointed out the importance of providing heavy weights (130 or more) events at our speed trial meets for mature horses and of limiting the distance of trials for two-year-olds to one eighth of a mile.

These are rather different from the schedules of present-day stakes and futurities. No doubt everyone would agree that the founders of the American Quarter Horse Association favored the Steel Dust, or bulldog, type. That type was the Quarter Horse.

To anyone with prescience perhaps the route the Quarter Horse has taken since 1940 would have been obvious. The clues were there. To begin with, there were the "ABC" classifications. At the start only pure dyed-in-the-wool bulldog Quarter Horses were to be registered; however, the officers of the new breed association soon came face to face with the cold fact that only a few Quarter Horses of the type they wanted were available for registry. The idea of a Quarter Horse association had been heartily supported by breeders and buyers, and many people were asking for Quarter Horses. In the end it was agreed to register a horse of the "correct" type with an "A" after its number, a horse that showed at least half-Quarter Horse characteristics was to have a "B" after its registration number, and half Thoroughbreds were to be registered "C." Very few breeders could boast of an "A" band of horses. Then came the annual meeting, where the majority ("C" breeders) abandoned the "ABC" classification, and all numbered horses were simply registered Quarter Horses.

One of the promoters of the "C"-type Quarter Horse was, in my opinion, the best horseman ever employed by the AQHA. His name was Jim Minnick. He frankly told the first executive committee that he was personally a "C," or half-breed-type, man. He preferred the Thoroughbred-Quarter Horse cross; his polo-playing experience had demonstrated to him that they were the best polo ponies. Jim was hired as the first inspector, and during the first years his selections provided the base stock for the breed. His choices set the pattern. He also judged most of the early official shows. His activities should have provided some clear indications how the association was going to go.

Other factors encouraged the move away from the bulldog. Since few breeders had horses of that type, it was popular to criticize them, and one generally heard the word "bulldog" coupled with "mutton-withered" or some other term of a disparaging nature. No doubt the criticism was often made sincerely. There are horses in all breeds that can be faulted, but that does not make every individual of the breed or type faulty, nor does it make all the "A"-type horses poor individuals. Many, such as Red Dog and Poco Bueno, were superb individuals.

Many breeders besides Jim Minnick preferred the half-breed horse. Some were directors of the new American Quarter Horse Association. Take Bob Kleberg, of the King Ranch, for example. In the early days the King Ranch provided a large share of the income of the new breed association, registering more horses than any other individual or corporation. But the Klebergs were not bulldog breeders, nor did they want to be. The King Ranch foundation stallion, the Old Sorrel, was half Thoroughbred, and the foundation dams, the Lazarus group, were all Thoroughbreds. Peppy, Wimpy, Macanudo, Hired Hand, and other basic stallions in the breeding program were not bulldogs of the Steel Dust stamp. They were ideal "C"-type Quarter Horses and great individuals; however, there were no Lobos, Tonys, Red Dogs, Joe Baileys, or Zantanons among them. Bob Kleberg explained his position in the first edition of the AQHA *Stud Book:* ". . . the Quarter Horse makes an ideal foundation on which to cross the Thoroughbred." He did it as well as anyone who ever lived.

One has to grant that the present Quarter Horse does not represent the type of animal that the registry was organized to perpetuate. One must also realize, however, that the breed organization as set up by the founders provided that the breeders themselves would run the association through electing its officials. If, as the years go by, the breeders wish the Quarter Horse to change, so be it.

For quite a few years conservative ranchers like Dan Casement, J. E. Browning, Helen and Maxie Michaelis, and Roy Parks were able to keep a brake on the "Thoroughbredization" of the Quarter Horse. Nevertheless, the drift was steadily toward the one-half, the three-quarters, and the seven-eighths Thoroughbred. Perhaps the events of the annual convention of 1957 did as much as anything else to make the trend of the organization clear. In the words of one who attended the convention, when John Ferguson's Go Man Go was proposed for registration, "We liked to have had blood all over the lobby." The executive committee had previously —and correctly, according to the rules—turned down Go Man Go. The board of directors decided to register him anyway, over the heads of the committee members. Leading the battle for registration were Johnny Ferguson and A. B. Green. Joe Huffington moved that the board of directors give Go Man Go a number, which they did.

Just in case some of my readers are unfamiliar with the great Go Man Go, a few words about him may be appropriate. The Klebergs bred River Boat, a Chicaro filly, to their great Thoroughbred Equestrian. This mating produced Top Deck. Bob Kleberg gave Top Deck to Ernest Lane, who later sold him to Johnny Ferguson. Johnny bred him to one of his half-Thoroughbred mares and came up with Go Man Go. That was in 1953. Go Man Go soon proved himself one of the very greatest running Quarter Horses and then one of the greatest sires. His speed was AAAT. He was a multiple-stakes winner. He was three times named World Champion Quarter Running Horse. He was also three times Champion Quarter Running Stallion and was Champion Quarter Running two-year-old and three-year-old stallion. At stud he sired two All-American Futurity winners, Hustling Man and Goetta. He became maternal grandsire of two others, Mr. Kid Charge and Rocket Wrangler. He was the leading sire of money earners in 1971, 1972, 1973, 1976, and 1977. At the end of 1979 his 774 starters had earned $7,468,123. The quality, performance, and prepotency of this marvelous stallion were such that to refuse to register him seemed incredible to those who were raising, training, and running Quarter Horses. He was registered No. 82,000.

A few words about Three Bars may also be appropriate. Had he not already been registered Thoroughbred, he too undoubtedly would have been registered as a Quarter Horse. Three Bars sired 558 foals, 424 of which started on the short tracks. In this group were 317 that made Racing Register of Merit; 212, AAA and AAAT; 90, AA; and 15, A. He was also the sire of 36 Show Register of Merit horses, 29 AQHA Champions and 4 AQHA Supreme Champions. His get accumulated 1,544 Halter points, 575 Arena Performance points, and 7,082 Racing points. His get earned $3,207,856 on the track. Every Quarter Horse breeder should have such a stallion.

So there are great Running Quarter Horse sires in the modern period just as there were in earlier times. Today the names of their sires may be Three Bars, Top Deck, or East Jet instead of Joe Bailey, Joe Moore, or Zantanon.

The Importance of the Dams to the Breed

In books, articles, and general conversation emphasis is placed on the sires, and indeed there are good reasons for that. The sire's influence, for good or bad, can easily extend through hundreds of offspring, while a dam's produce seldom exceeds ten. The King Ranch planned to breed 200 or 250 mares to each of two cutting-horse stallions during the spring of 1979. That included both pasture breeding and artificial insemination. If that was repeated for ten years, each stallion would have 2,500 get, a far cry from a dam's produce of ten. It is easy to see why a stallion's services are considered so important.

Even so, one should never underestimate the influence of the distaff side. A surprising majority of the best breeders sincerely believe that the lower side of the pedigree is the one to watch—that it is the more influential of the two.

Once while I was talking to that most knowledgeable horseman Jim Minnick, a discussion on the influence of the dam arose. Jim said that a breeder's reputation was made by the quality of his dams, not by the pedigree of his sire. He said that a good dam will drop good colts regardless of the sire. The reverse is not true. To emphasize this point, he mentioned by name several outstanding dams who had produced winners on the track or in the rodeo arena by more than one stallion. He then pointed out that even the best sires, when bred to large numbers of dams, are lucky if they have half a dozen winners in any given year. The more common the dams, the more important become the stallions.

Walter Merrick is considered by many to be the leading breeder of Running Quarter Horses. In the July, 1977, issue of *Speedhorse* he evaluated the relative importance of the dam and the sire in producing a foal, and he said that he considered the relationship 60 to 40 in favor of the dam. He went on to say that he believed one reason for this to be the close association of the dam and foal from the time of conception until the foal is weaned, at least a year and a half.

It is one of the regrets of the Quarter Horse historian that early-day breeders did not keep better records of their dams. Until the organization of the American Quarter Horse Association, records were kept haphazardly. Quarter Horse breeders recorded the sires, but if the dam was mentioned at all, it was generally just as a "such-and-such" dam, the "such-and-such" being the name of her sire. If she had been a great racing mare, perhaps her name was given. The reason for this is obvious but regrettable.

One interesting fact often overlooked is that until recently more mares than stallions were raced. Today's demand for good stallions has changed this. Not long ago Dash for Cash was syndicated for several million dollars. That would never have happened if he had not been an outstanding racehorse. When a horse becomes as valuable as that, breeders want to run their stallions in hopes that they too may be worth several million dollars.

In the days before pari-mutuel betting and organized race meets, most of the sprinters were mares, stretching from Miss Princess and Shue Fly right on back to Red Morocco and Eighty Grey. Mares are easier to train and handle. If a colt showed promise, he was generally gelded, though there were always exceptions, such as Clabber, Steel Dust, and Cherokee.

In 1946, *The Quarter Running Horse,* published by the American Quarter Racing Association, listed the horses qualifying during the 1945-46 season for the Register of Merit kept by the association. The Register of Merit was the most prestigious honor that a Running Quarter Horse could receive. Of a total of 146 horses that became eligible, only 42 were stallions. Among the world's record holders by far the largest number of short records were held by mares. These records were the best times made during the existence of the organization at recognized tracks and at recognized distances. At 220 yards Lucky, a gelding, held the record; at 300 yards Miss Ona held the record; at 330 yards three horses shared the honor: Lady Lee, Nettie Hill, and Jeep B (the only stallion in the listings); at 350 yards the record was held by Miss Bank, Prissy, and Punkin, all mares; and at 440 yards the record holder was Queenie, also a mare. Clearly mares are capable of running as fast as stallions if they are trained as well. Even on the recognized pari-mutuel tracks one encounters outstanding mares, such as Pan Zarita and Genuine Risk, both of whom showed their heels to the best males. The first and greatest match race between a Quarter Horse and a Thoroughbred on a recognized track was the race in 1947 between Barbra B and Fair Truckle, a Thoroughbred stallion. She outran him.

II

Foundation Dams, 1700-1800

The foundation dams of the colonial Quarter Horses were either English running mares, imported or bred in the colonies, or what we will call, for lack of a better name, "native mares."[1] We know a lot about the English mares, but very little about the native mares, except in general terms. There were no native mares in the Americas, of course. The first were brought in by the English and Spanish settlers.

By the time *Janus was imported during the middle 1700s, native mares were in the hands of the common or poor classes of colonists. Only wealthy planters could afford to import good English running horses. Some of the native horses were obtained, legally or otherwise, from the southern Indians. The tribes in the Southeast had obtained their horses from the Spanish settlements in Georgia and Florida. The Chickasaw horses were especially prized by the Virginians and Carolinians. The Chickasaws (crossed undoubtedly with some common mares from the English colonies) formed the nucleus from which the average colonist developed his horses.

The Quarter Running Horse appeared in the thirteen colonies in the late 1600s, when a race was simply a contest between neighbors trying to see who had the faster horse. Since there were no racetracks, any open space, a field or a road, served the purpose. These short, often rugged paths called for sturdy-legged flying machines. As so often happens among horses and people, when the need arises, an individual appears to fulfill that need. In this case it was the imported

---

[1] See "Geographical Index of Breeders," in Robert M. Denhardt, *Foundation Sires of the American Quarter Horse* (Norman: University of Oklahoma Press, 1976)

14

stallion *Janus. He was stocky, strong-legged, and fleet, and he reproduced his conformation and speed with monotonous regularity upon almost any mare to whom he was bred. We can assume that they were the best mares the individual breeder had because *Janus always commanded a stud fee. His offspring became standards, or models, for future short horses until after the American Quarter Horse Association was formed. *Janus himself ran four-mile heats, but his progeny were seldom able to go over half a mile, and more often only a quarter or less. The first great dams of quarter racers were sired by *Janus, and those for which we have records were out of English dams. Those out of native dams were unrecorded. Most of the colonists, after seeing how good their *Janus colts were, took their best mares and fillies back to him. He was prepotent enough to produce blazing speed not only in his immediate get but also in his daughters and granddaughters. There are records of as many as six crosses of *Janus without skipping a generation. This tendency to concentrate *Janus blood was the reason for the strong breed characteristics. Good English mares, sired by *Silver Eye, *Monkey, *Jolly Roger, and *Fearnought, provided a vigorous safety outcross for the concentrated *Janus blood.

Imported Dams

Some of the English mares imported into the colonies had great influence on the developing Quarter Horse. They will be taken up in order, beginning with *Mary Gray and ending with *Castianira.

*Mary Gray was a smooth gray mare foaled in 1742. She was bred by an Englishman named Crofts, the same man who bred Morton's *Traveler. Crofts must have had a weakness for early speed, because many colonial Quarter Horses can be traced back to his horses. The Crofts breeding farm was at Raby, in Yorkshire.

*Mary Gray was brought to Virginia by Ralph Wormeley, of Middlesex County, in 1748. She had been sired by Roundhead, and her dam was Ringbone. Ringbone was sired by Crofts' Partner, who was also the sire of Morton's *Traveler.

*Mary Gray was not only a fast race mare but also the dam of well-known sprinters. Some who were by *Janus were Wyllie Jones's Blue Boar, Thomas Eaton's Club Foot, and John Goode's Poll Smiling. Other descendants include Polly Williams by Mark Anthony, Red Bacchus by Old Bacchus, and Polly Flaxen by *Jolly Roger.

*Selima was an even greater mare than *Mary Gray, as shown by the influence of her produce on the running Quarter Horse. *Selima was sired by the Godolphin Arabian and out of a Shireborn mare named Hobgoblin. She was foaled in 1746 and died in 1766. *Selima was an attractive bay mare with a small star and some white on her near forefoot. She was bred by Lord Godolphin and later sold to the American Benjamin Tasker, of Belair, Maryland. Tasker had her brought to America in 1750.

*Selima was a capital race mare in America. She was both raced and bred by her owner. One of her greatest rivals was *Jenny Cameron, who will be discussed below. *Jenny was owned by Tasker's friend and racing competitor John Tayloe II. *Selima had six foals while Tasker owned her. When he died, she was sold to John Tayloe, who took her to Mount Airy, his plantation and breeding establishment on the north side of the Rappahannock River, in Virginia. For Tayloe, *Selima had four more foals.

Although *Selima was a valuable race mare, her true worth was shown in the quality of her colts. She had three by Morton's *Traveler—Ariel, Bellair, and Partner. Other foals include Babraham by Jupiter and Black Selima by *Fearnought. Two of her best Quarter Horse foals were Spadille and Nancy Wake. She foaled Spadille when bred to *Janus. Spadille was her eighth foal and, as far as the Quarter Horse is concerned, her greatest. Wyllie Jones, of Halifax county, North Carolina, bought Spadille from John Goode, the last owner of *Selima. Some records show Jones as her breeder, though I have not been able to find when he owned *Selima, if he ever did. Another well-known sprinter foaled by *Selima was Nancy Wake. She was sired by John Goode's Babram. She shared the fate of several other fine Quarter Horses: she was drowned by the British during the Revolutionary War.

*Jenny Cameron and her daughter *Betty Blazella were two fine imported mares and, like *Selima and *Jenny, were topnotch racers. In fact, *Selima and *Jenny were archrivals on the track. In December, 1752, *Jenny ran against *Selima and lost. Both of these mares were raced before and after having foals.

*Jenny Cameron was imported by John Tayloe II with her daughter *Betty Blazella. *Jenny had been sired by Cuddly, a son of Fox, and her dam was the well-known Cabbagewise, who was owned by a man named Witty. She foaled *Betty Blazella before she left England. In American she produced Silver Legs and Lloyd's Traveler, both of whom were sired by Morton's *Traveler. Later she was bred to Tom Jones, and Smiling Tom was the result, and when she was bred to *Childers, she foaled Little David.

*Castianira was probably as great a mare as ever arrived in America from England. She was a smooth brown horse, foaled in 1796. She was sired by Rockingham and was out of Tabitha by Trentham. John Tayloe III imported her. Tayloe was the scion of a wealthy Virginia horse-breeding and racing family. In 1812, when the British burned Washington, D.C., the sumptuous Tayloe mansion, which had been spared, was turned over to President James Madison and Dolly. There they found considerably more luxury than anything the White House had had to offer.

One of Tayloe's closest friends and associates in the horse business was John Hoomes. Hoomes imported many English running horses, among them the great stallion *Diomed. Tayloe owned an interest in the stallion, and he was bred to *Castianira. Tayloe allowed another friend, one Archibald Randolph, to breed the mare on shares, and the foal that resulted from this breeding was jointly owned by Tayloe and Randolph. Eventually the colt came to be called Sir Archy, after Randolph. Sir Archy became one of the great foundation sires not only of the American Thoroughbred but also, through his sons, of the American Quarter Horse. He ranks second only to *Janus in this respect. He and *Janus had what it took to produce early speed. Sir Archy produced five sons whose progeny dominated the short tracks until well after the Civil War. They were Timoleon, Bertrand, Cherokee, Contention, and Muckle John.

*Castianira continued to produce outstanding foals. In 1806, the year after Sir Archy was foaled, she had Highland Mary by *Diomed; in 1807 she produced Hephestion, who was sired by *Buzzard. Hephestion proved to be a sire of sprinters as well as stayers. In 1808 she foaled Castania by Archduke, and in 1809, Birgo by Sir Peter Teale. In 1810 she had Noli-Me-Tangere by Top Gallant. She also had a bay filly by *Mufti.

*Janus Dams

*Janus is generally spoken of as the progenitor of the Quarter running horse because he was the single most important early sire of the breed. The early short-horse breeders concentrated on him because his colts were so successful. If *Janus was the hub of the wheel, certainly his mares were the spokes without which the wheel would have never turned. It was the *Janus fillies who saw to it that his breed characteristics and early speed were passed down to his grandchildren and great-grandchildren into the twentieth century.

A great many of his fillies were rebred to him, and this did much to set his characteristics. Almost invariably their foals had his compact musculature, a characteristic that denotes the sprinter. Fortunately for the historian of the Quarter running horse, Patrick N. Edgar had a soft spot in his heart for the sprinter. As a result we know a lot about *Janus and his fillies.

The names of about thirty *Janus mares have come down to us, primarily because of their exceptional speed and their produce. These fillies were bred back to *Janus or to such sires as *Jolly Roger, Morton's *Traveler, *Fearnought, and Mark Anthony, and they produced a gene pool that breeders reached into for many years when they wanted sheer blinding speed. The descendants of these fillies were responsible for much of the early speed found in Shad, Peacock, Spadille, Babram, Jupiter, Bacchus, Celer, Twigg, Paddy Whack, One Eye, Moggy, Garrick, and Dappled John.

One of these fillies was a stocky but trim gray mare named for her breeder, George Kirkindall, of Virginia. The sire of her dam was the well-known English stallion *Silver Eye. Her second dam was sired by *Monkey. She was probably *Janus's first offspring dropped in America. She was born in or around 1757. Kirkindall is listed in both of the two first American studbooks, but only Edgar points out that she was a famous short-race mare.

Another early filly sired by *Janus was the fine race mare Nancy Willis, who was foaled about 1758. Her dam was by Morton's *Traveler. She was bred and raised by Joseph John Alston, of Halifax County, North Carolina, one of the premier breeders of his time.

One of the grand dams of the early Quarter Horse was Puckett's Switch. She was a sorrel, barely 14 hands high, foaled in 1765. She was bred by Shippey Allen Puckett, who lived in North Carolina. Later she was owned by John Goode, Sr. Virginia and North Carolina were the two early centers of Quarter Horse breeding, and they shared *Janus as well as their love of short races. As a young mare Switch was almost unbeatable when she ran less than 400 yards. She was too short-legged to run a good half mile, though she won many races at that distance. Switch was by *Janus and out of a *Janus mare. Her second dam was also a *Janus mare. Her

19

breeding shows two things, *Janus's prepotency and the respect the colonial breeders had for him.

When she proved to be fast on the tracks, John Goode (who tried to buy every good Quarter Horse) purchased her. She was four years old at the time. Goode bred her back to *Janus. He got Twigg, one of the best sprinters and sires of his age. Twigg was very highly inbred, but he showed no weaknesses on the track or in the stud. He was taller than his sire or dam, standing 14-1 hands.

A few years later Jacob Bugg bought Switch, and still later she was owned by Henry Delony. She was raced and bred, sometimes both at the same time. In addition to Twigg, she also foaled Holman's Babraham and a very fleet filly by Meade's Celer.

John Goode had another good *Janus mare, Miss Alsop. She was bred by Thomas Field, of Mecklenburg County, Virginia. She was foaled in 1772, and her dam was by *Fearnought.

For some curious reason the name Polly or Poll was a favorite of Quarter Horse breeders of the Revolutionary period. There were Polly, three Polly Williamses, Poll Pitcher, Poll Flaxen, Poll Smiling, and the reverse, Smiling Poll. Poll Pitcher may have got her name from Moll Pitcher, the alleged witch who achieved fame for carrying water to the American soldiers during the Battle of Monmouth in 1778.

One of the three Polly Williamses, according to Edgar, was by *Janus and out of a *Janus mare. The others were by Flag of Truce and Mark Anthony; I will tell more about them later. The Polly Williams sired by *Janus was a great brood mare as well as one of the fastest Quarter Horses of her day. Some of her descendants were the Johnson Medley Mare, Roanoke, Variety, Reality, Carolinian, Bonnets-o-Blue, and Slender— certainly a mellifluous list of appellations. Polly Williams was bred by Marmaduke Johnson (not an insignificant cognomen itself), of Warren County, North Carolina.

Poll Smiling was listed in Edgar's studbook as a Celebrated

American Quarter Running Mare. She was a red sorrel with a blaze and two white hind feet. Like most of *Janus's other fillies and colts, she was small. She stood only 13-2 hands. Both her sire and her dam were by *Janus. She was foaled in 1774, bred by the master breeder John Goode, of Mecklenburg County, Virginia. Her dam was undoubtedly Sweepstakes, the *Janus mare later owned by Wyllie Jones, of Halifax, North Carolina.

Poll Smiling had a half sister equally well known named Smiling Poll. She too was a sorrel, and she was one year younger than her famous sister. She was by *Janus and out of a *Jolly Roger mare and had been bred by John Goode. When put into training, she showed rare speed and was soon purchased by Goode's friend, neighbor, and sometime racing competitor Henry Delony. Delony raced her for a time and then sold her to another Quarter Horse enthusiast, William Davis, of North Carolina.

Poll Pitcher was an incredibly fast *Janus mare. She was raised by Joseph John Alston, of Halifax, North Carolina. Alston was a friend and racing rival of Wyllie Jones, Henry Delony, and John Goode. For some reason Poll Pitcher is mentioned by Edgar only as the dam of two other fast mares, Sweeping Tail and Broomtail. Poll was by *Janus and out of a mare by Mark Anthony.

Sweeping Tail and Broomtail were also sired by *Janus. They became Celebrated American Quarter Running Mares, and are so listed in Edgar's studbook. Joseph Alston bred and raised them, as he did their dam. They were dropped in the late 1770s, and listings for both are found in Bruce and in Edgar.

The last *Janus filly to be discussed in some detail here is the mare commonly known as Bynum's Big Filly. As can be guessed, she got her name from her breeder, her size, and her sex. Her breeder was Turner Bynum, of Northampton County, North Carolina. One of her outstanding features was her size. Almost all of *Janus's progeny were small horses, from 13 to a little over 14 hands. The Big Filly was 15 hands and heavily built. Her dam was a *Jolly Roger mare, and her second dam was by *Silver Eye. She was very closely related to Smiling Poll.

When the Big Filly was put into training, it soon became apparent that she possessed more than her share of early speed. Bynum's father-in-law, Jeptha Atherton, was visiting the Bynums one day, and Atherton persuaded Bynum to let him take the Big Filly and race her. That is why Atherton's name appears many times in accounts of her races.

One of the great races of the century involved the Big Filly and a horse named Paoli. Paoli was also by *Janus, as were almost all the other fast short horses running at the time. Paoli's dam was a daughter of *Janus. Paoli had been bred and raised by Captain E. Hayes, also of Northampton County. Paoli was large for a *Janus colt, and, once he had shown his speed, he was purchased by the racehorse man Wyllie Jones. Both Atherton and Jones were having trouble getting a match for their horses. Other men with sprinters knew that they did not have much of a chance of beating the Big Filly or Paoli.

Now the one man that Wyllie Jones most delighted in beating was the shrewd old racehorse man Henry Delony. It was not easy to beat Henry, because matching and racing short horses was about all that Delony did. One day the two men met and, of course, got to talking about racehorses. They decided that they would match a race, sight unseen. Each could run any horse he owned or could borrow. Wyllie Jones knew that the only horse that had a chance of beating his Paoli was the Big Filly, which Atherton was running. Right after they shook hands, Wyllie went to Atherton and got him to agree (or at least he thought he did) that he would not lend Delony the Big Filly. On the other hand, Delony was pretty sure that he could borrow the Big Filly, because Atherton owed him a favor.

When the day of the match arrived, Jones went to the track

and had a talk with his trainer. He was most surprised to find that Delony was there with the Big Filly, ready to run. At this point, with the race only a couple of hours off, he had little choice but to run or forfeit the race. He decided to run.

Jones had a quick-witted jockey, who saw that the Big Filly's rider would not allow her off the mark until he had the advantage. The horses were so nearly equal in ability that just the slightest edge would mean victory. To throw off the other jockey, Jones's jockey took one foot out of the stirrup to make it appear that he was not ready to start. That way he got a little jump on the Big Filly and won by a few inches.

Non-*Janus Dams

Every important breed has been created by combining desirable traits and concentrating the best available blood. Great care is taken to see that mated individuals complement each other. Weaknesses must not be doubled up; strengths always should be.

When the colonial breeders began taking *Janus fillies back to their sire, any that did not complement him were undoubtedly discarded, for the offspring would not be successful. Those whose strengths were enhanced became the Puckett's Switches, the Poll Smilings, and the Poll Pitchers of the breed. Regardless of the statements above, however, no breeding program—whether carried out deliberately under controlled conditions or haphazardly by individuals seeking early speed—gained much prominence without resorting to some outcrosses. Good outcross dams halt a tendency toward defects caused by blood concentration. When blood is concentrated, as it was with *Janus, added care must be taken to be sure that masculinity does not develop. That could be the reason why Bynum's Big Filly had masculine features and was never able to reproduce successfully. Loss of libido is often the result of overconcentration of blood. Outcross mares provided the stability necessary for the colonial short horses of *Janus descent.

Some of the dams that provided outcross blood for the sprinting *Janus clan were long mares, some were short, and some ran both long and short. Brandon was one of those superior dams that come along occasionally to provide an ideal outcross. She was the kind of mare that makes a breeder famous, not because of anything he does—except feed and water her—but because of the quality of her offspring. Everard Mead was the fortunate horseman who bought her. He purchased her from Benjamin Harrison, the father of the ninth president of the United States, who had bred and raised her. Her dam was by *Whittington, and her sire was *Aristotle, who was by the Cullin's Arabian.

When he bought Brandon, Mead had a small farm in the southern part of Amelia County, Virginia. Brandon made him a wealthy man. He sold eight of her offspring for 14,000 pounds sterling. The excellence of Brandon's produce was not due to a fortunate "nick" with a certain stallion. She was bred to seven different stallions and had seven outstanding foals. The credit for their excellence is primarily hers.

In 1774, Brandon had her first foal sired by *Fearnought. In the following years she was bred to Celer, Cloudius, Buckskin, Tippo Saib, Chevalier, Quicksilver, and Partner. According to most records, Brandon had only one filly, but her blood, through her other produce, occurs again and again in Quarter Horse lines.

Not all the records concerning Brandon agree. John Lawrence O'Connor, in *Notes on the Thoroughbred from Kentucky Newspapers* (excerpt dated March 12, 1810), said that Speckleback, the dam of Kentucky Whip, was out of Brandon. Between 1830 and 1870, Whip blood was used extensively in the breeding of sprinters throughout the states. The greatest gift (with the possible exception of Speckleback) that Brandon made to the short-racing fraternity was Celer. He is generally referred to as Mead's Celer, to distinguish him from other stallions of the same name. Some consider Celer second only to *Janus as a sire of early Quarter Horses. Brandon's foals Cloudius, Buckskin, and Quicksilver also begot many speedy sons and daughters. Brandon must rank as one of the truly great dams in Quarter Horse history.

Another non-*Janus mare that contributed much to the early American sprinter was Jane Hunt. She was a beautiful bay mare, foaled in 1796. She was bred by Daniel Hunt, of New Jersey. When Hunt's daughter married John Harris, of Kentucky, Hunt presented the new couple with one of his best filly prospects, one he called Jane. Jane had been sired by General Wade Hampton's good stallion Paragon, and she was out of Moll by Figure. After she arrived at her new home, she was always referred to as Jane Hunt to distinguish her from another Jane owned by Harris.

Jane Hunt spent the rest of her life in the South. According to a letter Harris sent to the *Franklin Farmer,* a Kentucky paper published near Harris's home, Jane Hunt was kept for a number of years and then sold in 1809 or 1810. The quotation from the letter published by the paper reads as follows: "In 1809 or 1810 I parted with Jane Hunt to the late Judge Todd. She afterwards produced Grecian Princess, Tiger, and Little Tiger, all by Cook's Kentucky Whip."

As was common, Jane Hunt was both run and bred. During those days many horseman believed that a mare would never reach her racing potential until she had had at least one foal (this belief is still held by some breeders today).

In 1802, Harris raised a filly out of Jane Hunt sired by Columbus. In 1803, Jane produced another filly by Speculator. After running for a year, she was bred to *Sterling and had her first colt, named Express. The following year she again had a filly, named Sally Sneed, who was by *Buzzard.

Both of the Tiger colts out of Jane were worthy sires of speed, and both were outstanding individuals. Tiger blood (with Whip blood), became almost synonymous with early speed, and many of the good Quarter Horses of the nineteenth century carried his blood. Grecian Princess also made a mark in the racing world. After running well, she was sold to William Buford, whose descendants still raise Quarter Horses. Buford lived in Woodford, Kentucky. He raised four good foals from Grecian Princess: Sir William Wallace, Charlemagne, Milam, and Titus. Grecian Princess also had three good fillies: Helen Max, Ann Merry, and Steamboat.

The Polly Williams sired by Mark Anthony was the fastest horse of her generation, except perhaps for Twigg. She was foaled in 1774. According to one record she was somewhat rough, a dusty-red sorrel with a high goose rump, ragged hips, and very narrow quarters. She sported a blaze and had socks or stockings on all four legs. Her dam was a *Janus mare. She was bred by Peter Williams, of Dinwiddie County, Virginia, but raced by William Davis, of North Carolina. She met an untimely death when she was shot to prevent a match race. When the owner of the other horse learned that she was the mare his horse was supposed to race, he had her shot to save the forfeit money. Polly had beaten all of her competition except Twigg. She was matched against him several times and only beat him once. It is said that William Davis and his backers lost 200,000 pounds of prime tobacco in her losses against Twigg.

There was a third Polly Williams, in addition to the one by *Janus and the one by Mark Anthony. This Polly was a gray mare foaled in 1780 (?) and probably bred by John Goode. She was by Flag of Truce and out of a Twigg mare.

As mentioned above, Henry Delony spent most of his time matching and running short races, but he also raised a few horses. One was an exceptionally good mare named Poll. A Celebrated American Quarter Running Mare, she was sired by Skipwith's Black and All Black and out of a fine *Janus mare named Figure. She was foaled in the early 1790s. After Delony was through racing her, he sold her to John Goode, Sr.

The Pumpkin Filly was another fine quarter mare. She was bred by Thomas Goode, of Chesterfield County, Virginia. She was by Blue Boar and out of a *Janus mare. If the quality of her owners is any indication of her worth, she must have been a good one. She was owned at different times by the following Quarter Horse men: John Goode, Sr., Henry Delony, Shippey Allen Puckett, and Wyllie Jones.

Linnet was by Baldwin's Friday and out of the Pumpkin Filly. She too, like her dam, was bred by Thomas Goode. Wyllie Jones liked her looks and bought her to run. Later he sold her to William McGeehee, of Person County, North Carolina. McGeehee bred her to Bellair, and the colt, while owned by Edmunton, became known as Edmunton's Janus. Edgar said that he was a beautifully formed horse and a successful quarter-mile racer. Edmunton's Janus stood 14-1 hands, about normal for a Quarter running stallion of the time.

Another good race mare was Coelia (sometimes spelled Caelia). She was once matched against her own fleet daughter Harlot for $10,000, and racehorse folk gathered from far and near to see the race. The race was held at Oxford, North Carolina, and the "dollars" were really Spanish pieces of eight (reals), commonly referred to at the time as dollars. (The colonies had no money system of their own. In the late 1700s, owing to an action of the Bank of England, a large number of the Spanish coins were released, all counterstamped with the head of George III. Many came to America in payment for tobacco sold in England.)

Coelia was a well-formed sorrel mare, sired by John Goode's Babram and out of a mare by *Fearnought. Her daughter Harlot, sired by Goode's Bacchus, was equally well known as a race mare. It is not known who owned Coelia when she was bred, but it must have been either Charles R. Eaton or Hugh Snelling, of Granville County, North Carolina. Harlot was probably foaled around 1770. She also had an outstanding quarter foal, Black Snake, by *Obscurity in 1788.

One of the best sires of Revolutionary times was the great Paddy Whack, sometimes called Little Twigg. He was foaled in 1778 and died in 1786. He was bred by John Goode, Sr., of Mecklenburg County, Virginia. His dam was probably Sweet Mary, and she was a capital racer. She was by *Jolly Roger and out of a mare by *Shock. She was gray and a little larger than the average quarter mare, standing 14-3 hands. She was bred by Henry Davis, a neighbor of John Goode, who later purchased her. It was while Goode owned Sweet Mary that Paddy Whack was foaled. It seems more than likely that the sire of Paddy Whack was *Janus, whom Goode owned at the time, not *Jolly Roger, as Edgar contends.

Polly Flaxen was out of the imported mare Mary Gray, discussed earlier. She was sired by *Jolly Roger and was bred by Captain Thomas Turner, of Powhatan County, Virginia. She is sometimes referred to as Poll Flaxen and also as Dolly Flaxen. She produced Camden by *Janus, Fleetwood by *Janus, and the great sire Brimmer. Brimmer, generally referred to as Goode's Brimmer to distinguish him from other horses bearing the same name, was by Harris's Eclipse by *Fearnought and was foaled in 1775.

Other good outcross mares were making their mark at this time, most of the better ones sired by Mark Anthony, *Fearnought, or *Jolly Roger. Mark Anthony, the only native-born stallion of the three, deserves a further word. He was foaled on the banks of the James River, in Virginia. His sire was Partner, and his dam was an imported mare. He was coal black with two white hind feet and stood a full 15 hands, large for a stallion of that period.

To the mares mentioned above that were sired by Mark Anthony, Rosetta and Deer Legs can be added. Rosetta was by *Obscurity and out of a *Jolly Roger mare. They were both fast mares.

Other important non-*Janus dams include Wild Goose. She was by *Fearnought and out of a *Janus mare. Betsey

Dancey was a well-known short mare sired by Twigg and out of a mare by Spadille. Still another celebrated racer was Dash. She was by *David and out of a *Janus mare. Edgar listed Fan Tail as a Celebrated American Quarter Running Mare. She was sired by Old *Shock.

These mares, and others similarly bred, provided the outcross necessary to stabilize the concentrated blood of *Janus.

III

Foundation Dams, 1800-1875

By 1800 the running Quarter Horse had become a recognized type and, in a loose sense, a breed. A breed can be defined as a group of domestic animals related by descent and similar in characteristics. In its strict sense a breed must have a registry and a studbook. Neither the Quarter Horse nor the Thoroughbred had a studbook until after the Civil War. The studbook maintained by the Jockey Club for the American Thoroughbred was begun in 1868. As related earlier, the Quarter Horse studbook was not established until 1940, but both the Thoroughbred and the American Quarter Horse were breeds in the sense described above by the early 1800s.

When Edgar and Bruce began compiling pedigrees of American running horses, they included both stayers and sprinters. The sprinters were the Quarter Horses; the stayers, who ran one to four miles, were to become known as the Thoroughbreds. As short racing lost its popularity in the East, the short horses who could not run long went west and were no longer considered Thoroughbreds. When Bruce started the American Thoroughbred studbook, he registered in an appendix many early Quarter Horses and, in his words, horses whose pedigrees were reported too late for classification, as well as those whose dams had no names (for example, "*Janus mare") or whose pedigrees were not authenticated as pure Thoroughbred.

One source of confusion in establishing the identity of the Quarter Horse is that the Quarter Horse man has never hesitated to breed to any Thoroughbred that has early speed to contribute to his short horses. That is why Thoroughbreds such as *Janus, Kentucky Whip, Brimmer, Timoleon, Printer, Cherokee, Bertrand, Tiger, *Bonnie Scotland, Chicaro, and others were accepted by the Quarter Horse breeders. The appendix of Bruce's studbook provides a most valuable source of information for those tracing Quarter Horse pedigrees. There one can find the names and partial pedigrees of many of the Quarter Horses running during the last half of the nineteenth century. A surprising number were actually registered as Thoroughbreds, with the sire or dam inaccurately reported. Not all short horses were relegated to the appendix. Some, like Haynie's Maria, could run both long and short and had the bloodlines to qualify for registry in the main section of the studbook. They could be considered Thoroughbred or Quarter Horse. For that reason both registered Thoroughbred and Quarter mares are discussed in this chapter. This period, 1800-75, is the last period during which large numbers of Quarter Horses were bred in Virginia, North Carolina, and Kentucky. It seems only fitting that the last mare discussed in this chapter, Paisana, though foaled in Kentucky, became materfamilias of some of the greatest Texas Quarter Horse families.

Dams of the Southeast

Young Speckleback was a bay filly foaled about 1800. According to most reports she was bred and raised by John Patrick, of Charlotte County, Virginia. Her sire is given as Randolph's Celer, and her dam, Old Speckleback by Meade's Celer. As happens so often, however, there is another version of her breeding. John O'Connor believed that Young Speckleback was foaled by the great mare Brandon. In his book of excerpts from Kentucky newspapers he has two entries. According to an advertisement in the March 12, 1810, excerpt, the dam of Whip (Speckleback, by Celer) was out of Brandon. Again on April 1, 1811, the dam of Whip, Speckleback by Celer, is said to be out of Brandon. Kentucky Whip, also called at various times Whip, Cook's Whip, and Blackburn's Whip, was one of the all-time great sires of Quarter Horses, and Speckleback must be considered one of the breed's outstanding foundation dams.

Kentucky Whip's only contemporary rival as a sire of speed was Sir Archy's great son Bertrand. Eliza was Bertrand's dam, and Sir Archy his sire. Eliza was foaled in 1804. She was bred by Colonel William Alston, of South Carolina, a relative of both J. J. Alston and Gideon Alston, who lived in North Carolina. The whole family showed a liking for sprinters. Eliza was sired by *Bedford, and her dam was Mambrina by Mambrino. Bertrand was foaled in 1821. Later she produced Gray Girl by *Buzzard and Pacific by Sir Archy.

Haynie's Maria was an outstanding mare, a fact agreed upon by both Thoroughbred and Quarter Horse enthusiasts. Even as great a mare as Polly Williams had to take a back seat to Maria, because she could run just as well long as she could short. She could and did run 100 yards or 4 miles and beat her competition.

Maria was bred by Bennett Goodman, of Virginia. He took one of his best mares to *Diomed to be bred. *Diomed was by then thirty years old. Only four years earlier *Castianira had been bred to *Diomed and had subsequently foaled Sir Archy. Maria's dam was sired by Tayloe's Bellair and out of *Selima. Maria's second dam was Symme's Wildair.

After breeding his mare to *Diomed, Goodman moved to North Carolina, where Maria was foaled. Goodman did not find what he was looking for in North Carolina, so he packed up his belongings and drove his horses on into Tennessee. In Tennessee he sold the filly Maria to Captain Jesse Haynie, of Sumner County. Haynie bought her as a running prospect, and he never made a better purchase. Maria was by this time almost three years old and had grown into a beautiful piece of horseflesh. She was a dark liver chestnut, 15 hands high, and one person who saw her said she seemed to radiate strength, muscular power, and symmetry. James Douglas

Anderson said that Maria was a most extraordinary race-horse at all distances, and as good as any racer that had appeared in America.

Maria was trained by the most famous trainer of his day, Green Berry Williams. He never matched her to run without sufficient time and always trained her for the distance of the match. General Andrew Jackson tried repeatedly to beat her, both long and short, but was never able to get the job done. Maria and her trainer were reportedly the only ones able to beat General Jackson in every match race they ran.

The blood of a sire called Cherokee appears in many Quarter Horse pedigrees. It was especially popular during the first three-quarters of the nineteenth century. The first important Cherokee was foaled by the good mare Roxana. Roxana was sired by Hephestion and out of a mare by *Marplot. Hephestion, also out of *Castianira, was a half brother of Sir Archy. According to Bruce, Roxana's dam was owned by a Dr. Hayward when she foaled Cherokee. O'Connor says that the mare was owned by a Colonel Single-ton. In any case, Cherokee was foaled in 1821, out of Roxana and sired by Sir Archy. Cherokee was rich in the blood of the great mare *Castianira. Several sons of this horse were also called Cherokee.

The greatest of all the short horses carrying the name Cherokee was foaled in 1847 and died in Council Bluffs, Iowa, in 1872. He was undoubtedly sired by a son of Roxana's Cherokee. His dam, according to Bruce, was by Kentucky Whip. Some of both his male and his female descendants were called Cherokee. At least half a dozen Cherokee mares lived during this time, and most produced fast colts. A bay Cherokee mare was owned by Colonel Buford, who sold her to R. J. Breckenridge. Another Cherokee mare was given a slightly different spelling: Sherokas. She was a bay, foaled in 1827, and she was the dam of a stallion named Whip. She was owned by George Keene, of Fayette County, Kentucky.

Kentucky was a hotbed not only of Quarter Horses bearing the name Cherokee but also of some with more original names, like Blinkey and Paisana. Blinkey (also called Mary Porter) was one of the finest mares to come out of Kentucky. She was a beautiful chestnut, foaled in 1834. She was sired by Muckle John by Sir Archy and out of a Printer mare. This Printer was a grandson of *Janus. She was bred by J. C. Mason, who owned her until her seventeenth year and then sold her to Webb Ross, of Scott County. At the time she was sold, she was in foal to Gray Eagle and in good health, and Ross hoped to get a colt or two more out of the old mare. She foaled Sweet Owen soon after she arrived at the Ross Farm. Webb then bred her to Wagner, and the next spring she foaled Wagner, Jr. He then bred her to Gray Eagle, and this time she foaled Bay Printer. That was in 1853. The following year, her twentieth, she had Viley by Gray Eagle.

Gray Eagle was highly regarded by the sprinting-horse breeders. He was by Woodpecker by Bertrand, and he had been bred in Kentucky by Major H. T. Duncan. Blinkey's colts by Gray Eagle were all good Quarter Horse sires, especially Bay Printer. Blinkey had had only two foals when she was bought by Webb Ross. She had spent many of her earlier years racing under the name Mary Porter. Her two earlier foals were Flying Dutchman by Gray Eagle (foaled in 1845) and Rheube by Boston by Timoleon (foaled in 1848).

Blinkey's performance in producing top foals until she was twenty was a considerable feat, but the last mare to be discussed in this chapter had an even more remarkable record. Her name was Paisana, and she, like Blinkey, was foaled in Kentucky, probably on Webb Scott's farm. Paisana is credited with nineteen foals, all good ones, and she lived for thirty years. It must have been the water.

We do not know what name she was originally given, but she became Paisana in Texas. So many records are found on her at different times and different places that the general outlines of her movements and owners can be traced, though until she came into the hands of William Fleming in south Texas, there were some nebulous periods during her life.

As far as the records can be interpreted, Oliver and Bailes, of Guadalupe County, Texas, bought her from Frank Lilly, of Thorp Springs, Texas. There is also great probability that E. Shelby Stanfield, of the same settlement, took her to Texas from Kentucky. Stanfield had many racehorses and contacts in all the racehorse states. We know that he brought other mares from Kentucky. As mentioned, Lilly sold Paisana to Oliver and Bailes, who continued racing her. When they dissolved their partnership about 1866, she was sold to William Fleming. Her pedigree is firmly established, as are her progeny. Fleming's records are complete.

Paisana was foaled in the spring of 1856. She was by Brown Dick and out of a Belton Queen by Guinea Boar. When she was three years old, she had her first foal, a colt named Anthony by Old Billy. She had been put in training but was accidentally bred, and Anthony was the result. After Anthony was weaned, she was again put into training and raced for about nine years. In 1868 she foaled Whalebone by Billy. She had Old Joe in 1870. Old Joe was followed in turn by Pine Knot, Jennie Oliver, Artie, Dora, Red Rover, and Alice, all sired by Billy. She was then bred back to her son Whalebone and foaled Yellow Wolf in 1868. The next year she was rebred to Billy and foaled John Crowder. After John Crowder she was again bred to Whalebone, and the resulting foal was Chunky Bill. Then came Sweet Lips, Little Brown Dick, Blaze, and in following years Joe Collins, Kitty, Cuadro, and Pancho, most of them by Billy or Whalebone.

Such longevity and fecundity seem almost incredible, but the records seem to leave little doubt. The names of her produce are all familiar because they formed the foundation for the Quarter Running Horse in south and west Texas. Only Jenny and Della Moore came close to Paisana in their influence on the breed.

Dams of the Trans-Mississippi West

As long races became more popular along the Atlantic Coast, short races and Quarter Horses moved farther west and north.

The states and territories north of the Ohio and west of the Mississippi became the new home of the Quarter Horse. Most of the short horses were brought in by settlers looking for new land and new homes. From Louisiana and Texas north through Missouri, Arkansas, and all the way into Illinois the Quarter Horse became king. The settlers brought with them some of the best horses available, mares and stallions carrying the blood of Whip, Bertrand, Printer, Tiger, Cherokee, and Lightning. They skipped over the Great Plains and settled Oregon and California, and these far-western states also received Quarter Horse blood. This chapter will discuss a cross section of the mares racing and producing in the new western settlements of the United States after the Civil War.

June Bug is a fine example to begin with. She was foaled in Greene County, Illinois, sometime during the Civil War. Her sire was Harry Bluff, so she was a half sister of Steel Dust. Harry Bluff was by Short Whip, who carried the blood not only of Kentucky Whip but also of Timoleon. June Bug's dam was Munch Meg by Snow Ball (Alford), and she was out of the good mare Monkey by Boanerges, who was by Old Printer. June Bug carried some of the best sprinting blood in her veins.

Two well-known horses were out of June Bug: Nannie Reap, foaled in 1870, and Cricket, foaled in 1875. Then June Bug was bred to Jack Traveler, a son of Steel Dust. The result was an extremely fast mare called Butt Cut, so named because of a racing accident; her real name was Lady Bug. Butt Cut was foaled in 1876. She was as fast a mare as the Watkins family, of Petersburg, Illinois, ever bred or raised. On a dare Samuel Watkins once raced her when she was twenty years old. She was run against a stallion named Famous, by *Bonnie Scotland. The race was run on a half-mile "bull ring." She had always been run straightaway. She started not to turn and had to be pulled up, but then she really began to run, and she nipped Famous at the finish line. Butt Cut was also the dam of well-known horses. In

1886 she foaled Honest Abe by Voltigeur (TB), in 1887 she foaled Dan Tucker by Barney Owens, and in 1891 she foaled Hi Henry by Big Henry (TB). Dan Tucker was the sire of Peter McCue.

Sam Watkins was so impressed by the colts sired by Barney Owens that he went to Berlin, Illinois, and purchased him from his friend James Owen. Until then the stallion was known as Barney. Barney's dam, Nettie Overton, was one of the great mares of her day. She was also the dam of Bob Wade, who held the world's record for the quarter mile, 21¼ seconds, set at Butte, Montana. It stood until modern times.

According to one report Nettie Overton was foaled in the late 1860s; however, her sire, Roan Dick, is elsewhere said to have been foaled in 1877—two dates, that barring divine intervention, are clearly incompatible. Perhaps she was sired by Roan Dick's sire, Black Nick. Moreover, Bob Wade was foaled in 1886, when Nettie would have been rather old to have a foal. The date could be a typographical error for 1880, or there could have been two Nettie Overtons, perhaps mother and daughter. Whatever the explanation, the horses and their records are given in *Goodwin's Annual Turf Guide*, in *The American Stud Book*, and in newspaper reports.

Nettie Overton was bred by John Hedgpeff, of Joplin, Missouri, as was Barney Owen. Grant Rea, of Carthage, Illinois, bought Nettie and Roan Dick at a public auction. Robert T. Wade, of Plymouth, Illinois, owned Nettie when she foaled Bob Wade.

Samuel Watkins had many good mares besides Butt Cut. One such was Kitty Clyde. Kitty was foaled in Kentucky in 1860 and died sometime after 1880. She was by Star Davis and out of Margravine by *Margrave. Watkins bought her from C. B. Carpenter, of Talona, Illinois. Her breeder was Thomas Bryan, of Fayette County, Kentucky. She produced Bird by Jack Traveler in 1882, Nora M by Voltigeur (TB) in 1880, Kittie Watkins by Jack Traveler in 1877, and Kitty

Menard by Marion in 1872. She was apparently in Texas in 1872 when she foaled Kitty Menard, though it is possible that her owner, Tom Gay, who lived in Menard, Texas, sent her to Illinois to be bred.

Kitty Clyde, according to one record, was taken to Ohio in 1864 to race Ida Mae, a local champion. Ida Mae had won so many races that her owner had challenged the world, excepting only Comet, the California sensation who was breaking track records wherever he went and had already beaten Ida Mae once. A man named Clark accepted the challenge for $2,000, put up forfeit money, and left to find the right racehorse. He was given six months. He ran into many difficulties, none pertinent to this account, but eventually arranged for Ida Mae to run against Kitty Clyde. The story is told in *Spirit of the Times*.[1] Bets were placed at 220, 440, and 660 yards. Ida Mae led at the 220, the two were neck and neck at the 440-yard marker, but from there on it was all Kitty's race. Ida Mae's best time was made at San Antonio, Texas in 1892, where she ran a quarter in 21½ seconds. Kitty Clyde died soon after Bird was foaled in 1882. It is hard to reconcile some of her dates, especially the date when she ran her 21½-second quarter. She should have been at least thirty years old in 1892. At this late date it seems impossible to come up with an explanation. The stories of her foals will be found in chapter 4.

Kitty Menard, a sorrel, was foaled in 1872. She was by Marion by Lexington and out of Kitty. As mentioned above, her breeder, according to the appendix of *The American Stud Book*, was T. A. Gay, of Menard, Texas. Kitty Menard entries in *The American Stud Book* are good examples of the difficulties the compilers faced when they registered Quarter Horses. In volume 3, she is in the appendix, where she belongs (p. 363). She was listed there because her dam, Kitty Clyde, was not a clean-bred Thoroughbred but a Quarter mare. She and her progeny ran so well, however, that by

[1] *Spirit of the Times and New York Sportsman* (New York, 1864), 9:290.

the time volume 4 came out her backers had worked hard enough that she was listed in the main registry (pp. 263-64). She stayed in the main registry in volumes 6 and 7, though some of her close relatives remained in the appendix.

Some good mares were foaled on the Pacific Coast during this period. The bloodlines were familiar, of course. Hennie Farrow (also known as Betty Maney) foaled the Thoroughbred Shannon (also called Tuesday). Shannon, sired by Monday, was foaled in 1872. He is mentioned here along with Hennie Farrow because he got some of the fastest short horses on the Pacific Coast. When John Adams, of Woodland, California, owned Shannon, he became the premier breeder of speed horses on the coast. Adams also bought Hennie from Arthur Turner, who lived in Modesto.

John Adams owned another well-known race mare, Bess. She was a sorrel, foaled the same year as Shannon. Her sire was Oregon Charlie, and her dam was by Pilgrim. When retired from racing, Bess proceeded to foal some of the classiest speedsters in California. In 1881 she foaled Ella T by Shannon. In 1885 she foaled Uncle Billy by Joe Hooker. In 1886 she foaled Beppo by Joe Hooker, and in 1888, Yolo by Joe Hooker. All of these horses, especially Ella T, were fast, and the fillies became good brood mares.

Kansas also had top mares during the period, none better than Grasshopper and Cherokee. In fact, only a handful of Quarter mares have produced as well as these two wonderful mares. Grasshopper was bred and raised by Joe Lewis, of Hunnewell, Kansas. Cherokee Maid, her half sister, was later bought by Mike Smiley, of Sylvan Grove, Kansas. Mrs. H. A. Trowbridge (as good a breeder of Quarter Horses as lived during this period) also had some horses of this blood. All these mares were by Cold Deck, all could fly, and all were good producers. Mrs. Trowbridge also had horses sired by Jack Traveler, Barney Owens, Harry Bluff, and Marion (by Lexington). Uriah Eggleston, of Garden City, Kansas, raised horses of similar breeding.

Grasshopper was bred shortly before 1875. Her sire was Cold Deck, and her dam was Alice, a full sister of June Bug. Alice was by Harry Bluff and out of Munch Meg by Snow Ball (also called Alford). Her produce sounds like a who's who of the Quarter Horse world during the last quarter of the nineteenth century. She was bred several times to her full brother Bobby Cromwell. She foaled Joe Lewis by Bobby in 1878, Rolling Deck by Bobby in 1879, and Doe Belly by Bobby in 1880. Later in 1887 she foaled her best son, Sykes Rondo, by McCoy Billy. He became famous in the hands of Joe Mangum, of Nixon, Texas.

Cherokee Maid, Mike Smiley's mare, was sometimes referred to as the Old Gray Mare. She had been foaled in 1875, sired by Cold Deck. She may have been out of a mare owned by Joe Lewis, who took her to Arkansas to be bred to Cold Deck. Mike Smiley bought her to race and, when she was four, bred her. She foaled Little Steve by Pony Pete in 1879. In 1884 she foaled Johnny Corbett by Pony Pete. She had Printer Tom by Pony Pete about 1888 and Guinea Pig by the same sire around 1892. These dates are educated guesses, and somewhere in between she foaled Mountain Maid and Croton Oil, who will be brought up again a little later.

Cherokee Maid was undoubtedly Smiley's best mare, but he had several others almost as good. Mike made north-central Kansas as famous for running Quarter Horses as Mrs. Trowbridge made southern Kansas. Mike always gave Sylvan Grove as his address because it was the best post office, though it was well south of his farm, which was much closer to Ash Grove. His ranch was a beautiful sight in the green, rolling hills, with its limestone-block buildings gleaming white in the Kansas sun. As of this writing they are still standing but, being empty, are rapidly falling into ruin. Mike was a familiar and welcome figure in the racing circles of Kansas, Colorado, Oklahoma, Missouri, and Arkansas. Whenever he heard of a fast horse, he would arrange a match, and he generally won.

Texas, too, had its share of fine horses during this period. Mittie Stephens is a good example. She was a smooth chestnut mare, one of those who could produce a winner from any good stallion. She was bred to five different stallions and had outstanding foals from each. She was foaled soon after the Civil War and is listed in the appendix of *The American Stud Book*. She was sired by Shiloh, Jr., by Shiloh. Shiloh, Jr., was owned by Charles R. Haley, of Sweetwater, Texas, who was also her breeder. Her dam was Nellie Gray by Dan Secres. Dan Secres was by Joe Chalmers and out of Mary Cook by Printer. Shiloh, Jr., was out of Old Puss by Freedom. Mittie's first foal was Shelby, sired by Tom Driver. He was foaled in 1878. In 1880 she had Lock's Rondo by Whalebone. In 1888 she foaled General Ross by the Thoroughbred Havre. Following this she had two good fillies by Blue Dick, Heeley, foaled in 1889, and Sally Johnson, foaled in 1890. Her last foal was Dead Cinch, by Silent Friend. J. F. Newman, of Sweetwater, liked Heeley's looks and bought her from Haley. After running her, he bred her, and she produced Simple Sam, Kid Weller, Minyon, and Red Nellie.

Mittie Stephens's first foal, Shelby, became an outstanding stallion for the man for whom he was named, E. Shelby Stanfield, of Thorp Springs, Texas. Her second foal, Rondo, was raced by Jim Brown, of Giddings, and then used as a stud by W. W. Lock, of Kyle, Texas. He was one of the four outstanding south Texas sires of his day.

One more mare is of interest, not because of her produce but because of her associations. She belonged to the celebrated outlaw Sam Bass, of Denton, Texas. Her name was Jenny, but during her racing days she was generally referred to as the Denton Mare. She was a granddaughter of Steel Dust, who had been stabled in Lancaster, a neighboring town. Jenny was foaled in 1874. Will Williams said that her dam had been stolen out of Kentucky by Henry Underwood, who became one of Sam Bass's gang. When he arrived in Denton, Underwood turned her loose on the prairie. She was then considered "estrayed" (a loose horse with no known owner), and she was "bought in" by Moss Taylor. This was a common ploy used by horse thieves to gain title to a stolen horse. Underwood then got the mare from Taylor and had legal ownership of the mare he had stolen. This was the mare that became Jenny's dam.

Sam Bass bought the mare's filly from Underwood, and when she grew up, she could run. She lost only one race in the Denton area, and that was to a horse named Rattler, owned by Buck Tomlin. Soon after this race Bass became an outlaw, and we lose track of Jenny, the Denton Mare.

IV

Foundation Dams, 1875-1900

The West in 1875 was anyplace north of the Ohio River and west of the Mississippi. Ohio, Illinois, Arkansas, Missouri, and Kansas may not now seem so far west, but they, with Texas, were the West during this period. As California and Oregon became more important, the states mentioned above came to be called the Middle West to distinguish them from the Far West.

By 1875 the Quarter Horse was widely considered the common man's racehorse. While the Thoroughbred was raised and raced, it continued to be a rich man's horse, and the tracks and breeding centers of the long horses were in or near populated centers, where enough bettors could be gathered to ensure the success of pari-mutuel betting.

Quarter Horse breeders and racing could be found in any hamlet, and the races were held on county roads, on the main street, or in someone's pasture. No expensive equipment was needed, and only the two who matched the race needed to be present. When two well-known Quarter Horses were matched, however, a surprising number of people often showed up, some even coming from neighboring states. The point is that, unlike the Thoroughbred purse races, which depended on a large turnout of people to ensure the success of the pari-mutuels, the Quarter Horses could run anywhere, any-time, as long as there were two trainers or owners, two horses, and two riders.

This basic difference in short match racing and organized purse racing helps explain why the best blood of the Quarter Horse was scattered far and wide and why the best Thoroughbred blood was concentrated in certain areas, such as around Lexington, Kentucky. Thoroughbreds were raced for a few years and then put in the stud. The mares were usually brought to them and tended to be clustered in the area where the stallions and the racetracks were. Before the days of trucks, airplanes, and artificial insemination, only an exceptional mare was led or ridden more than a hundred miles to a stallion. The Quarter Horse stallion, on the other hand, was run as long as he could win his share, and after the race he was available to breed. In their search for a match race owners of the better stallions had to travel far and wide. We find the names of the same Quarter Horse stallions appearing in the sporting journals and in *Goodwin's Turf Guide* in Illinois, Oregon, Montana, Arizona, California, and even Juárez, Mexico.

Another interesting fact that becomes clear with some research is that the very best stallions and mares were raised by a relatively few breeders. These breeders often lived in the same neighborhoods. Examples that come immediately to mind are the Watkinses and the Owens of Illinois; the Trowbridges, the Smileys, and the Lewises of Kansas; the Haleys, Newmans, and Stanfields of north Texas; and the Hedgepeffs and the Stocktons of Missouri. Most of the fastest horses were raised by these small groups of breeders, all clustered within small areas.

Other factors—perhaps not all that surprising when one thinks about it—were that the breeders used almost identical bloodlines and that they bought or traded stallions or mares among themselves. These breeders knew that good mares were the key to success.

Illinois

The last quarter of the nineteenth century was probably the high point for Quarter Horse breeding in Illinois, though some good horses were foaled in the early 1900s. They were bred primarily by the Watkins family, of Petersburg and Oakdale; Robert Wade and Grant Rea, around Plymouth; and James Owen, of Berlin. Three of the best Watkins mares were foals of one mare, Kitty Clyde, discussed in the last chapter. One was Kittie Watkins (Kiddie Waddell); another, Bird; and the last, Nora M.

Kittie Watkins was a smooth bay, foaled in 1877. She was by Jack Traveler and out of Kitty Clyde. Kitty Clyde was owned at that time by C. B. Carpenter, of Talona, Illinois. Carpenter still owned her in 1881, when she was again bred to Watkins's Jack Traveler and foaled Bird. When Watkins realized how good a mare Kitty Clyde was, he bought all three, Kittie Watkins, Bird, and Kitty Clyde.

Bird, a sorrel, was foaled in 1882, and a full sister of Kittie Watkins, as mentioned above. Both she and her two sisters could run, as could their dam.

Kittie Watkins had the following foals: Dobbins by Famous in 1888, Tom Harding by General Harding in 1889, Sealum by Famous in 1890, Tom D by Duke of Highland in 1895, Kitty Hero by Hero in 1896, and Dry Camp by Hero in 1897. It is pretty obvious that Watkins knew how much early speed *Bonnie Scotland produced, because Famous was sired by Frogtown, who was by *Bonnie Scotland. Both Hero and Duke of Highlands had dams sired by *Bonnie Scotland.

Kitty Clyde's Bird was even more productive than Kittie Watkins. In 1887 she had a filly by Voltigeur (TB). The following spring she dropped a filly, called Frankie C, sired by Spinning, a grandson of *Bonnie Scotland. In 1890 she foaled Log Cabin by Dan Tucker, and in 1891, Pat Tucker by Dan Tucker. In 1893 she foaled Bird of the Highlands by Duke of the Highlands, and in the following two years she had two more foals by him, Harry N and Pira. In 1901 she dropped Lucretia M by Hero. Most of Bird's and Kittie's offspring went out and raced.

The third mare of the group was Nora M. A bay foaled

in 1880, she was the dam of Peter McCue. She was registered in *The American Stud Book* as sired by Voltigeur, and that breeding probably should be accepted, though Helen Michaelis claimed to have proof that she was by Dan Tucker. There is also strong evidence that Watkins bought the mare Owen, from James Owen, of Berlin, Illinois. The ownership problems arise because authors of sports articles are often non-horsemen who do not know that the breeder is considered to be the owner of the mare at the time of service. Another confusing fact is that mares in foal were sold and that the foal that came the following year was often credited to a new owner who had nothing to do with the breeding. Besides Peter McCue, whom she foaled in 1895, Nora M also produced Briggs by Dan Tucker and Millie D by Tennyson. Millie became the dam of Nona P. In all she had eight foals.

The records show that Nora M was raced by Hap Mitchell when she was two years old. Mitchell lied in Ashland, Illinois, a few miles north of Berlin, where James Owen lived. Undoubtedly Mitchell knew all about the filly and her parents and realized that she was a good prospect. He named the filly for his daughter Nora. She was not fast enough for top company but ran a consistent 49 seconds in the half mile and won her share of races. Nora M was fourteen when she was bred to Dan Tucker and produced Peter McCue. She died a few years later giving birth to twins.

Watkins had some other mares that should be mentioned. Two were later sold to George Clegg, of Alice, Texas. When Sam Watkins died, his widow decided to sell his horses, and that is when George Clegg bought Hattie W and Lucretia M, along with a few other horses. Clegg knew that Mrs. Watkins was selling Sam's horses because a jockey he sometimes used told him so. The jockey's name was Pap Rebo, and he had exercised horses for Watkins and even ridden a few of them. Clegg knew Peter McCue and Harmon Baker and wanted a colt of the same quality. He made arrangements to buy four horses: Hickory Bill, Hunter, Lucretia M, and Hattie W.

Hattie was by Hi Henry and out of Katie Wawekus. She had ten foals in Illinois and two in Texas. One of her Texas foals was Sam Watkins by Hickory Bill. According to Mrs. Watkins, Hattie ran a scored quarter in 21 seconds.

Two other mares owned by Illinois breeders are well worth mentioning. One was Puss B, a bay, foaled in 1882. She was owned and probably bred by James Owen. She was sired by Tom Flood, who was by Voltigeur. She was out of Reap by Dr. Cash. Reap, who was also known as Nannie Reap, was a daughter of that grand old mare June Bug, by Harry Bluff. There are some indications that Puss B, or at least her dam, Reap, was bred by James Owen's cousin (?) W. C. Owen, of Smithville, Missouri. In 1894, Puss B foaled a bay called Flush, sired by Fib. In 1895 she produced the filly Katie Flanger, also by Fib.

Robert Torian Wade, of Plymouth, Illinois, also raised fast Quarter Horses, including the world record holder, Bob Wade. Bob Wade's record (21¼) held for eighty-odd years, until Dash for Cash ran a quarter in 21.17 in 1977.

One of the fastest mares bred in Plymouth was Nettie S, a gray, foaled in 1885. She was sired by Roan Dick and probably bred by Robert Wade, though she was raised by Mose Toland, of Hancock County. After she began running, her ownership became confused. Various people entered her in races, she was claimed and then bought back, and reports often listed as her owner the man who entered her in a race. The following account is complete and accurate, I believe, as far as it goes. Mose Toland bought Nettie S from Wade and sold her to J. P. Sutton. Sutton ran her in Illinois and Missouri until no one wanted to run against her. He then took her to Montana, where the proceeds from copper mines were lining many men's pockets. He also took Bob Wade, her half brother. After a few races Nettie S came into the ownership of Barker and Parrot, of Anaconda, Montana. She then set what was reputed to be a world's record for 600 yards: 30¼ seconds. She also ran a quarter mile at Helena, Montana, on

August 23, 1890, in 21¾ seconds. In the famous race in which Bob Wade set the world's record for a quarter mile, she was second by a scant neck. After she was through racing, Nettie was bred to her sire, Roan Dick, and produced Bay Billy.

The Roan Dick family was the only one that could be compared with Dan Tucker's. Jim Miller, another son of Roan Dick, set a quarter-mile record at Deer Lodge, Montana, running the distance in 21½ seconds, a record which held until it was broken by his half brother Bob Wade. Silver Dick, another son of Roan Dick, also set records. Roan Dick's daughters were also fleet, as were his grandsons and granddaughters. Jim Miller sired Dolly Miller, Jim Miller II, Miss Miller, Roan Beauty, and Young Jim Miller. Dolly equaled the world's record for a three-quarter mile. She was owned and raced by the Quarter Horse man John Hancock, who lived at Twisp, Washington. She was never beaten when matched at distances over 300 yards.

While Jim Miller's get were showing their heels to the best sprinters in the West, another Miller, a filly whose first name was Nellie, was also making waves. Nellie Miller, a gray, was foaled sometime in the late 1880s—or perhaps in the early 1890s, since she did some of her fastest racing in those years. Her story goes like this:

Earl Kelly claims that W. J. (Bill) Miller, an early settler in the Texas panhandle, saw two good-looking gray mares pulling a milk wagon in Kansas City. He bought the one called Nellie, whose mouth showed her to be a five-year-old. It was said that she was born in Kentucky (any horse was automatically worth twenty-five or fifty dollars more if it was claimed that she was born in that state). She looked to be a Thoroughbred. Bill Miller, who owned the J D Ranch at Sweetwater, Oklahoma, had her shipped there. When he died soon afterward, his son, Zack Miller, inherited Nellie, who by now was called Nellie Miller.

Milo Burlingame told me that he used to ride Nellie Miller in her races. Milo obtained her half sister, who was named Fly (she was the other mare pulling that Kansas City milk wagon).

One of Nellie's first races was against Gold Dust, a Cold Deck mare whom she beat. Then she was matched against Jane Baker in Mobeetie, Texas. Again she won. Milo said that except for Peter McCue she was the fastest horse that he ever rode. She was rematched against Gold Dust for a half mile in Kansas City in 1893 and was successful. She was a quarter mare but could run three-eighths or a half mile. She ran a quarter mile against Flossie at Canadian, Texas, in 22 seconds flat.

Nellie was a stubborn horse and hard to start. Something happened to all her colts. She was bred to Idle Boy several times. She had a filly, then Luke Dunn, then Dot, all of whom were grays.

In the spring of 1892 a big roan mare named Jane was led into Mobeetie behind a wagon. She had come to match Nellie Miller, who was stabled in Mobeetie. A match was soon arranged for May 5, 1892, to be run for $5,000 a side. It attracted wide attention, not only because of the size of the purse but also because both mares were well known and respected. Nellie won by almost a length. Years ago Milo told me that he then took Nellie to Kansas City for some races and ran into Roan Jane again. It was then that he learned that she was by Cold Deck. Nellie and Roan Jane ran in a race that included Gold Dust, Gray Ollie, Rabbit, and Dora Mae. Nellie won again, with Roan Jane a close second. From Kansas City, Milo took her to Marshall, Missouri, for several races, then on to Saint Louis. In Saint Louis she ran against top competition, including April Fool, Log Cabin, Sheriff, and several other fast Quarter Horses. A double race was matched by Frank James, Jesse's brother. He matched Log Cabin against Sheriff for a quarter mile; Nellie was to race the winner. Sheriff won, but James paid the forfeit so that he would not have to run against Nellie. It was at this race meet that Milo first rode Peter McCue.

Nellie appears in *Goodwin's Turf Guide*, where she is reported as winning a half-mile race on March 23, 1894, at Hot Springs, Arkansas, in 53½ seconds. Others in that race,

49

in order of finish behind Nellie, were Jack Thomas, a chestnut gelding by Cold Deck; Headlight, a gray gelding by Little Mike and out of a Cold Deck mare; Lady Tom, a bay mare by Rebel Morgan and out of Texas Belle; and Little Joe, a sorrel gelding by Sykes Rondo and out of Jenny Oliver.

Nellie Miller may or may not have been related to the Jim Millers, but she could run in their company (which was the best) and win. She was sired by Gray Cold Deck by Cold Deck and out of a Thoroughbred mare whose breeding is unknown.

Kansas

Kansas was another breeding center for good quarter mares during the last fourth of the nineteenth century. There were Mike Smiley, of Sylvan Grove; Mrs. H. A. Trowbridge, of Wellington; Joe Lewis, of Hunnewell; and Uriah Eggleston, of Garden City and Minco. Like the Illinois breeders, all these breeders are mentioned in the previous chapter because their operations began after the Civil War and extended to the twentieth century.

Cherokee Maid was discussed in the previous chapter. She was owned by Mike Smiley, and two of her last foals were Croton Oil and Mountain Maid. Mountain Maid was campaigned all over the West and later in life was sold to C. A. Underwood, who sold her to Foxhall Keane. Mountain Maid became the dam of Red Texas when bred to Little Conductor, a Thoroughbred. Both of these mares also ended up in the ownership of Foxhall Keane, who played polo and needed their speed for his teams.

Mrs. Trowbridge had the following outstanding mares: Vergie, a bay mare foaled in 1886 by Cold Deck and out of Cherokee Belle; Belle H, a bay mare foaled in 1887 by Spinning by Voltigeur and out of a Jack Traveler mare; and Deck, a sorrel mare foaled in 1883 by Barney Owens and out of Lucy by Marion. These last two mares were raised by James Owen. Belle H had been raised by Sam Watkins.

Another good Trowbridge mare was Miss Murphy, a sorrel, foaled in 1882. She was by Grand River Chief by Satanta and out of a Harry Bluff mare.

Vergie was the dam of Mrs. Trowbridge's good running horse and breeding stallion Little Danger. He was a brown, foaled in 1894, by Okema. Okema, although a registered Thoroughbred (shown as out of Maggie), had the quarter mare Cherokee Belle for a dam, the same Cherokee Belle who was the dam of Vergie. Cherokee Belle was probably a full sister of Cherokee Maid and was also a close relative of Grasshopper, all raised by Joe Lewis, of Hunnewell.

California

There was a fine mare in California at this time named Pearl. She was a large bay, foaled in 1874. She was sired by Brick, a sorrel foaled in California by Oregon Charlie, a Printer stallion. John Adams, of Woodland, in northern California, owned both Pearl and Brick. He had bred Brick to one of his best mares, Nellie, who was by Walnut Bark and out of a full sister of Choctaw by Obe Jennings.

Pearl was raced all up and down the Pacific Coast, but she was only a 23-second mare. In 1884, Adams put her in with his brood mares. Her first foal was Miss Mitford by Joe Hooker, a Thoroughbred owned by a sometime neighbor and friend Theodore Winters. Miss Mitford, a sorrel, was foaled in 1885. She turned out to be one of the fastest mares on the coast in the late 1880s. Pearl's second foal was Steam Beer. He was sired by Uncle Billy, a son of Joe Hooker. Pearl's third foal was Ben Martin, also by Uncle Billy. He was a bay, foaled in 1888. He too could run.

Oklahoma

Oklahoma has been one of the best producers of Quarter

Horses since the last half of the nineteenth century. M. S. ("Small") Baker was always raising one or two fast horses to match. His home was near Peggs, but he raced in all the surrounding states. One top mare he raced was a gray mare foaled in 1886 (?) by Cold Deck. She was out of a Lightning mare. Foss Barker, who owned Cold Deck at the time and lived in Van Buren, Arkansas, was a good friend of Baker's. They specialized in Cold Deck, Lightning, and Brimmer blood in their running horses. Cold Deck was by Steel Dust, Lightning was by Lexington, and their Brimmer blood came from the Tennessee Brimmer. Foss Barker raised the gray mare whom Baker called Jennie and who was also called Gray Jennie. She was running in Saint Louis in 1894, according to *Goodwin's Turf Guide.*

Herb McSpadden told Helen Michaelis that they never knew Jennie could run until one day she ran away pulling a double shovel and the shovel only hit the ground twice in the first quarter mile. That is undoubtedly one of those interesting stories. It hardly seems likely that a racehorse man like Small Baker would buy a good mare from a top Quarter Horse breeder like Foss Barker and never train her or expect her to run. Let's go on with Herb's story, however. When they saw the gray mare take off with the fresno, they knew she could run, so Small's daughter took Jennie to the tracks and won a lot of money with her.

Another Oklahoma Nellie that could run some was Nellie Hart. She was a bay, foaled in the late 1880s or early 1890s. She was by Pid Hart and out of Queen Victoria by Lock's Rondo. Queen was out of Margie by Cold Deck. C. B. Campbell, of Minco, owned Nellie Hart's dam and gave her to the Armstrong boys, who took the filly west.

Later she was owned by W. J. Francis. Nellie Hart had two fine colts, Catch Me and Hermus. Catch Me stood only about 14 hands, yet he ran his quarter mile in 22 seconds and a little. He was by Bob Peters. The other fast colt was Hermus by Tom Campbell. He was foaled in 1910.

Texas

As may be assumed, Texas had its full quota of good mares during this period. Some of the best were owned by W. W. Lock, of Kyle. Mary Lee, a dun, was foaled in 1877. She was by Lock's Joe Lee and out of a dun race mare of questionable breeding. Joe Lee, also known as Joe II, was by Joe Hamilton by One-Eyed Joe. Mary Lee produced two outstanding foals when bred to Lock's Rondo. In 1888 she had Blue Jacket and in 1892 Minnie Lee. Minnie Lee was a dun like her dam. She was rather small, weighing only 900 pounds in good flesh, and had a black stripe down her back. She was, of course, bred and owned by Lock. She had an excellent racing record and ran the quarter in 22 seconds and the three-eighths in 35½. She was sold, along with Bonnie Bird II, in Roswell after a race meet.

Bonnie Bird II was foaled in 1891 and was out of Daisy L. Daisy L was also out of Mary Lee, and her sire was Project (TB). Her second dam was Nellie. W. W. Lock, in a letter to Helen Michaelis dated August 13, 1942, said that Daisy L was foaled on May 15, 1882. He added that she was a dun with a white right hind foot and that she had a snip. She ran a scored 440 in 22½ seconds. There are records of four foals of Daisy L. In 1890 she had Texas Chief by Lock's Rondo; in 1891, Bonnie Bird II by Rondo; in 1892, a sorrel filly who destroyed herself in a barbed-wire fence; and in 1893, a dun colt who was shot in 1897 because he was vicious.

Bonnie Bird II was a dun like her dam. She stood 14-2 hands and weighed over 1,100 pounds. She was branded L O on her left shoulder. As mentioned above, she was sold in Roswell, New Mexico, to Bob Burns, of Hope, New Mexico. J. A. Locklear bought Bonnie from Burns in 1913. She was run for a number of years and had a record of 22 seconds flat for the quarter mile. When her racing days were over, she was bred. In 1913 she produced June Bug by Tommy Twigg (TB), and in 1916, California Filly by the same sire.

Lock was in the racehorse business, and he had many running mares. One of his best was Red Bird. Red Bird was a sorrel, sired by Lock's Rondo. In one of her most famous races she was matched against a horse belonging to Jim Brown. Jim outran her with a mare he had named Blue Bird. Red Bird lost that race, but there were rumors that it had been set up so that she would lose.

Besides Lock's Red Bird there was another Red Bird running about the same time. She was apparently sired by Shelby Stanfield's Bill Garner by Steel Dust. This is the Red Bird who later foaled Idle Boy.

Jim Brown's Blue Bird was a gray mare, foaled in 1883. Brown bred, raised, trained, and raced her. He ran her in New Orleans in 1886. In Kansas City's Exposition Park she ran a two-out-of-three-heat race for a half mile. She won both heats, running the first in 48 seconds and the second in 48½. In that race she was matched against H. A. Trowbridge's Hattie. Hattie was by Little Danger by Cold Deck and out of Miss Murphy.

Jim Brown also owned and raced Jenny Oliver. Jenny, a black, was foaled in 1881. She was sired by Billy and out of the famous Paisana, mentioned earlier. Jenny Oliver was bred by Bill Fleming, of Belmont, Texas. While Fleming was racing Jenny in San Angelo, he matched a race with Pat Garrett. When Jenny won, Jim Brown, who was at the race, bought her. She ran a 22-second quarter mile. When she was through racing, John Wilkins, of San Antonio, bought her from Brown and bred her. Jenny had Brown Alice by Whalebone in 1888 and Mamie B by Sykes Rondo in 1890. Brown Alice later became the dam of Ollie by Barnes and Dr. O. G., also by Barnes. Mamie B was brown like Brown Alice. She is listed in the appendix of *The American Stud Book* and in *Goodwin's Turf Guide*, as are so many of the other good Quarter mares of the period. Jim Brown owned another good Fleming mare. Her name was Dora. She was a sorrel, foaled in 1882, sired by Billy and out of the one and only Paisana.

Shelby Stanfield enjoyed a short race, but he was more than just a race fan. He was a superb breeder. In fact, he was one of the half-dozen best in the United States. An example of the excellence of his breeding program was Jenny Capps. She was a sorrel, foaled in 1882 (?), sired by Dash. She was out of Bay Puss, mentioned earlier, and had both Shiloh and Steel Dust up close in her pedigree. By the stallion Shelby she had in order Pid Hart, Anti-Pro, and Eureka. No one could ask for more.

Another royally bred Texas mare was Mamie Sykes. She was foaled in 1894 (?) and was sired by Sykes Rondo and out of the great May Mangum. She was May's last foal, though some have written that Baby Ruth was May's last foal. Mamie was run often but not always wisely. She lost a match race with Judge Thomas at Sonora. The race was rematched, and she won. She also lost to Blue Jacket. C. L. Patterson said that she was matched by N. N. Patterson in December, 1896, against the Bob Wade owned by Johnny Johnson. Later Truston Polk and Bill Nack took her to Louisiana and matched a cajun horse. Mamie pulled a leader, and they sold her there at Abbeville. Her only Texas offspring was Major Gray, by Uncle Jimmy Gray.

Mention of Judge Thomas in the preceding paragraph brings up his dam, Fanny Pace. Fanny was bred by "Trump" Pace, of Baird, Texas. She was later owned and run by C. C. Seale, also of Baird. Her sire was Gulliver. Her produce, besides Judge Thomas, were Judge Welch and Buster Brown, all by Traveler. Pace had been driving her hitched to his icewagon when Seale bought her.

The stallion Anthony was mentioned earlier. He was used by both Fleming and Sykes. He was by Billy and out of Paisana. He was raised and owned by Fleming, whose horse ranch was near Belmont, a few miles east of San Antonio. Two of the fastest mares ever to come out of south Texas were full sisters, Fashion, foaled in 1887, and Lemonade, foaled in 1888. Both were out of Silentina, a mare owned by their breeder, Tom King, of Belmont. King sold them to Wade McLemore, of Dallas. When they were running, Tom Lipscomb was their trainer.

Fashion, although meeting an untimely death, ran many races. S. C. Riggs said that he rode her in fifty-six races and she won them all. Two of her times on recognized tracks were three-eighths mile at Lampasas in 1891 in 38 seconds and a half mile at New Orleans in 1892 in 48 seconds. She was in Helena, Montana, in 1892, and ran three-eighths mile in 33 seconds. She also broke the bull-ring record for three-eighths mile at San Angelo, running on the half-mile circular track in 34 seconds. It was a circular track that caused her death. She ran over the fence at New Orleans and had to be destroyed. Her only produce was Sam, sired by her half brother Priest Bob and foaled in 1901.

Fashion's sister Lemonade was a brown mare. Like her sister Lemonade raced as a Thoroughbred on the larger tracks, and a different pedigree was sent in from the one given here. They are both in the appendix of *The American Stud Book* and in *Goodwin's Turf Guide*. She was not quite as fast as Fashion but plenty fast enough to win many races. She had three known foals, Phil King by *Gallantry (TB), a brown colt foaled in 1902; Marge, a sorrel mare by Isaac Lewis (TB), foaled in 1896; and Enze, a bay mare by Galen (TB), foaled in 1895.

The last mare discussed in this section is one of the all-time great south Texas mares, May Mangum. She was great because of her outstanding progeny. She too was sired by Anthony by Old Billy, and her dam was Belle Nellie by a son of Tiger by Kentucky Whip. She was owned by Dow and Will Shely, of Alfred, Texas. The list of her progeny sounds like a who's who of south Texas Quarter Horses. She was a bay, foaled in 1882. She foaled six fillies and four colts, all by Syles Rondo. The fillies were Nellie, Jenny, Mamie Sykes, Nettie Harrison, Kitty, and finally Baby Ruth. May's Jenny will be discussed at some length in the next chapter, for she was the dam of Big Liz and another Baby Ruth.

May Mangum's four colts were Little Joe (a gelding), Blue Eyes, Dogie Beasley, and Blaze, all by Sykes Rondo. Dow Shely used Blue Eyes, and Jap Holman used Dogie Beasley. As a producer May is in the class of the very greatest Quarter mares.

The following lists give some idea of the speed of the early-day Quarter mares running a quarter-mile.

Fast Times by Quarter Mares, 1880-1903
(Scored start)

Mare	Site of Race	Date of Race	Time, Seconds
Queen T	Butte, Montana	August 9, 1902	21.50
Nettie S	Helena, Montana	August 23, 1890	21.75
Belle	Galveston, Texas	July 3, 1880	21.75
Queen T	Butte, Montana	August 18, 1902	22.00
Rosie	San Bernardino, California	October 29, 1891	22.00
Plowmare	Fresno, California	July 4, 1886	22.50
Lady Blanch	Visalia, California	October 6, 1891	22.50
Nettie S	Deer Lodge, Montana	July 22, 1890	22.50
On-the-Lea	Lexington, Kentucky	September 1, 1890	22.75

Fast Times by Quarter Mares 1940-44
(Standing start)

Mare	Site of Race	Date of Race	Time, Seconds
Shue Fly	Eagle Pass, Texas	October 22, 1942	22.20
Ginger Rogers	Junction, Texas	1939	22.20
Shue Fly	Tucson, Arizona	February 15, 1941	22.40
Rosita	Eagle Pass, Texas	October 25, 1942	22.60
Shue Fly	Tucson, Arizona	December 7, 1941	22.60
Squaw H	Eagle Pass, Texas	October 29, 1944	22.80
Maggie	Eagle Pass, Texas	October 29, 1944	22.80
Mae West	Eagle Pass, Texas	October 25, 1944	22.80
Free Silver	Eagle Pass, Texas	October 25, 1944	22.80
Rosita	Eagle Pass, Texas	October 31, 1943	22.80
Shue Fly	Tucson, Arizona	February 15, 1942	22.80

V

Foundation Dams, 1900-1940

The years between 1700 and 1940 saw the breeding centers of the Quarter Horse shift farther and farther west. Starting in the 1700s in Virginia and North Carolina, they traveled ever westward, moving into Kentucky and Tennessee, then on to Missouri and Arkansas. By 1900 the primary breeding centers were in Texas and Oklahoma. There were, of course, centers in certain peripheral states, such as Ohio, Illinois, and Kansas, but Texas and Oklahoma furnished most of the Quarter Horses registered in the early years of the association. The period from 1900 to 1940 can be called the "early modern period," because by 1940 the Quarter Horse had a breed association and a registry of its own, entirely independent of the Thoroughbred.

The mares discussed in this section are taken up alphabetically by state. It should be pointed out again that some mares and foals overlap from one period to the next. A mare and her produce can easily cover a span of forty years.

Arizona

Toward the close of the 1800s, John Crowder, a son of Paisana and Old Billy, sired one of Arizona's best mares. Her name was Birdie, or Birdie Hopkins, as she was occasionally known. She was foaled in 1890 (?) out of a mare listed simply as a Blackstone mare, probably a reference to the individual or ranch that raised her. In any case, she found her way into Arizona. Some claim that she was taken to Arizona by Van Hastings on one of his trips from Texas. All accounts agree that she was sired by John Crowder. Birdie could run, as she showed in a match race at Phoenix in which she ran the quarter mile in 22.2 seconds. Her greatest claim to fame, however, came from two of her offspring, Dottie and Mamie. Both were sired by No Good by Barney Owens. No Good was bred by Tom Trammel, of Sweetwater, Texas, and was sold to Jim Kennedy and Mark Dubois, both of Bonita, Arizona. While No Good was in Arizona, he sired Dottie and Mamie.

Dottie became the dam of the famous Arizona stallion Red Cloud when bred to Jim Kennedy's Possum. Possum was, of course, the Texas King, full brother of Little Joe, a son of Jenny. Later Dottie became the dam of Doc, also by Possum. Mamie, not to be outdone, foaled Guinea Pig when bred to Possum in 1921.

Another illustrious Arizona family was established by the mare Silver, foaled in 1928. Her dam's pedigree is open to discussion, though all agree that she was a top individual. Silver's sire was Blue Eyes by Possum. Blue Eyes was foaled in 1910, bred by Mayburn Gardner. He was sold to Fred Mickel, of Cottonwood, and spent his last days with Whitey Montgomery at Rimrock.

Silver's owner, Chester Cooper, of the Tonto country, was a short-horse man who bred, raised, and raced sprinters. Cooper settled near Roosevelt when that country was still just halter-broke. In 1932, Cooper bred Silver to his stallion Doc, mentioned above. Doc was a half brother of Blue Eyes, sired by Possum. Cooper bought Doc from Doc Pardee, of Phoenix, from whom Doc got his name.

The cross of Silver and Doc was a good one. The 1933 foal was named Peggy C. She became a top roping and racing mare. In 1935, Silver foaled Duchess by Doc. After a few years under the saddle Peggy C and Duchess were bred. Right then Arizona began producing some top Quarter running horses. For example, Peggy C foaled Sleepy Dick by Colonel Clyde, Tonta Gal by Clabber, Little Wolf by the same sire, and War Chance by Red Man. Duchess foaled Prissy when bred to Colonel Clyde, Buster when bred to Clabber, Twilight by the same sire, Miss Atomic by Red Man, and Betsy Ross by Joe Reed II. Few mares have passed their ability through their offspring better than Silver. Whom they were bred to made little difference in the excellence of their offspring.

Chester Cooper had many good mares besides those mentioned above. An example was his Lady C. She was by Guinea Pig and out of a Bulger mare. Bulger was a Texas-bred horse sired by Traveler and owned in Arizona by Jim Kennedy. It was Cooper's claim that Lady C was never beaten from one-eighth to one-quarter mile while running in Arizona and California. When she was bred later, she became the dam of Chester C. A. A. Nichols owned her at that time.

Ernest Browning also had some excellent mares. His primary interest was in raising roping and cow horses, but all of his stock had speed too. He combined the blood of Casement's Balleymooney with his Billy Byrne and the blood of Possum. Billy Byrne was out of Natalie by New Mexico Little Joe. Later he used Billy the Kid, a Billy Byrne and Possum bloodlines cross.

Colorado

Three Colorado mares have been selected to represent that state in the period. First was Stockings, foaled soon after 1910 and bred and owned by Coke T. Roberds, of Hayden. Among her outstanding colts were Buck Thomas by Peter McCue; Prince (Coke T) by Brown Dick; Goldie by Fred S, a Thoroughbred; and the Brown Dick Mare by Deering Doe, also a Thoroughbred. Fanny White was another exceptional mare. She was bred by George White, of Mancos, but was owned most of her life by Kirk Williams. When Fanny was crossed on Williams's good Texas racehorse stallion Billy Caviness by Brown Dick by Billy, the results were outstanding. Two of the best were Billy White and Silver Dick, racehorses of the first quality. The last mare selected was Pet, bred and owned by Coke Roberds. She was sired by Old Fred, and her best foal was the well-known Sheik 11 in *The Quarter Horse Stud Book.*

One more item on Colorado mares: Sometimes a stallion comes along that seems to sire mares that produce great horses. One such was Little Joe, of New Mexico. He was a grandson of Harmon Baker. Dan and Jack Casement bought or traded for a half-dozen Little Joe mares. Cinnabar foaled Red Dog, Christabel foaled Red Cloud, Natalie foaled Billy Byrne, Christina foaled Frosty, and another mare foaled Buckshot. Most of these New Mexico Little Joe mares had Uhlan (TB) blood.

Illinois

One of the more interesting running mares of the early 1900s was Carrie Nation. She could really run, and for a time she held the world's record for five-eighths mile. Few horses living during her racing days were able to beat her at a half mile. Because of her speed Thoroughbred papers were obtained for her, which allowed her to run at the organized tracks.

She was registered in *The Thoroughbred Stud Book* (7:874). According to the entry she was foaled in 1899, named Belle of Oakford and out of Trixie W. Trixie W was raised by Sam Watkins's friend James Owen, of Berlin, Illinois. She was by Owen's stallion Fib, who was by Story, both registered Thoroughbreds. Her sire is shown as Bowling Green, an Illinois Thoroughbred. When racing on the long tracks, she ran as Belle of Oakford. Most authorities agree that her sire was Peter McCue; many different stories are told about the identity of her dam.

Oakford is a little town north of Petersburg, where some of Sam Watkins's brothers and nephews lived. They too were short-horse men. Sam leased Peter McCue to one of them, and while he was in Oakford, Peter McCue sired not only Carrie Nation but also Harmon Baker and several others of his well-known colts.

In a booklet honoring Oakford's past, the section about the Watkinses and their horses was written by Eugene Boeker. Since this booklet has had limited circulation, it seems worthwhile to summarize it here. Boeker begins by saying that in recording Oakford's history he had to reserve a chapter for the great Quarter Horses that were Oakford's claim to fame at the turn of the century. He then talks about the Watkinses. He says that Thomas and Joseph Watkins came to Clary's Grove from Kentucky about 1821, bringing with them their quarter racing horses. Seven descendants settled in the Oakford area.

Joseph Watkins had a son, Samuel, the best known of the Watkinses. He married Mary Walridge and had eight children. His best-known son was Walter. Other Watkinses, all descendants of the original two, were Beverly, William, Eli, Kay, Charlie, Hugh, and George.

When Peter McCue was a yearling, Sam Watkins leased him to his nephew Charlie, a son of his brother William. Charlie lived a few miles east of Oakford. Charlie trained Peter McCue, and when he found out that he was fast, he registered him and took him to the big track in Chicago. They followed the circuit throughout Illinois, Indiana, and Michigan and into Windsor, Canada. Peter was then returned to Sam Watkins. After more racing, he was leased to George Watkins, Charlie's brother. George stood Peter for a few years at the south edge of Oakford, in Harmon Baker's barn. George was living with Baker at the time. It was during those years that the following great horses were sired: Carrie

Nation, Buck Thomas, Harmon Baker, Cricket Ray, Oakford Queen, Bridget, and the Chase Mare.

The story of Carrie Nation, according to Boeker, is as follows: When Peter McCue stood at Oakford, Ed King, a groceryman, used a mare to pull his wagon through the county. Her filly by Peter McCue was named Carrie Nation. Joe Bennett, a farmer west of town, got the filly but later lost her to pay a gambling debt to one of Jim Thomas's boys. Jim Thomas had opened the main saloon of Oakford, which he operated until his death in 1891. His son continued to operate the business until the town voted itself dry in 1908. Jim Thomas liked to race. He had great luck with a gelding he called Dobbin. He challenged Sam Watkins's horse Dan Tucker. Although previously retired, Dan Tucker was returned to the tracks and defeated Dobbin. Jim Thomas's boys continued his love of short horses and ran Carrie Nation successfully until Jim sold her, and she was taken to Texas.

In Texas she was owned by J. F. Newman and John Wilkins, of San Antonio. Ott Adams, of Alfred, Texas, received a letter from Wilkins in 1919, when he bought one of Carrie Nation's colts, Billy Sunday. The letter said in part that "the sorrel colt Huyler [the Thoroughbred name for Billy Sunday] is by Horace H, a very fast horse for ½ mile. I bought him from F. Newman and gave $1000 for him. . . . the dam of Huyler was Belle of Oakford, nicknamed Carrie Nation, who was the fastest Quarter Horse I ever saw." Undoubtedly Newman owned Carrie Nation before Wilkins did. Carrie Nation also foaled Edgar Uhl by Horace H while she was owned by Wilkins.

One of the Watkinses' best mares during this period was Nona P. Nona P's sire is listed as the Thoroughbred Duke of the Highlands. Helen Michaelis, after considerable research, which included correspondence and personal conversations with older horsemen of this period, decided that, like Peter McCue, she was sired by Dan Tucker. This is really not an important point, for the Duke was a sire of early speed whose maternal grandsire was none other than *Bonnie Scotland.

Nona P's dam was the good mare Millie D, who was by the Thoroughbred Tennyson and out of the superb mare Nora M. As mentioned earlier, Nora M was by Voltigeur and out of the speed burner Kitty Clyde.

Nora spent her early days on Sam Watkins's Little Grove Stock Farm, near Petersburg, Illinois. When she was between two and three she was leased or loaned, along with Peter McCue, to George Watkins, a nephew of Sam Watkins and a son of Bill Watkins. Earlier Sam had leased Peter to Charlie, George's brother, who had raced Peter, as mentioned above. George lived at Oakford. Nona P's first foal at Oakford was Tot Lee, who was sired by Peter McCue. Her next foal was Buck Thomas, who was gelded and raced. He won forty-nine of his first fifty races. The next foal was a colt. George named him Harmon Baker for a friend. Buck Thomas was named for a hired hand.

In 1907 John Wilkins, of San Antonio, Texas, went to Petersburg to buy some of Watkins's horses. He bought Peter McCue, Harmon Baker, Buck Thomas, and Nona P. Peter McCue was later sold to Milo Burlingame, and Harmon Baker was sold to William Anson. Wilkins ran the gelding Buck Thomas.

After 1907 all of Nona P's colts were foaled in Texas. They were Hattie Jackson, San Antonio, and Edee Ree. Edee Ree was to become the dam of Rainy Day when bred to Lone Star. She produced some of the best, in Illinois as well as in Texas.

The last of the Watkins mares to be mentioned here is Lucretia M. Her greatest influence was on the Quarter Horses of south Texas. Lucretia's dam was the great Watkins mare Bird. Lucretia, along with a few others, was sold to George Clegg, of Alice, Texas. The other horses sold were Lucretia's Hickory Bill, Hattie W, and Hattie's offspring, Hunter, by Hi Henry. Hickory Bill was by Peter McCue.

Lucretia M was a bay, registered by the Jockey Club for racing purposes only. The register shows that she was sired by Hero and out of Bird. She was foaled on March 11, 1901. Mrs. Watkins wrote George Clegg about these horses. She claimed that Hattie W could run a quarter mile in under 22 seconds. While she did not mention Lucretia's speed, she said that Hickory Bill, Lucretia's son, could run a quarter in 21 seconds—that undoubtedly would be a scored quarter. She also said that Hickory Bill ran the half mile in 46 seconds. As a two-year-old, she said, he ran an eighth in 10 seconds flat. This claim has some authenticity because the race was against Never Frets, who at the time held at least a track record (according to Mrs. Watkins, the world's record) for the half mile in 46 seconds. Also, the race was well attended, and several watches were on both horses.

George Clegg bred his Watkins mares to Little Joe. Lucretia's first colt was called Joe D (sometimes spelled Jodie). He proved to be a real racehorse, even beating Della Moore. Hickory Bill also sired some good colts. One of his best known was the Old Sorrel, the foundation horse of the King Ranch Quarter Horses.

Louisiana

Della Moore would have been a great mare in anybody's book. She was born in Louisiana, probably in 1905 or very close to that date. Not only was she one of the fastest mares of her period, but two of her sons created separate Quarter Horse families—Joe Reed and Joe Moore.

Della was foaled near Scott, Louisiana, on the farm of Ludovic Stemmans. Ludovic, like so many other French-Louisianans, loved horses and short racing. The best and fastest mare he ever owned was Bell. She was a daughter of Sam Rock, who some claim was Thoroughbred. Although he is not listed in *Sires of American Thoroughbreds* (published by the Blood Horse in 1938), he could have been clean-bred.

When it came time to breed Bell, Ludovic planned to take her to Dewey, the fastest stallion in Louisiana. Dewey should have been a good one. He was by *Sain and out of a Luke Blackburn mare, and Luke Blackburn was by *Bonnie Scotland and out of a Lexington mare. Luck ruled otherwise, however. Dewey was matched against a horse called Dedier, who beat him at his best distance, 256 yards. So Bell went to Dedier instead of Dewey.

The following spring Della Moore was dropped. Little is known about Dedier, her sire. Helen Michaelis concluded after much research that he was probably sired by the Thoroughbred Henry Star and that his dam was a Quarter running mare whose name has been forgotten.

Misleading or forgotten breedings are the bane of anyone trying to work out pedigrees. It was not just the Louisiana short-horse men who forgot the breedings of their racehorses. Quarter horsemen have always been willing to give you a race but slow to give you the breeding of the horse they plan to run. The simple fact is that a horse of unknown pedigree is easier to match than the son or daughter of a well-known sire or dam. Also, a racehorse man would buy a horse just to match. They were much more interested in the horse's speed than in his ancestors.

Della Moore ran her first race when she was still a suckling foal. These baby races were called "milk races" or "milk runs," and they served a dual purpose. By watching their young stock run, the owners could get a line on their future prospects and at the same time indulge in their favorite pastime, betting. The way they did it was to take the mare and foal to the nearest straightaway track. At the starting line men would hold the foals while the mothers were led up the track to a predetermined spot. While the babies were calling their mothers, and the mothers were nickering in return, the foals were released. The first across the line, which was a few yards short of where the mothers were being held, was the winner. Della was an easy winner in her milk race.

Della had several good races in her by the time she was a two-year-old. Cajun jockeys began riding at eight or nine years of age and were veterans before they were teenagers. Their light weight made these early races possible. Della was so fast that before long none of Ludovic's racing buddies cared to match her. She was also well known in the various parishes surrounding Lafayette. Ludovic let Demonstran Broussard race Della because he did not wish to leave home. Broussard hired Boyd Simar to train her. Boyd campaigned her throughout Louisiana and soon had to go into Texas to get any worthwhile competition. Boyd Simar was from Abbeville, and short-horse racing was all he or his son Paul ever knew.

Della was later sold to Henry Lindsay, of Granger, Texas. In 1920 she was stabled in San Antonio while she was in training for a race. Next to her was the greatest sprinting Thoroughbred stallion of the time, Joe Blair. Joe Blair held several records but gained the greatest attention for his races with Pan Zarita at Juárez, Mexico. Incidentally, the mare Pan Zarita beat him in a race that in some respects was a forerunner of the Barbra B-*Fair Truckle match held about thirty years later, with the Quarter mares winning. Curiously the time for the quarter was the same for both mares, 21 3/5. Barbra B carried only 110 pounds, as did *Fair Truckle. Pan Zarita was carrying 120 pounds when she made that time against Joe Blair.

While Della was stabled next to Joe Blair, she was bred to him. One unauthenticated story has it that the stable boys were playing poker and Della was in heat and Joe Blair was kicking up such a fuss that they decided to let him breed her so that they could go on with their game. Why they were mated will never be known, but the next spring her first foal, Joe Reed, was dropped. A book could be written about Joe Reed and his get.

In 1922, Della Moore was purchased by Ott Adams and taken to his ranch at Alfred, Texas. He had been following her career and had decided that she was the dam to furnish him a son to replace Little Joe, who was getting old. Her first foal was a filly that Ott named Aloe. John Dial bought Aloe. Ott rebred Della to Little Joe, but she did not stick. She came in regularly but just would not get settled. Over the years Ott learned that for some reason she only had a foal every other year, regardless. In 1925, Della foaled Grano de Oro, and again John Dial bought the colt. On March 23, 1927, Della Moore produced a foal that suited Ott Adams to a T. He called the little fellow Joe Moore after his sire, Little Joe, and his dam, Della Moore.

Ott kept Joe Moore all of his life as his breeding stallion. Joe Moore proved to be equal in all respects to his half brother Joe Reed. In 1929, Della Moore foaled Panzarita by Paul El. She died in 1930. If any other mare produced two such different, yet outstanding, sires of early speed as Joe Reed and Joe Moore, she does not readily come to mind. Della was a true matriarch of the sprinting Quarter Horse.

Oklahoma

Oklahoma was the home of some excellent mares during the early years of the twentieth century. Just as he had been during the last of the nineteenth century, Charles Campbell, of Minco, was still the premier breeder, but new ones were appearing farther west around Cheyenne, Sayre, Elk City, and Foss. Western Oklahoma became an active breeding center and established a tradition that is still carried on today.

One especially outstanding mare was Bettie Campbell. She was bred and raised by that master breeder C. E. Campbell, of Minco. Campbell's contributions to the Quarter Horse extended over a period of almost forty years. He was a wealthy rancher whose main holdings were in Grady County, southwest of Oklahoma City. He also ran horses and cattle on Indian lands covering a vast territory. He is probably best remembered for stallions like Pid Hart, Bob Peters, Tom Campbell, Uncle Jimmy Gray, and Bonnie Joe. His mares were equally outstanding. Bettie Campbell was just one of his many mares.

Bettie was foaled in 1900 or 1901. Her sire was Bob Peters, a Campbell-raised stallion. Campbell had sent one of his good mares about two hundred miles north to Kansas to be bred to Mike Smiley's Pony Pete. He and Mike were good friends and racing rivals. The resulting foal was named Bob Peters. Bettie's dam was a Pid Hart mare. Pid Hart had been bred and raised by another friend of Campbell's, Shelby Stanfield, of Thorp Springs, Texas. As a short-horse breeder Stanfield was in a class with Smiley and Campbell. Pid Hart was by Shelby and out of Jenny Capps and had been a noted racehorse.

Charles Campbell was a lot like Tom Burnett in that he would try to buy any horse that beat him in a race. He also had learned that Bonnie Joe, son of Faustus and out of a daughter of *Bonnie Scotland, could be bought. Bonnie Joe was a bay stallion, foaled in 1894. His dam, Bonnie Rose, was one of *Bonnie Scotland's better daughters.

Campbell bred his new stallion, Bonnie Joe, to Bettie Campbell, and in 1906 a brown colt was dropped. Campbell named the little fellow after a trusted employee who was in charge of his breeding program, a man everyone called Uncle Jimmy. His last name was Gray, so the new foal became Uncle Jimmy Gray. He grew into a first-class racehorse and eventually was sold to the Army Remount Service. He was used by the service for many years. The last man to stand him for the army was Henry Pfefferling, who ran a public stable in San Antonio. Uncle Jimmy Gray proved to be a sire second only to Flying Bob as a producer of early speed in the 1920s to 1940s. Bettie Campbell had other good foals, most of them fillies, though the colt Minco Jimmy became almost as well known as his brother Uncle Jimmy Gray.

C. B. Campbell also bred Useeit. *The American Stud Book*

shows that she was a bay, foaled in 1917, sired by Bonnie Joe and out of Effie M by Bowling Green. Effie M was a half sister of Miss Blair. Miss Blair was the dam of Joe Blair. Many horsemen who took the trouble to run down the breeding of Useeit—some while she was still alive—claimed that her dam was one of Campbell's Quarter mares. These horsemen, as widely diverse as Quentin Reynolds, the writer, and Helen Michaelis, onetime secretary of the American Quarter Horse Association, agree on her dam's Quarter Horse blood.

Useeit's foal Black Gold, by Black Tony, won the Kentucky Derby. Even without Quarter Horse blood, Black Tony, with Peter Pan and Ben Brush up front in his pedigree, would have the speed necessary to win the Derby. Useeit also foaled Catchme by Jenkins's Bob Wade, and U Tell Um by the same stallion.

So much for Campbell. There were other good breeders in Oklahoma. The Meeks, of Foss, had an exceptional mare in Kate Bernard. She was a sorrel foaled in 1910. Her sire was Santa Claus by Red Buck. Alden Meek later sold Red Buck to his brother-in-law, Reed Armstrong. Kate Bernard was raced by Jim and Ralph Avant, who lived in Clinton. Later she had two outstanding foals, Kate Blair by Joe Blair and Kate Jones by Casey Jones.

There were two Oklahoma Queens, mother and daughter. The first Queen was foaled around 1910. She was sired by Tom Campbell by Bob Peters and out of Brunk's Queen by the Thoroughbred Quartermaster. She was bred and owned by John Harrel, of Canute. In 1920 she was bred to A. D. Reed and foaled the second Oklahoma Queen, sometimes referred to as Oklahoma Queen II. Among the first Oklahoma Queen's other progeny were Jack Dempsy by Big Boy. Oklahoma Queen II became the dam of Duck Hunter by A. D. Reed and Scarecrow by the same sire.

Babe Dawson was from an entirely different line of Quarter mares. Successful racehorses leave records, and infor mation is available about them. Quarter Horses, used for cow work and rodeo, do not receive as much publicity and so are soon forgotten—but not Babe Dawson. She was a brown, foaled in 1925. She was sired by Little Earl, Jr., by Little Earl and out of Queen by Little Earl. Little Earl was by Missouri Mike. All her foals were athletes and had good speed. Many became well known for cutting, roping, and dogging, as well as for occasionally matching a race. Some of her foals include Pet Dawson; Baldy (Troy Fort's great roping horse); Pistol Dawson; Oklahoma Star, Jr.; Little Babe; and Buckskin Dawson. All of them were bred by her owner, John Dawson, of Talala.

Texas

Texas seems to have had more than its share of both breeders and mares. W. W. Christian, Eugene Schott, Matt Renfro, Will Shely, Ott Adams, and Shelby Stanfield were no better than Campbell, of Oklahoma; Smiley, of Kansas; or Watkins, of Illinois; it just happened that there were more of them in the Lone Star State. This has been true from the time of Steel Dust and Shiloh right up to the present.

One of the Texas mares of this period was Old Mary. She was a dun, foaled in 1908. She was sired by Ben Burton and was out of Mandy by the Old Dutchman. She was bred by Dick Baker, of Weatherford, Texas. Jim McFarlane, a rancher who bought one of her sons, Yellow Wolf, verified this pedigree. Mary produced three great colts, all yellow duns, named Yellow Wolf, Yellow Bear, and Yellow Boy. The first two were by Weatherford Joe Bailey, and the last was by Burnett's Yellow Jacket.

Farther south a stallion named Traveler gained considerable fame, not entirely unjustified but certainly exaggerated. He would probably have been unheard of but for his get from two mares, Jenny and Fanny Pace. Fanny Pace had

Judge Thomas, Buster Brown, and Judge Welsh when bred to Traveler; Jenny had Little Joe, King (Possum in Arizona), and Black Bess.

Jenny is well worth mention. As is to be expected, Jenny had a great dam, May Mangum, discussed in the last chapter. It is not clear whether May was bred by Billy Fleming, of Belmont, who owned her sire, Anthony, or whether Will Shely took a mare to Belmont to be bred to Anthony. In either case the Shelys owned May during her productive years. Jenny's breeding was spotless.

Jenny, a brown, was foaled soon after 1890, at Alfred, in south Texas. Her sire was Sykes Rondo. When the Shelys sold her, Ott Adams, of Alfred, bought her, as well as Mamie Crowder, Julie Crowder, Moselle, and Little Kitty. These mares and their foals were the foundation on which Adams's successful breeding operations were carried out until his death in 1963 at the age of ninety-four.

Jenny foaled Little Joe in 1904 and King in 1905; both were, of course, by Traveler. King, or Possum, was her last foal; she died soon after his birth. Her bloodlines proved potent. Besides being the dam of Little Joe and King, she was the granddam of Zantanon and the great-granddam of Jess Hankins's King P-234. She was the granddam of Joe Moore and the great-granddam of Stella Moore. She was also the granddam of Ace of Diamonds, Dutch, Grano de Oro, Cotton Eyed Joe, Little King, Guinea Pig, and Red Cloud.

Another mare that Ott Adams bought from the Shelys was Mamie Crowder. She was born about 1900 and was sired by John Crowder by Billy and out of a Blue Eyes filly. Blue Eyes was by Sykes Rondo. In her younger days she was raced extensively. She ran a quarter mile in a match race against her half brother Ples Walters at the Dallas Fair in 1904. She won. Later, in a rematch at Kerrville, they tried to stretch her out by matching her for three-eighths, but she outran him at this distance also. Her two best-known foals were Captain Joe by Traveler and Ada Jones by Little Joe. More will be said about Ada Jones later.

Mamie Crowder had a close relative on the tracks at the same time that she was running. This mare was called Free Silver. She was a sorrel, foaled in 1902. She was by Rondo and out of a John Crowder mare. She was owned and raced by Cornelius Bass, of Eagle Pass and Piedras Negras. She was extremely popular in Mexico and was never beaten in that country. Helen Michaelis said that she was so popular that her picture was hung in Sanbourne's, in Mexico City. Even her brand showed plainly: a 7V connected. In Juárez she ran a 220 in 10½ seconds carrying 114 pounds. In another race in the same city she ran three-eighths in 33 seconds flat. She died of colic before she could be bred.

Katy Flyer, another mare with an interesting history, was foaled in 1914. Her breeder was F. G. Senne, of Hondo. Her sire was Paul Murray, and she was out of a Sleepy Joe mare. Her foal of note was Black Streak, by Uncle Jimmy Gray.

Katy was being used for farm work. One day when she was eleven years old, she was pulling a walking plow. Something frightened her, and she bolted. A mounted rider was nearby, but he could not get close to her and the plow. The witnesses decided maybe she could run. In 1926, at twelve years of age, she was sold to George Miller for $450, with the agreement that if she could not play polo he would get back $150. She could and did. Miller sold her the next year for $1,000 to a Judge Staddler, of Brackettville. It must have been a welcome change for her to be pampered with the other polo ponies after life as a plow mare.

The next three mares are good examples of how the best ones transmit their ability to their produce. The first was Annie May. She was a bay, foaled in 1898 or 1899. She was by Eureka and was bred by Shelby Stanfield, of Thorp Springs. He sold her to Webb Christian, of Big Spring. She ran successfully and could win from a quarter to three-eighths mile.

She was the dam of Barney Lucas by Traveler, foaled in 1910.

Now the filly foal. Annie T was named for her dam with the T for Traveler (her sire) added. She carried on the family tradition. Annie T ran and then produced Wandering Jew by Palm Reader (TB) in 1908 and Leman by Dr. Curtis (TB) in 1909. Christine C was her filly. She was sired by Palm Reader (TB). Christine C ran a little and then produced Lenox by Bobby Lowe, Money Back by Recluse (TB), Sam Sparks by Dr. Curtis (TB), and Jackie Boy by Barney Lucas. Just these three mares could have kept a man in the short-horse business.

Pan Zarita is considered by many racehorse historians the equal of any sprinter who ever lived. There is no doubt that she had no equal during her days on the tracks. Her wins and her world records prove that. Her dam was probably Caddie Griffith. Caddie was bred and owned by Jim Newman, of Sweetwater. Her sire was Rancocas (TB). His dam was Ontario by *Bonnie Scotland. Caddie's dam was Boston Girl, whose dam was Sally Johnson by Blue Dick.

Caddie Griffith foaled Pan Zarita in 1910. The sire was Abe Frank, a Thoroughbred sired by Hanover whose dam, Bourbon Belle, was also sired by *Bonnie Scotland. Pan Zarita matured into a rather good-sized sprinter, standing 15-2 hands high and weighing 1,000 pounds in running shape. She was a deep sorrel. Jim Newman, of Sweetwater, bred and raised both her dam and her. Newman raised his best sprinters using Thoroughbreds with early speed and crossing them on his good Quarter mares. He bought Abe Frank, a favorite in the Kentucky Derby of 1902, from George Bennett, of Memphis, and he bought Rancocas from P. Lorrillard in 1885.

There has been considerable discussion about the distaff side of Pan Zarita's pedigree. Helen Michaelis decided that Caddie Griffith was by Peter McCue. Walter Trammell, whose father raised horses with a relative, Jim Newman, wrote to me on December 20, 1939, telling me that Pan Zarita was out of Minyon by Rancocas. Minyon's dam was Heeley, who was by Blue Dick and out of Mittie Stephens. The Jockey Club has her entered as out of Caddie Griffith by Rancocas. Any of this blood could have produced Pan Zarita, though none seems more reasonable to me than the pedigree given by the Jockey Club.

Pan Zarita could fly. At Juárez, Mexico, on February 10, 1915, carrying 120 pounds, she ran five-eighths on a circular track in 57 1/5 seconds. It has been considered both a track and a world's record. She ran many of her best races at Juárez, including her famous match race with Joe Blair. She was so popular at the fairgrounds in New Orleans that after her unexpected death she was buried in the infield, as was Black Gold. (It is poignant that two sprinters, both raised by top Quarter Horsemen, one in Oklahoma, and one in Texas, should lie today side by side, far from their southwestern homes.) No other sprinter, filly or colt, has appeared since to rival the flying feet of the sorrel Pan Zarita.

Bettie Campbell's great son Uncle Jimmy Gray passed on her excellence to a whole series of fast mares. A classic example was the sorrel mare Manosa, foaled in 1925. She was by Uncle Jimmy Gray and out of Meanie by Possum. She was bred either by Carol Thompson, of Devine, or by Jim Roach, of Big Foot, probably by the latter. She could run, and she had seven outstanding foals. They were Cyclone by Alamo (a son of Uncle Jimmy Gray) in 1928, Jack Mystery by My Texas Dandy in 1929, Tommy's Pride by My Texas Dandy in 1930, Ginger Rogers by My Texas Dandy in 1932, Jimmy King by Captain White Sox in 1938, Carol Dandy by My Texas Dandy in 1939, and Chain Lay by My Texas Dandy in 1941. In 1936, Carol Thompson bought Manosa from Roach.

Ginger Rogers, mentioned in the preceding paragraph, was a running mare if there ever was one. She was bred by Jim Roach. In 1938 she was purchased by J. D. Raines, of

Mexico City, who went to Texas to buy the fastest mare he could find. She had been racing all through Texas and Louisiana, and it is doubtful that he could have found a faster short mare than Ginger Rogers. In 1937, E. F. Lovelace had campaigned her in Oklahoma and Texas and had won eighteen consecutive match races. The only time for her that can be accepted without doubt was made in a race she ran at Junction. The track was chained, the distance was exact, and there were three reputable men with watches on her. Although she was not pushed, she ran the quarter mile in 22.2 seconds.

Chain Lay, a full sister of Ginger Rogers, was sorrel, foaled in 1941. C. R. Thompson, of Devine, bred her. She was incorrectly registered with the Jockey Club as being by Tommie Gray and out of Donna Tuck. She ran on tracks recognized by the American Quarter Racing Association, and one of her best times was 330 yards in 17.7 on a slow track, carrying 120 pounds. She was almost impossible to beat in a two-horse match race. She also had electrically timed races of 220 in 12.4 and a quarter in 23 seconds flat.

Still another daughter of Uncle Jimmy Gray was Lady Speck. She was a sorrel, bred by John Kenedy, of Sarita. She won fame by beating the good King Ranch horse Don Manners in 22.6 on the Kingsville track. She also beat Cyclone at 350 yards in 18½ seconds. Both times were recognized by the American Quarter Horse Association.

Mentioning the King Ranch recalls some extremely good mares associated with Bob Kleberg and the King Ranch. If there was one foundation to this sprinting family, it was Ada Jones. Ada was foaled at the close of World War I on Ott Adams's ranch in south Texas. She was certainly no beauty, being a rather plain red roan with a big bald face, a white hind leg, and many more white hairs than red on her lower chest and belly. A close examination, however, would show short, alert ears; a deep, wide chest; and knees and hocks close to the ground. She had long, powerful legs from hip to hock and from shoulder to knee. Her neck was a little short and straight, but she had a clean throatlatch. Her sire was Little Joe; her dam, Mamie Crowder, mentioned earlier. Ada was taken to the tracks as a two-year-old, and her first race made her a marked mare. The race was run at the Kenedy Fair in 1920. As Ott Adams told me the story, she defeated a fast bunch of horses, traveling three-eighths on a heavy track in 39 seconds. This race was held only thirty days after a saddle was put on her back for the first time. Ott loved to raise fast horses and to watch them run, but he never raced any himself. He sold Ada. She was raced by several men, and when her racing days were over, John Dial, of Goliad, bought her.

Dial raised several colts by Ada, but it was her foal Chicaro Hallie that is of interest here. John Dial had purchased Chicaro, a Thoroughbred sired by *Chicle and out of Wendy by Peter Pan. Chicaro was Hallie's sire; Ada, her dam. Bob Kleberg, of the King Ranch, stopped in at John Dial's place looking for some Little Joe blood. He bought Ada and her daughter Chicaro's Hallie, and, almost as an afterthought, he bought Chicaro too. That was in 1934, when Ada Jones was sixteen years old.

Ada Jones and her daughter Chicaro's Hallie founded a dynasty of sprinters for Bob Kleberg. Hallie was a winner as a two-year-old. Like her mother she won her first outing. Hallie's daughter Bruja was to do the same thing a few years later. Then the fourth in a line, Miss Princess, also won her first outing, all in the family tradition. Ada Jones, her daughter Chicaro's Hallie, her granddaughter Bruja, and her great-granddaughter Miss Princess all were winners, and all were outstanding. It was Miss Princess who finally was able to take the world's championship away from the fabulous Shue Fly.

Miss Princess was not the only fast daughter of Bruja. Encantadora set a world's record for 5 furlongs of 57 seconds flat. Haunted ran 4½ furlongs at Golden Gate Fields in 52 flat, and Mickie ran 350 yards in 18 flat. Miss Princess equaled the world's record for 2½ furlongs running it in 27 1/5 and set the then-modern record for the quarter mile in 22 flat.

When Ada Jones arrived at the King Ranch, she was bred to the Old Sorrel, and her fillies returned to the brood-mare bands to add an infusion of Little Joe blood. Consequently none of her offspring foaled after she was taken to the King Ranch reached the short tracks.

Another interesting King Ranch mare was Chicaro Jane. Although she was registered in the Jockey Club, as were Chicaro's Hallie, Bruja, and Miss Princess, Chicaro Jane was a half-breed Quarter mare. She was out of the good Little Joe mare Plain Jane and was sired by Chicaro. She became the dam of Don Manners when bred to Lovely Manners. Plain Jane's dam was Mamie Roberts, who was by Ace of Hearts.

One more Texas mare should be mentioned, Little Fanny. She was a bay, foaled in 1937, sired by Joe Reed and out of Fanny Ashwell, a Thoroughbred. She was bred by J. W. House, of Cameron, and bought by Bert Wood, of Tucson. Little Fanny foaled one of the great sires of speed-producing females of the century, Leo, by Joe Reed II. Little Fanny was also the dam of Bell Reed, Ashwood, Tick Tack, Tucson, Little Sister W, and Sassey Time.

VI

Guidelines Used in Compiling This Volume

One thing that the reader of this book must remember is that pedigree research is not an exact science. Newspaper accounts, studbooks, even entries in the same studbooks can vary. Often a primary source provides only a vague outline, which must be filled in. Sometimes it is not difficult to arrive at a satisfactory fact, figure, or pedigree. For example, you know that a certain horse was foaled in 1810 but have no dates for its dam. You know that the dam was probably at least two years old and probably no more than twelve or thirteen at the time the foal arrived. You guess halfway—that she was seven; therefore, the dam was born, according to your estimate, around 1803. That is usually close enough for reasonable research—even though the odds are over-whelmingly against the mare's having been foaled in precisely 1803. When a date is arrived at in this fashion, a question mark appears after the date.

Again, supposedly primary accounts may differ. For example Barney Owens was foaled in or near 1870, and Bob Wade was foaled in 1886. Both were out of Nettie Overton, who was supposedly foaled in the late 1860s. Now comes the enigma. Roan Dick is given as the sire not only of Bob Wade but also of Nettie Overton. Where do you go from there? It is impossible at this late date to make all these details fit.

Thoroughbreds, and how to treat them in a Quarter Horse book, are also a problem. The fact that a number of the successful ones were falsely registered compounds the problem. Others, like *Bonnie Scotland and Kentucky Whip, were purebred and proved to be outstanding sires of sprinters, as good as or better than many of those that slipped in the back door. The decision was to indicate that they were Thoroughbred if they were relatively unknown, but horses such as *Janus, Sir Archy, Kentucky Whip, and Three Bars are not specifically identified. One can easily look up any that are unknown in *Sires of the American Thoroughbred* or in the companion volume to this book, *Foundation Sires of the American Quarter Horse.*[1]

In the registry that follows, pedigrees for stallions are often omitted, especially if they appear in *Foundation Sires of the American Quarter Horse.* The principal interest here is in the bloodlines of the dams. No doubt I will be questioned for occasionally giving a different pedigree for a Thoroughbred from that found in *The American Stud Book* or the Jockey Club records. When a different pedigree is given, however, it is the result of several different sources, all of an original nature, such as owner's or breeder's statements. All the Jockey Club had was an application, probably filled out by the horse's trainer, who wanted to get the horse on the recognized tracks. The Jockey Club always has the benefit of the doubt if only one other reference shows a different pedigree.

Another unfortunate fact is that many good Quarter mares who were not run on recognized tracks left no records that I could uncover. That was especially true of the good cow horses, cutting horses, rodeo horses, and ranch horses. By its very nature racing, like baseball, is a sport that keeps records—either in the appropriate association or in newspaper and sports-journal accounts. That is the reason why many mares who foaled great Quarter Horses not intimately connected with racing are left out. There was no information available to me beyond a name.

[1] Norman: University of Oklahoma Press, 1976.

VII

Key for Finding Dams

Horses are listed alphabetically by first name in the registry; for example, *Ada Jones*, not *Jones, Ada*.

The owner's name, if commonly used, is found after the name; for example, *Switch, Puckett's*, not *Puckett's Switch*.

The adjective "young," "old," "big," or "little" is found after the name; for example, *Mary, Old*, not *Old Mary*.

Color is considered part of the name; for example, *Gray Alice*, not *Alice, Gray*.

A commonly used second name appears in parenthesis; for example, *Fair Chance (Verna Grace)*.

A secondary name is cross-referenced; for example, *Verna Grace*, see *Fair Chance*.

An unnamed mare, referred to by her sire, is listed under the sire; for example, *Arch Oldham Mare*, not *Mare, Arch Oldham*.

Available information is generally given in the following order: (1) name and color, if known, (2) foaling date, (3) date of death, (4) physical characteristics, (5) pedigree, (6) breeder, (7) owner or owners, and (8) other pertinent facts.

VIII

Foundation Dam Registry

A

ADA JONES. Ada Jones was foaled in 1918 and died in 1941. She was a red roan with considerable white on her face. She was by Little Joe and out of Mamie Crowder. Ada was bred by Ott Adams, of Alfred, Texas. She was raced, and finally ended up in the hands of John Dial, of Goliad, Texas, who sold her to Bob Kleberg, of the King Ranch. That was in 1934. Some of her better-known get include Hallie by Chicaro (TB), Cambiada by Chicaro (TB), John Dial by Chicaro (TB), and a number of fillies by the Old Sorrel. For more on her prepotent family, see CHICARO'S HALLIE.

ADALINA. Adalina was foaled in 1926 (?) and was sired by Little Joe and out of Black Bess. She was bred by Ott Adams, of Alfred, Texas. She was the dam of Cotton in 1934, of Pauleta in 1931, and of Chaparita in 1930 (?), all by Paul El.

ADELAIDE. Adelaide was foaled in 1865 (?) and died in 1890 (?). She was a sorrel, sired by Pudhomme (TB) and out of a good Martin short mare. She was bred by Marion Martin, of Corsicana, Texas, She was the dam of Navarro by Peacock by Flying Dutchman.

AFTON. Little is known about this mare except that she was sired by Harmon Baker and was owned by Matt Renfro, of Sonora, Texas. She was the dam of Pee Wee by Everett (TB).

AGATE. Agate was foaled in 1915 (?) and died in 1930 (?). She was sired by Joe T and bred by Harry Clark, of Boise City, Oklahoma. In the 1930s she became the dam of Nabob, a bay colt sired by Brave Bob (TB).

AGGY. Aggy, a chestnut, was foaled in 1817 (?), sired by Eaton's Little Janus and out of a Dare Devil mare. She was bred and owned by James Sommerville, of North Carolina. In 1822 she produced the chestnut colt Tickler by Timoleon.

ALAZAN, see ALLIE SAN.

ALICE. Alice was foaled in 1880 (?) and died in 1895 (?). She was sired by Grindstone and bred by John N. Nasworthy, of San Angelo, Texas. One of her foals was Hal Fisher, a brown colt foaled in 1887, sired by Buck Walton (TB).

ALICE. Alice was foaled in 1873 (?) and died in 1890 (?). She was sired by Old Billy and out of Paisana. She was bred by William Fleming, of Belmont, Texas, and raced extensively by Jim Brown, of Giddings, Texas. She is only known to have produced one foal, Maud by Billy. Brown bought her at a race meet in San Angelo and lost her in a match race in the Indian Territory of Oklahoma.

ALICE. Alice was foaled in 1858 and died in 1880 (?). She was by Harry Bluff and out of Munch Meg. She was bred by Joe Lewis, of Hunnewell, Kansas. She was a half sister of Steel Dust and a full sister of June Bug, and was sometimes referred to as Sister of June Bug. In 1872 she foaled Bobby Cromwell by Cold Deck, and in 1874 Grasshopper by Cold Deck.

ALICE (MLLE DENISE). Alice was sired by Arch Oldham and out of an Army Remount (TB) mare. She was bred at the Fort Robinson, Nebraska, station. She foaled Archer, a bay colt, in 1921 by Cannon Shot.

ALICE, BIG. Big Alice was foaled in 1906 (?) and died in 1924 (?). She was sired by Pid Hart and was out of a

83

Meek Quarter mare. She was bred by Milo Burlingame, of Cheyenne, Oklahoma. Her best foal was John Wilkes, by Peter McCue. Big Alice's dam was by Good Enough by Ned Hanger. She weighed 1,325 pounds.

ALICE, LITTLE. Little Alice, a bay, was foaled in 1917. She was sired by Baby by Alex Mitchell and out of Old Alice by Little Buck by Buck Walton. She was bred either by Barry Ketchum or by Jim Harkey, of Fort Stockton, Texas.

ALICE McGILL. Alice McGill was by Little Hickory Bill by Hickory Bill and out of a mare by Mac by Little Rondo. The Mac mare was bred by A. L. East, of Sarita, Texas. Alice McGill was bred by the McGill brothers, of Alice, Texas, and later owned by Horace Wilson, of Forth Worth, Texas. She is primarily remembered as the dam of the racehorse Horace Wilson (Jimmie Allred) by Joe Hancock.

ALICE WOOD. Alice Wood was foaled in 1892 (?) and died in 1912 (?). She was sired by Peter McCue and was out of Dora Wood. She was bred by Fred T. Wood, of Abilene, Texas. She foaled the bay colt John MacKay when bred to Dan Tucker in 1900.

ALICIA. Alicia was foaled in 1928 and died in 1945 (?). She was sired by Pancho Villa and out of Alice by Billy Sunday. She was bred by Joy Weakley, of Wharton, Texas. She could run, as could her foal Lightning Weaver by Tony McGee.

ALLIE, OLD. Allie was foaled in 1923 and died in 1940 (?). She was sired by Peter McCue and was out of Flaxie O'Neal. She was bred by William Francis, of Elk City, Oklahoma, and also owned at one time by Frank Malek, of Rosenberg, Texas. She is listed in *The Half-Breed Stud Book* as by Peter McCue and out of a Quarter mare. Some of her produce include Oklahoma Shy by A. D. Reed, Red Bird by Scotsman (TB), and Rainy Day (Gray) by Midnight.

ALLIE SAN (ALAZAN). Allie San was foaled in or around 1928 and appears to have died about 1940. She was sired by Lone Star and bred by Josephine Davenport, of Center Point, Texas. She foaled Hill Cat in 1935 when bred to Goldie II (TB).

ALLINE D. Alline D was foaled in 1918 (?) and died in 1932. She was sired by Withers and bred by Joe Parker, of Gorman, Texas. She is remembered as the dam of Billy Dawson by Barney Lucas, who was foaled in 1927.

AMANDA MILLER. Unfortunately little is known about this great mare, and many details of the information we do have conflict. It seems most likely that she was foaled around Plymouth, Illinois, in or about 1880. In 1885 she foaled Jim Miller by Roan Dick. He held the world's record for a quarter mile before Bob Wade. All her produce were racehorses of the very top class.

ANGELINE. Angeline, a bay, was foaled in 1881. She was sired by Pickpocket and out of July. She was bred by H. Pickrel, of York, Nebraska, and raised by C. R. Pickrel, of the same town. Her produce include a bay filly named Very Soon, foaled in 1887; a bay colt called Tom Edwards, foaled in 1888; and another called Oscar, foaled in 1890.

ANN. Ann, a sorrel, was foaled in about 1900. She was by Traveler and out of a mare carrying the blood of Rondo. She was a full sister of Texas Chief, and she was bred by W. W. Lock, of Kyle, Texas. Her best-known foal was Sutherland by Hickory Bill.

ANNA STATIA. Anna was by Peter McCue, and she was foaled shortly after 1900. In 1924, while she was owned by John Wilkins, of San Antonio, Texas, she produced Maru San by Uncle Jimmy Gray.

ANNA VETO. Anna Veto, a sorrel, was foaled in 1873 and died in 1885 (?). She was sired by Veto and out of Idaho. She was bred by either John Spark or C. M. Hutchinson, of Liberty, Missouri.

ANNIE HAWTHORNE. Annie Hawthorne's dam was purchased by William Anson when he was buying horses for the Boer War. He bred the mare to Jim Ned, and the resulting filly was Annie Hawthorne. Anson lived at that time at Christoval, Texas. Annie became the dam of Foster's Billy Anson and of Whitehead's Billy Anson, both of whom were by Harmon Baker.

ANNIE L. Annie L was foaled in 1928 (?) and died in 1945 (?). She was sired by Billy Sunday and was out of Lady by Little Joe. She was bred by Ott Adams, of Alfred, Texas.

ANNIE LEE. Annie Lee was foaled in or about 1880. She was called a Quarter mare, but her breeding is not recorded. She was owned by Wade McLemore, of Belmont, Texas, and by Tom King, of the same town. In 1890 she foaled Sam Jones, a sorrel colt by Buck Walton (TB).

ANNIE, LITTLE. Little Annie was foaled somewhere around 1900. She was crippled but was nonetheless a dainty sorrel with three white stockings. She was sired by Jeff C. by Printer and out of Bess (Bessie). She was raised by Jim Cooper, of Hammon, Oklahoma, or by one of the Trammells, who lived in the same general area. Her best known foal was Chief by Peter McCue. Her last owner was Claude Stinson, of Claude, Oklahoma.

ANNIE MAY. Annie May, a bay, was foaled in 1898 and died in 1912 (?). She was sired by Eureka and out of a good Stanfield Quarter mare. She was bred by E. Shelby Stanfield, of Thorp Springs, Texas, and later purchased by D. W. Christian of Big Spring, Texas. She ran successfully at distances from a quarter to three-eighths mile. She was bred to Traveler and between 1902 and 1911 produced Jacquette, Anne T, Mary T, Barney Lucas, and Ola N.

ANNIE SPRING. Annie Spring was foaled about 1900 and died about twenty years later. She was black and had been sired by Democrat, a Standardbred stallion. Her dam was a good Quarter mare owned by her breeder, Andrew Spring, of Seguin, Texas. She produced Coley, a black stallion sired by Little Jack by Anthony in 1908.

ANNIE T. Annie T was foaled in 1903 (?) and died in 1920 (?). She was sired by Traveler and was out of Annie May. She was bred and owned by D. W. Christian, of Big Spring, Texas. Among her produce were Leman by Dr. Curtis (TB) in 1909, Christian C (f.) by Palm Reader (TB) in 1906, and Wandering Jew by Palm Reader (TB) in 1908.

APRIL FOOL. Little is known about April Fool except that she must have been a good individual or Coke Roberds would not have owned her. Roberds lived at Hayden, Colorado. She was the dam of Jiggs, a palomino colt by Fred Litze, foaled in 1925. Chances are that she was by Old Fred and that she was bred by S. Dawson.

APRIL FOOL. April Fool was foaled in 1868 and was an attractive bay mare. Her sire was Waterloo (TB), and her dam was Fanny Daily by Blacknose. She was bred by Dr. W. H. Henderson, of Saint Louis, Missouri, and raced by Sprague and Akers, of Kansas. When she was no longer raced, she was purchased by J. J. Trask of Walla Walla, Washington. For Trask she produced Victoria Viney, Valley Tan, and Kittie Van, all by Vanderbilt.

APRON FACE. Apron Face was foaled in 1900 (?) and died in 1919 (?). She was a bald-faced mare sired by Little Danger and out of a mare by Jeff C. She was bred by John Armstrong, of Elk City, Oklahoma, and later owned by his brother, Reed, who lived at Foss, Oklahoma. She is best remembered as the dam of Dr. Blue Eyes by A. D. Reed.

ARCH OLDHAM MARE. The Arch Oldham Mare was owned by Crawford Sykes, of Nixon, Texas. She was by *Gallantry (TB), and she was foaled in 1890 (?). In 1916 she foaled Prince Oldham (Prince Odem) by Rex Beach (TB).

ARTIE. Artie, a bay, was foaled in 1870. She was by Billy and out of Paisana. Artie was bred by W. B. Fleming, of Belmont, Texas, and became the dam of Alex Gardner by Anthony.

AUNT JOE. Aunt Joe was foaled in 1895. She was sired by Sol Cleveland and out of Heeley. She was bred by J. F. Newman, of Sweetwater, Texas. In 1904 she foaled the sorrel colt Kari Koff by Rancocas (TB).

AURY. Aury was foaled in 1886 (?) and was sired by Old Dutchman by Lock's Rondo. She was out of a mare by Little Brown Dick by Old Billy. She was undoubtedly bred by C. R. Haley, of Sweetwater, Texas. She foaled Susie McQuirter when bred to Little Ben.

B

BABE. Babe was sired by Wildcat by Jim Ned and was owned by Ben Savage, of Steamboat Springs, Colorado. She was the dam of Roman Gold by Old Nick, foaled in 1924.

BABE ANSON. Babe Anson was by Harmon Baker. She was bred by William Anson and owned by Tom Henderson, of El Dorado, Texas. She was the dam of Herren's Hardtack by Chip by First Chip (TB).

BABE COOK. Babe was sired by Nedwood by Possum and out of Lady by Guinea Pig. She became the dam of Buck Clayton, a sorrel stallion foaled in 1937 by Red Joe of Arizona.

BABE DAWSON. Babe Dawson, a brown, was foaled in 1925 and lived until 1946. She was sired by Little Earl, Jr., by Little Earl and out of Queen by Little Earl. She was owned, and perhaps bred, by John Dawson, of Talala, Oklahoma. She was an outstanding producer. Among the many colts she had were Pet Dawson by Jeff, Oklahoma Star, Jr., by Oklahoma

Star, and Baldy (Troy Fort's roping gelding), Pretty Lady, Bay Babe, and Flapper Dawson, all by Red Buck.

BABE LOWRY. Except for the fact that she was sired by Yellow Jacket about 1925, little is known about Babe Lowry. Clyde Lowry, of Cedar Vale, Kansas, obtained her from a man named Borrum while he was foreman of Borrum's ranch. Borrum bought her in Fort Worth in 1930.

BABIE STALKS. Babie Stalks was by Stalks by John Wilkins and out of a mare by Charles Berry (TB). She was owned by S. B. Morse, of McLean, Texas, and was the dam of Bud Thomas, a sorrel stallion foaled in 1939.

BABY GIRL. Baby Girl was sired by Red Cloud and out of Nellie Girl by Baby King. She was the dam of Dreamy by Delmor.

BABY HELMS, see BOBBIE HELMS.

BABY KING. Baby King was sired by Possum and out of a Quarter mare. She was owned by J. T. McKinney, of Willcox, Arizona. She was the dam of Mack by Delmor (TB).

BABY RUTH. Baby Ruth was May Mangum's last foal, dropped in 1904. She was sired by Sykes Rondo. She was bred by the Shelys, of Alfred, Texas, and later owned by Mangum and Sykes, of Nixon, Texas. She had three good foals by Cotton Eyed Joe, Madam Murray, Billy Mangum, and Joe Ratliff; and Paul El by Hickory Bill.

BALD-FACED MARE, THE. The Bald-Faced Mare was by Hickory Bill and owned by George Clegg, of Alice, Texas. She was the dam of Red Chief by Little Rex.

BALL. Ball was sired by Hero (TB) and bred by Hugh Watkins, of Oakford, Illinois. She was the dam of Duck Hunter, who was sired by Peter McCue and foaled in 1901.

BARBEE DUN. Barbee Dun was foaled in 1881 (?) and was by Lock's Rondo and out of Mary Lee. She was bred by W. W.

Lock, of Kyle, Texas, and later owned by Jim Barbee, of Kyle, Texas, and still later by John Parks, of the same town. She was the dam of Yellow Jacket by Little Rondo, foaled in 1908.

BARNES' BLACK MARE. Barnes' Black Mare was by Billy McCue and owned by John Burson, of Silverton, Texas. She was the dam of Choctaw by Line Up (TB).

BATHSHEBA. Bathsheba was by Balleymooney and out of Betty by Madrigalian (TB). She was bred and owned by Dan D. Casement, of Manhattan, Kansas. She foaled Manhattan Red in 1939 after being bred to Deuce.

BAY KATE. Bay Kate was foaled in 1874 (?). She was sired by Norfolk (TB) and was out of Big Gun (Kate George). She was bred by Theodore Winters, of California and Nevada. She was later sold to T. J. Knight, of Beatrice, California. She had four outstanding running horses by Joe Hooker (TB), Tom Atchison in 1882, Ukiah in 1884, Walter Overton in 1885, and Isabella in 1887.

BAY ORPHIE. Bay Orphie was sired by Senator and raised on the 7-11 Ranch at Hot Springs, South Dakota. She was the dam of Billy Sunday by Tom Sunday (TB).

BAY PUSS. Bay Puss was by Mounts and was foaled in the late 1860s. She was bred and owned by E. Shelby Stanfield, of Thorp Springs, Texas. She was the dam of Jenny Caps, foaled in the early 1880s.

BAY TIGER MARE. The Bay Tiger Mare was sired by Tiger by Kentucky Whip and out of an unpedigreed short-race mare. She was bred by James Keith and later owned by George Thomas, both of Kentucky. She was the dam of Brown Kitty by Birmingham, of Nellie Harden by Boston, and of Model by Wagner.

BEAUTY. Beauty was by Captain Joe by Traveler and out of a King Ranch mare by Blue Eyes. She foaled Albert by Alamo in 1929.

BEAUTY. Beauty was by Billy Mason. Neither breeder nor owner is known to me. She was the dam of Rex K by Tad H (TB).

BEAUTY ROSE (TB). Beauty Rose is listed here only because of the quality of two foals she had when bred to Barney Lucas. They were George Duke, foaled in 1927, and Honest Dick, foaled in 1928.

BELL, see BESS.

BELLE. Belle, a bay, was foaled in 1897 and died in 1915. She was by Bell Punch by Whalebone and out of Judy by Bell Punch. She was bred by M. G. Michaelis, of Kyle, Texas. She foaled Dot by Kalamus (TB) in 1908 and Belle Wood by Honest Bob in 1912.

BELLE, ZERENGUE'S. Zerengue's Belle, a fast Quarter mare, was sired by the Louisiana Dedier. She was raced and owned by Noah Zerengue, of Abbeville, Louisiana. When John Dial, of Goliad, Texas, was taking Chicaro to Texas, he spent the night in Abbeville, and Chicaro was bred to Belle. Flying Bob was the resulting foal in 1929.

BELLE H. Belle H, a bay, was foaled in 1887. She was by Spinning and out of a mare by Jack Traveler. Spinning was by Voltigeur (TB). She was bred by Samuel Watkins, of Petersburg, Illinois. She was raced by James Owen, of Berlin, Illinois. Later she was sold to H. A. Trowbridge, of Wellington, Kansas. She foaled Queen of Berlin by Fib (TB) and also Billy Duff and Miss Patrick by the same stallion.

BELLE NELLIE. Belle Nellie, a bay, was foaled in 1875 (?). She was sired by a son of Tiger who was by Kentucky Whip (TB). Tiger's son was a black horse owned by a man named Fannin, of Gonzales County, Texas. Belle Nellie was the dam of May Mangum by Anthony.

BELLE OF KILBORN. Belle of Kilborn was by Peter McCue and was owned by George Newton, of Del Rio, Texas. She was the dam of Little Penny by Barnsdale (TB) in 1913.

BELLE OF OAKFORD, see CARRIE NATION.

BELLE REDMOND. Belle Redmond, a sorrel, was foaled in 1883 by Uncle Tom and out of Crazy Jane by Little Pete by Pony Pete. She was owned by G. Landon, of Elkhorn Grove, Illinois, and probably bred by John Day, of Asawata, Kansas.

BELLE STAR. Belle Star was by Big Danger by Berry's Cold Deck and was bred and owned by Coke Blake, of Pryor, Oklahoma. She was the dam of Red Devil by Idle Jack and of Red Man by Idle Jack. Idle Jack was by Tubal Cain.

BELLONA. Bellona was by Belle Aire (TB) and became the dam of Muckle John by Sir Archy.

BELLONA (WISE MARE). Bellona was foaled sometime in the 1860s and was sired by Franchie. She was owned by John M. Mathewson, of Lowell, Michigan. She was the dam of Odd Fellow by Bay Printer by Sweet Owen and of Franchette by the same stallion.

BELTON QUEEN. Belton Queen was by Guinea Boar and owned by Oliver and Bailes, of Seguin, Texas. She was the dam of Paisana. Like her daughter, she was probably foaled on Webb Scott's farm in Scott County, Kentucky. She was taken to Texas from Kentucky by E. Shelby Stanfield, of Thorp Springs, Texas.

BERTHA. Bertha was by Morris (TB) and out of Franchette by Bay Printer. She was bred and owned by John M. Mathewson, of Lowell, Michigan. She was the dam of One Dime, a bay colt foaled in 1888 by Afton (TB), and of Burnese, a sorrel mare foaled in 1890 by the same stallion.

BESS. Bess, a sorrel, was foaled in 1872, bred and owned by John Adams, of Woodland, California. She was sired by Oregon Charlie and out of a Pilgrim mare. Her second dam was a sister of Choctaw by Abe Jennings. She was a full sister of Brick. She had one filly and four colts; all could run. They were Ella T by Shannon (TB) and Uncle Billy, Beppo, Yolo, and Gasser, all by Joe Hooker (TB). Shannon and Joe Hooker were both by Monday.

BESS (BELL). Bess, a brown, was owned and bred by John Adams, of Woodland, California. She was foaled in 1889 by Uncle Billy and out of Lou B by Jim Douglas. Her second dam was Star by Brick.

BESS (BESSIE, OLD BESS). Bess, a bay, was foaled about 1900. She was owned by Claude Stinson, of Hammon, Oklahoma, who bought her from Jim Cooper, also of Hammon. She foaled Little Annie and Nettie Stinson when bred to Jeff C.

BESS, OLD, see BESS.

BESSIE, see BESS.

BESSIE KEOUGH. Bessie Keough was by Peter McCue, and was owned by Joseph Brown, of Petersburg, Illinois. She was the dam of Johnnie Brown by Starr McGee (TB) and of Peter Brown by the same stallion.

BESSIE MacKEN. Bessie MacKen, a gray, was foaled in 1897. She was by *Gallantry (TB) and out of Betty W. She was bred and owned by O. G. Parke, of Kyle, Texas. She was the dam of MacKen by Bannockburn (TB) and of Dorothy Duncan by Thrive (TB).

BESSIE McCUE. Bessie McCue was sired by Jack McCue and out of Marguerite by Barlow by Lock's Rondo. She was bred by W. J. Francis, of Elida, New Mexico.

BESSIE TAR TAR. Bessie Tar Tar was sired by a son of Tar Tar. She was owned by John Adams, of Woodland, California. She was the dam of Adams's stallion Walnut Bark by Blevin's Little Tom.

BESS McCLAIN. Bess McClain was by Joy by Jeff and out of Old Black Hill by Slasher. She was owned by Jack Hodgson, of Sayre, Oklahoma.

BETSEY DANCEY. Betsey Dancey was foaled in 1795. She was a popular colonial race mare sired by Twigg and out of a mare by Spadille. She was probably bred by William Moody, of North Carolina. She is found in Edgar and is also listed in Bruce.

BETSY. Betsy was by Henry Star and out of a Dedier mare. Gabriel Strauss said that she was out of a mare that came to Louisiana from Montreal, Canada. Ab Simpson said that she was raised around Abbeville, Louisiana. Elmer Hepler said that she was a Dedier mare. All could be right. She was the dam of Black Annie by Texas Henry.

BETSY. Betsy was sired by Kid Weller and bred by J. F. Newman, of Sweetwater, Texas. She was owned by Kenneth Montgomery, of Reydon, Oklahoma. She was the dam of Billy the Tough by A. D. Reed.

BETSY BAKER. Betsy Baker was by Wildon's La Branch. She was bred and owned in Oregon. She was the dam of Obe Jennings.

BETSY BOBBIE. Betsy, a brown, was foaled in 1926. She was sired by Rex Beach (TB) and was out of Emma Hill by Peter McCue. She was bred by John Dial, of Goliad, Texas, and owned by Cornelius Haby, of Riomedina, Texas. She foaled Gold Wing by High Prince (TB) and Gran Ortiz by Pride of India (TB).

BETTIE CAMPBELL. Bettie Campbell, a bay, was foaled at the turn of the twentieth century, sired by Bob Peters by Pony Pete and out of a Pid Hart mare. She was owned, and perhaps bred, by Charles B. Campbell, of Minco, Oklahoma. She was the dam of Uncle Jimmy Gray and Minco Jimmy, both sired by Bonnie Joe. They were foaled in 1906 and 1909, respectively. Jimmy Gray was registered as a Thoroughbred (the dam is given as Mary Hill) so that he could race on the organized tracks. Neither he nor his offspring could run a mile, however.

BETTY. Betty, a bay, was foaled in 1899 (?). She was a short mare bred by the McGonigals, of Midland, Texas. Later she was purchased by Albert Harrington, of Correo, New Mexico, and was also owned by Virgil Harrington, of Albuquerque, New Mexico. Her first foal, a filly named Miss Texas, sired by Rocky Mountain Tom, was born in 1903. Then she had two fillies and a colt, Rita, Trixie, and Little Boy, all by Jack Harrington.

BETTY LANE. Betty Lane was by Oklahoma Shy by A. D. Reed and out of a Thoroughbred mare named Virginia. She was owned by C. A. Lane, of Sunray, Texas. She was the dam of Little Abner, foaled in 1939.

BETTY LOU. Betty Lou was by Bubbling Over by Rainy Day and out of Star by Bobbie Burns (TB). She was owned by Melville H. Haskell, of Tucson, Arizona. She was the dam of Starbright and of Redwing, both sired by Red Joe of Arizona.

BETTY MANEY, see HENNIE FARROW.

BETTY W. Betty W, a sorrel, was foaled in 1887. She was by Silent Friend (TB) and out of Betty Bass. She was bred and owned by O. G. Parke, of Kyle, Texas. By four different Thoroughbreds she had six good foals: Fanny Wilson (1893), Trebor (1895), Pearl Barner (1896), Bessie MacKen (1897), Jack Poulton (1898), and Captain Terg Kyle (1900).

BETTY WHARTON. Betty Wharton was by the Thoroughbred Othello, and her best foal was Rebel. Rebel was in Texas from 1872 to 1887. Whether he died or was taken out of the state is not clear. He was owned in Texas by C. S. West and by John Hancock, of Austin. He may well have been named for, and sired by, Jim Brown's Rebel by Steel Dust. Betty

Wharton's Rebel is in Bruce, but that book shows his sire as Socks.

BEULAH BURNS. Beulah Burns was by Black Joe by Little Joe and was owned by L. J. Burns, of Yoakum, Texas. She was the dam of Chicaro, a black colt foaled in 1938 by Chicaro Bill by Chicaro (TB).

BIDDY. Biddy was by Smuggler and out of a roping mare. She was owned by Everett Bowman, of Hillside, Arizona. She foaled Snooper by Oklahoma Star and Sonny Boy by Ben Hur.

BILLY CAUTHORN'S MARE. This mare was by Dogie Beasley and was owned by C. R. White, of Brady, Texas. In 1932 she foaled Silver Streak, who was sired by Wag by Yellow Jacket.

BIRD. Bird was foaled in 1902 (?) and was a red sorrel. She was sired by Jack Traveler and was out of Kitty Clyde. She was bred by Sam Watkins, of Petersburg, Illinois. Later C. B. Campbell, of Minco, Oklahoma, bought her. She had twelve known foals, five of whom were Hattie V by Voltigeur (TB), Log Cabin by Dan Tucker, Pat Tucker by Dan Tucker, Bird of the Highlands by Duke of the Highlands (TB), and Lucretia M by Hero (TB).

BIRDIE (HOPKINS). Birdie, a bay, was foaled in or around 1890. She was by John Crowder and out of a Blackstone mare. She was taken from Texas to Arizona by Van Hastings, and she was later owned by J. J. Kennedy, of Bonita, Arizona. She ran a quarter mile at Phoenix in 22.2 seconds. Two of her produce were Dottie by No Good by Barney Owens and Mamie by the same sire.

BIRD OF THE HIGHLANDS. Bird of the Highlands was by Duke of Highlands and out of Bird by Jack Traveler. Her second dam was Kitty Clyde.

BISHOP'S MARE. Bishop's Mare was sired by Little Ace of Hearts and owned by J. S. Holman, of Sonora, Texas. She foaled Peter Pan in 1924 when bred to Ben Hur.

BLACK ANNIE. Black Annie was by Little Joe and out of Jeanette by Billy by Big Jim. She was bred by Ott Adams, of Alice, Texas.

BLACK ANNIE. Black Annie, a bay, was foaled in 1928. She was sired by Texas Henry and out of Betsy. The above breeding was given by Elmer Hepler. According to Robert Strauss, a Cajun jockey, her dam came into Louisiana from Montreal. In a letter to Helen Michaelis, Hepler said that Black Annie was by Rodney by Young D. J. and out of Betsy by Texas Henry. Her exact breeding will probably never be known.

BLACK BEAUTY. Black Beauty was foaled in 1890. She was sired by Joe Collins and out of Gray Alice by Steel Dust. She was owned by Jim Brown, of Giddings, Texas.

BLACK BEAUTY, OLD. Old Black Beauty was by Kansas King, Jr., by Kansas King and out of a mare by Buck Dawson. She foaled Goldie Dawson in 1926 when bred to Kansas King, Maud Dawson in 1928 when bred to Oklahoma Star, and Black Beauty Dawson when bred to Old Red Buck.

BLACK BELLE. Black Belle, a black, was foaled in 1883. She was by Langford (TB) and out of Bay Kate. She was bred by Theodore Winters, of Woodland, California. In 1888 she foaled Calamity by Joe Hooker.

BLACK BESS. Black Bess was a well-known race mare on the Pacific Coast. She was foaled in 1897 (?) in Oregon by Black Prince by Captain Jinks. She raced extensively in Oregon in 1902 and before that in California. She is listed in *The Half Breed Stud Book*.

BLACK BESS. Black Bess was foaled about 1915. She was sired by Captain Sykes, and her dam was Jenny. She was bred by Ott Adams, of Alfred, Texas. Her three best-known foals were Cotton Eyed Joe by Little Joe, El Rey by Traveler, and Adalina by Little Joe.

BLACK BIRD. Black Bird was foaled around 1918. She was a dark-sorrel mare sired by John Wilkes and out of a Renfro running mare. She was bred by J. E. Renfro, of Menard, and later owned by Matt Renfro, of Sonora. She was the dam of Mushmouth, a sorrel colt of 1926 sired by Everett (TB) and of Rio, another sorrel colt foaled in 1927 by the same sire.

BLACK DIAMOND II. Black Diamond II was foaled in 1934, sired by Foregone (TB) and out of Jeanne Paynne by Peter McCue. She was bred by R. C. Miller, of Fluvanna, Texas. She is listed in *The Half Breed Stud Book.*

BLACK EYED SUSAN. Susan, a brown, was foaled in 1821. She was sired by Tiger by Kentucky Whip and out of a mare by Albert. She was bred by George Burbridge and raced extensively by Burbridge and Gillespie and by George Viley. She was a Kentucky-bred mare. One of her most famous races was against Cherokee in 1825. She was bred to some of the best sprinting sires of her day. She produced Catharine by Bertrand, Richard Singelton by Kentucky Whip, Mistletoe by Cherokee, and Emily Johnson by Bertrand.

BLACK GEORGE. Black George, a black, was foaled about 1890, sired by Morland by Steel Dust. She was owned by either Walter Trammell or J. F. Newman, of Sweetwater, Texas. Her two foals of note, both by Barney Owens, were Easter and Danger.

BLACK GIRL. Black Girl, a bay, was foaled in 1883. She was sired by Cold Deck by Steel Dust and out of Mollie Hubert. She was bred by W. Tissley and later owned by J. A. Cook, of Oklahoma City. She foaled a black filly, Fears Me Not, by Nebraska in 1892 and Miss Rippy by the same stallion in 1893. In 1894 she produced Rendon by B. G. Bruce (TB).

BLACKIE. Blackie was sired by Pancho Villa by Little Joe and out of a Benevides Quarter mare. She was bred and owned by Manuel Benevides Volpe, of Laredo, Texas. She was the dam of Cuatro de Julio, a sorrel colt foaled in 1936, sired by Zantanon.

BLACK MARIA. Black Maria was a California short mare sired by the Thoroughbred Belmont. She was bred by J. Buckley and foaled the brown colt Osceola when bred to Norfolk in 1868.

BLACK PATTY. Black Patty was foaled in 1928 (?) and died in 1937. She was sired by Little Dick and out of a mare by Porte Drapeau (TB). Her second dam was Panmure (TB). She was owned by Albert May, of Wharton, Texas. She was the dam of Sally Rand by Tony McGee. She died while nursing Sally Rand, foaled in 1937.

BLACK SQUAW. Black Squaw was bred by Walter Trammell, of Sweetwater, Texas. Her breeding is unknown. She foaled Two Socks when bred to Old Joe Bailey.

BLAZE. Blaze was by Sykes' Rondo and out of May Mangum. She was bred by Crawford Sykes, of Nixon, Texas, and was the dam of Allen's Sykes by Sykes' Rondo in 1902.

BLAZE, LITTLE. Little Blaze was foaled in 1880 (?). She was a sorrel with a blaze, and she had a flaxen mane and tail. She was sired by Old Billy and was out of Paisana. She was bred by William B. Fleming, of Belmont, Texas, who sold her to the Corrigan brothers, of Beeville, Texas, who raced her. In a few years she broke down, and Fleming bought her back. In 1890 she foaled Little Hack by Anthony, and in 1891, Joe Murray by the same sire.

BLAZE, LITTLE. Little Blaze was sired by Possum and was an Arizona mare. She produced Top Kick by Brown Dick by Mose in 1890(?).

BLINKEY (MARY PORTER). Blinkey, a sorrel, was foaled in 1834 and died in 1854 (?). She was sired by Muckle John and out of a Printer Quarter mare (*American Stud Book*, 1:248). She was bred by J. C. Mason, of Kentucky, and later owned by Webb Ross, of Scott County, Kentucky. She had seven colts: Flying Dutchman by Gray Eagle (1845), Rheube by Boston (1848), Sweet Owen by Gray Eagle (1851), Wagner, Jr., by Wagner (1852), Printer by Gray Eagle (1853), Viley by Gray Eagle (1854), and Hempland by Yorkshire (1855).

BLONDIE S. Blondie S was by Lone Star by Gold Enamel (TB) and out of Emory Goldman by Captain Joe. There is some evidence that she was the dam of Clabber by My Texas Dandy. She was owned by Frank Smith, of Big Foot, Texas.

BLOSSUM. Blossum was by Billie Tom, and she was bred by J. M. Corder, of Sanderson, Texas. She was the dam of Gun Powder by Esquire (TB).

BLUE BELL. Blue Bell, a gray, was foaled in 1924. She was sired by Uncle Jimmy Gray and owned by D. Banard, of Tucson, Arizona. She ran three-eighths at Juárez, Mexico, in 1926 in 32 4/5 seconds. She was matched against Magician in that race. Magician ran the quarter in 21 4/5 seconds and led by a length, but after that Blue Bell caught up and won the race.

BLUE BIRD. Blue Bird was a 14-hand, blue-gray race mare. She was sired by Monkey, and her dam was by Lycurgus. She was probably bred by Edward Wyatt, Sr., of Virginia.

BLUE BIRD. Blue Bird, a gray, was foaled in 1883. She was reported to be by Old Billy, and may have been a full sister of Billy Fleming. She raced successfully in New Orleans, in 1886 and she beat Red Bird at Exposition Park, in Kansas City, in 1888. She ran two out of three heats in a half-mile match and won one in 48 seconds and the other in 48½. The other horses running were Hattie Trowbridge, second; Gray Goose, third; and Brown Dick, fourth.

BLUE GOWN. Blue Gown, a gray, was foaled in 1888 and died in 1900 (?). She was sired by Joe Collins and was out of Gray Alice by Steel Dust. She was owned by W. F. Jenkins, of Menard, Texas, and she foaled Rob Roy when bred to Chulo Mundo in 1898 (?).

BOBBIE HELMS (BABY HELMS). Bobbie Helms was foaled somewhere around 1895. She was sired by Silver Dick by Roan Dick and out of Mary S. She was a small mare, only weighing about 800 pounds. She was bred by Ross Koontz, of Illinois. For a time she was considered to be the fastest mare in the Middle West. She was a bad post mare and was eventually sold to a doctor in Montrose, Iowa.

BONNIE. Bonnie was by Nick by Old Fred and out of Wild Rose by Wild Cat by Jim Ned. She was bred by Coke T. Roberds, of Hayden, Colorado. In 1932 she foaled the black filly Fancy when bred to Red Bird by Scotsman (TB).

BONNIE. Bonnie was by Billy Mason and owned by Elmer Mourning, of Kiowa, Colorado. She foaled Wanderlust by Allen's Chorie (TB) in 1926.

BONNIE. Bonnie was by Billy Tom and was owned by Monty Corder, of Sanderson, Texas. She was sorrel, as were her three foals of note: Pickaninny by Red Seal (1923), Shooting Star by Red Seal (1925), and Red Gold by the Thoroughbred Esquire (1926).

BONNIE. Bonnie was sired by Captain Montgomery (TB) and bred by Dan Evans, of Stephenville, Texas. She foaled Pancho, a dun colt, in 1935, sired by Charm Peavine, who reportedly had American Saddle Horse blood.

BONNIE, OLD. Old Bonnie was by Red Rover. She was one of two Thoroughbred mares owned by Sam Harkey when he left home in 1895 and settled in Sheffield, Texas. She was the dam of Little Sister.

BONNIE BIRD. Bonnie Bird, a bay, was foaled April 22, 1890. She was sired by Lock's Rondo and out of Mary Lee by Joe Lee. She was a rather large mare, weighing 1,150 pounds. She was bred by W. W. Lock, of Kyle, Texas, and later owned by Ramon Moreno Zermeno, of Mexico. She could run a quarter in 22 seconds, and three-eighths in 34½.

BONNIE BIRD. Bonnie Bird was sired by Paul El and owned by Witherspoon and Sanders, of Hereford, Texas. She foaled Straight Shot by Line Up (TB) in 1935.

BONNIE BIRD II. Bonnie Bird II, a dun, was foaled in 1891 and died in 1912. She was sired by Lock's Rondo and was out of Daisy L by Project. She stood 14-2 hands and weighed well over 1,100 pounds. She was branded L O on her left shoulder. She was bred by W. W. Lock, of Kyle, Texas, and later sold to Bob Burns, of Hope, New Mexico. She was a full sister of Texas Chief. She foaled June Bug by Tommy Twigg (TB) in 1913, and three years later had California Filly by the same sire. She was said to be a 22-second mare.

BONNIE ROSE. Bonnie Rose, a gray, was a Thoroughbred who had considerable influence on the Quarter Horse. She carried the blood of *Bonnie Scotland, and she and her produce were bred to sprinters by her owner, C. B. Campbell, of Minco, Oklahoma. She was the dam of Bonnie Joe, the sire of Uncle Jimmy Gray.

BONNIE WILKINS. Bonnie Wilkins was sired by Peter McCue and out of Jarene.

BOOTS. Boots, a sorrel, was foaled in 1935. She was sired by Jimmy Sure Shot by Uncle Jimmy Gray and out of a mare by Yankee Star (TB).

BOSTON GIRL. Boston Girl, a brown, was foaled in 1896. She was by Boston Boy and out of Sally Johnson. She was bred by J. T. Newman, of Sweetwater, Texas. In 1900 she produced Review by Rancocas (TB), whose dam was by

*Bonnie Scotland, and in 1901 she foaled Caddie Griffith by the same sire.

BRANDON. Brandon, a colonial mare, was one of the truly great mares of all time. She was foaled about 1770 and died in 1785 (?). Her sire was *Aristotle, and her dam was by *Whittington. She was bred by Benjamin Harrison and later owned by Everard Mead, of Amelia County, Virginia. Mead sold eight of her colts for 14,000 pounds, which made him a wealthy man. John O'Connor, in his *Notes on the Thoroughbred from Kentucky Newspapers* (extracts for March 11, 1810, and April 1, 1811), shows that Speckleback, the dam of Kentucky Whip, was out of Brandon. Her produce were as follows: Pilgrim by *Fearnought (1774), Celer by *Janus (1776), Cloudius by *Janus (1778), Buckskin by Mark Anthony (1779), Tippoo Saib by Lath (1780), Chevalier by Celer (1782), Quicksilver by Mercury (1783), and Fritz by Partner (1784). One account says that she had a filly by Pilgrim in 1784. Celer had the greatest influence on the Quarter Horse, though all her produce got speed.

BRIDGET McCUE. Bridget McCue was by Peter McCue, and she was owned by Harry Stuart, of Lewiston, Illinois. She was the dam of Barney McCoy by Floyd K (TB), foaled in 1910.

BROOMTAIL. Broomtail was a celebrated colonial race mare and a full sister of the equally celebrated Sweeping Tail. She was foaled in the 1780s, and she was bred by Joseph John Alston, of Halifax County, North Carolina. She was sired by *Janus and out of Poll Pitcher, who was also sired by *Janus. She appears in Edgar's studbook (p. 127) and in Bruce's studbook (1:259).

BROWN ALICE. Brown Alice, named for her color, was foaled in 1888, and she was sired by Whalebone and out of Jenny Oliver. She was bred by Joe Mangum, of Nixon, Texas, and later bought by John Wilkins, of San Antonio.

In 1894 she produced Ollie W by Barnes (TB), and later Dr. O. G. by the same sire.

BROWN DICK MARE. The Brown Dick Mare was foaled in 1880 (?), and was by Brown Dick and out of a Haley mare. She was probably bred by Tom and C. R. Haley, of Sweetwater, Texas. In 1884 she foaled Ben Burton when bred to Blind Barney, and in 1886 she had Aury by Old Dutchman.

BROWN DICK MARE. The Brown Dick Mare (no relation of the Brown Dick Mare above) was foaled in 1930 (?) by Brown Dick by Deering Doe (TB) and out of Stockings by Old Fred. She was bred and owned by Coke T. Roberds, of Hayden, Colorado. She was the dam of Biddie McCue and of Mollie McCue, both by Champagne by Dundee.

BROWN JUG, LITTLE. Little Brown Jug was sired by Bert by Tommy Clegg and out of Old Boy by Waggoner's Rainy Day. She was owned by O. R. Snow, of Gilbert, Arizona.

BROWN KITTY. Brown Kitty was foaled in 1842. She was by Birmingham and out of Kit by Tiger. Her second dam was a Keith Quarter mare. She was bred by George Thomas and owned by Keene Richards, of Scott County, Kentucky. *The American Stud Book* (1:525) says that she was a fine mare at all distances, and her records bear this out.

BRUJA (TB). Bruja was a registered Thoroughbred. She was owned and bred by the King Ranch, of south Texas. She was the dam of Mickie (Witch Brew) and of Miss Princess (Woven Web). Miss Princess ruled the quarter-mile tracks from 1945 to 1948 and at one time or another held most of the records from 300 to 440 yards. See also CHICARO'S HALLIE and ADA JONES.

BUCK. Buck was by Old Fred, and she was owned by T. D. Jenkinson, of Glenwood Springs, Colorado. She was the dam of Glenwood Springs by Cruzard (TB), foaled in 1932.

BUCK EYE. Buck Eye was by Sheik and was bred and owned by Quentin Semotan, of Clark, Colorado. She was the dam of Chief by Saladin in 1935.

BULGER. Bulger was by Traveler and out of Pancha by Billy. She was owned by J. J. Kennedy, of Bonita, Arizona. She was the dam of Strawberry by Possum (King).

BURNIE BUNTON. Burnie Bunton, a sorrel, was foaled in 1898. She was sired by Rancocas (TB) and out of Dead Cinch, a full sister of Clara Berry. She was bred by C. R. Haley, of Sweetwater, Texas.

BUTT CUT, see LADY BUG.

C

CADDIE GRIFFITH. Caddie Griffith was foaled in 1901. She was sired by Rancocas (TB), whose dam was by *Bonnie Scotland. Caddie's dam was Boston Girl. Her second dam was Sally Johnson by Blue Dick by Wade Hampton. In 1910 she foaled the great sorrel filly Pan Zarita. She was bred and owned by Jim Newman, of Sweetwater, Texas.

CADDO MAID. Caddo Maid was by Joe Chalmers, and she was bred and raised by Tom Haley, of Sweetwater, Texas. She was the dam of Dash by Little Jeff Davis in 1877.

CAELIA, see COELIA.

CALLISE. Callise was by Abe Frank (TB) and out of Minyon by Rancocas (TB). Her second dam was Heeley by Blue Dick. She was bred and owned by J. W. Newman, of Sweetwater, Texas.

CAMDEN. Camden was raised by Webb Ross, of Scott County, Kentucky. She was the dam of Mike Sullivan by Sweet Owen, foaled in 1867.

CANDY. Candy was sired by Brown Tom by Baby King by Possum, and she was out of Old Lil by Lucky Mose. Her second dam was Mae by Fuzzy.

CANTALOUPE. Cantaloupe was by Old Joe by Harmon Baker and out of an Old Joe mare. She was owned by Jack Casement, of Whitewater, Colorado, and was the dam of Polly by Balleymooney.

CAPPATOLA. Cappatola was by Brother Compton (TB) and was owned by J. E. Renfro, of Menard, Texas. She was the dam of Kinch, a sorrel stallion foaled in 1927, sired by Everett (TB).

CARRIE. Carrie was by Chickasha Bob by Texas Chief and out of a Boren Quarter mare. She was owned by Blain Barnes, of Tulia, Texas. She was the dam of Barney Troutmen by Billy McCue.

CARRIE ESTHER. Carrie Esther, a bay, was foaled in 1872. She was by Hi Belden and out of Gipsy Girl. She was bred and owned by William Arnett, of Sharon, Illinois.

CARRIE NATION (BELLE OF OAKFORD). Carrie Nation, a sorrel, was foaled in 1899. Belle of Oakford was her registered name. She was by Peter McCue and out of Trixey W by Fib (TB). Her second dam was Lynn Lady by Leveller. She was bred by the Watkins family, of Oakford, Illinois, and later owned by John Wilkins, of San Antonio, Texas. In 1910 she foaled the bay filly La Cometa by Peter McCue; in 1912, Marian Mueller by Horace H; in 1913, Edgar Uhl by the same stallion; in 1914, Lady Wilkins by Horace H; in 1916, Billy Sunday (Huyler) by Horace H; and in 1917, Lily White by Horace H.

CARTRIDGE. Cartridge was by Jim Brown and out of Chestnut Belle by Norfolk (TB). Her second dam was Big Gun (Kate George). She was owned by George Hearst and J. S. Barbee, of Athens, Tennessee.

CASINO. Casino was sired by Peter McCue and was bred by Alden Meek, of Foss, Oklahoma. She was the dam of Jeff Self by A. D. Reed.

CASINO, BIG. Big Casino was foaled in 1874 (?) and died in 1889. She was sired by Steel Dust and out of Louise Herrington. She was owned by H. M. Harporter, of Florence, Kansas. She was the dam of Little Casino and of A. T. Tucker by Intrinsic (TB).

CASINO, LITTLE. Little Casino, a bay, was foaled in 1886. She was sired by Astral, a grandson of Lexington, and out of Big Casino by Steel Dust. She was bred by H. M. Herrington, of Florence, Kansas (*The American Stud Book,* 7:1220).

*CASTIANIRA (TB). *Castianira was a Thoroughbred foaled in England in 1796. She was imported by John Tayloe, of Virginia. She was by Rockingham and out of Tabitha. She was the dam of Sir Archy by *Diomed, Hephestion by *Buzzard, and several other well-known Thoroughbreds. Her greatest contribution to the Quarter Horse was Sir Archy.

CATCH ME. Catch Me, a sorrel, was foaled about 1900. She was by Bob Peters and out of Nellie Hart. She was bred by C. B. Campbell, of Minco, Oklahoma, and owned by the Armstrong brothers, who settled near Elk City, Oklahoma. The Armstrongs worked for Campbell, and when they left, they took several Campbell horses with them, including Nellie Hart, who was in foal with Catch Me. Catch Me had the shortest possible legs and yet could run a chained quarter in under 22 seconds. It became impossible to match her, so she was sold and taken to New York. Before leaving Oklahoma, she beat Frog, Fannie Nash, Rocky Mountain Tom, Figure 2, Bell, Blue Tail, Chickasha Bob, and a host of others.

CATCH ME (JENKINS'S). Catch Me was foaled around 1920 and was sired by Jenkins's Bob Wade and out of Useeit by Bonnie Joe. She was owned by Mathew Hooker, of White

Deer, Texas. She was a full sister of U Tell Um and the dam of Choteau.

CAW LADY. Caw Lady, a sorrel, was foaled in 1906 (?), sired by Lightning Conductor (TB) and out of Croton Oil by Pony Pete. She was bred and raised by Mike Smiley, of Sylvan Grove, Kansas. Ed Echols said that she was one of the greatest running mares he ever saw and that the only race he ever heard that she lost was one with Scooter by Lone Star.

CESS, BIG. Big Cess was a five-eighths mare owned by W. C. Watkins, of Oakford, Illinois. She was by Wawekus (TB) and out of a Quarter running mare. She was the dam of Emma Hill. (She may be the same mare as Big Ciss.)

CHAIN LAY. Chain Lay, a sorrel, was foaled in 1941. She was sired by My Texas Dandy and out of the good mare Mañosa by Uncle Jimmy Gray. She was bred by C. R. Thompson, of Devine, Texas, and raced by Jim Crutchfield. She was registered as a Thoroughbred, with her sire given as Tommie Gray. She was later owned by E. F. Lovelace, of Seguin, Texas, and later by the Gill Cattle Company, of Tucson, Arizona. She was an honest and consistent race mare. She was a full sister of Ginger Rogers and Carol Dandy.

CHAPARRITA. Chaparrita was by Paul El and out of Adalina by Little Joe. She was foaled about 1930. She was bred by Ott Adams, of Alfred, Texas. She was the dam of Canales Charro and of Hobo, both by Joe Moore.

CHARLOTTE HILL. Charlotte Hill, a bay, was foaled in 1833. She was by Hephestion and out of a Kentucky Whip mare. She was owned by John Fawcett, of Texas, in 1839, according to *The American Stud Book;* according to *The American Turf Register,* however, she was owned and raced by Major Shelby Smith.

CHEROKEE. Cherokee was by Cuter and raised by George Clegg, of Alice, Texas. She was the dam of Edes Horse by Hickory Bill.

CHEROKEE BELLE. Cherokee Belle was one of the best brood mares owned by H. A. Trowbridge, of Wellington, Kansas. Since she was not raced, details about her are hard to find. Her approximate dates are 1875 to 1890. There seems to be little question that she was raised by Joe Lewis, of Hunnewell, Kansas, and that she was a full or half sister of Mike Smiley's Cherokee Maid. She was the dam of Trowbridge's Vergie and her stallion Okema, though Okema was registered as out of Maggie B. B.

CHEROKEE MAID (OLD GRAY MARE). Cherokee Maid was foaled in 1876 and died in 1894 (?). She was a gray, sired by Cold Deck and out of one of Joe Lewis's best Quarter mares. Joe Lewis lived in Hunnewell, Kansas. Later she was purchased by Mike Smiley, of Sylvan Grove, Kansas. She was one of the greatest producing mares of all time. In 1879 (?) she had Little Steve; in 1884, Johnny Corbett; in 1888, Printer Tom; in 1889, Mountain Maid; in 1890, Croton Oil; and in 1891, Guinea Pig, all sired by Pony Pete. She was a half or full sister of Cherokee Belle.

CHERRY. Cherry was by Billie Tom and was bred by Monty Corder, of Sanderson, Texas. Her approximate dates are 1912 to 1928. She was the dam of Prince Albert by Red Seal. She was the dam of Skipalong Red, Starlight, and Prince Albert.

CHESTNUT BELLE. Chestnut Belle was foaled in 1880 (?) and was sired by Norfolk and bred by Theodore Winters, of Woodland, California. She was the dam of Millinette by Joe Hooker.

CHICARO JANE. Chicaro Jane, a bay, was foaled in about 1930. She was by the Thoroughbred Chicaro and out of the

Quarter mare Plain Jane by Little Joe. She was registered as a Thoroughbred (*The American Stud Book,* 16:438) out of Katie Dale, but both Ott Adams and George Clegg told me that she was out of Plain Jane.

CHICARO'S HALLIE. Hallie, a roan, was foaled in 1930. She was by the Thoroughbred Chicaro and out of the Quarter mare Ada Jones by Little Joe. She was registered in *The American Stud Book* (16:463) as out of Lady Eloise. Both her owner, Bob Kleberg, and George Clegg told Helen Michaelis and me that Ada was Hallie's dam. Hallie was the dam of Bruja, who was the dam of Miss Princess.

CHIQUITA. Chiquita was by Pacheco by Silver King by Possum and out of Chapita by Apache Kid. She was bred by M. H. Getzwiller, of Benson, Arizona.

CHIROMANEY. Chiromaney was sired by Palm Reader (TB) and out of a Christian Quarter mare. She was bred by Webb Christian, of Big Spring, Texas, and was later owned by W. R. Matsler, of Plainview, Texas. She was the dam of Hudson, Jr., by Bobby Lowe (1913) and of Fortune by Barney Lucas (1915).

CHOCTAW'S SISTER. Choctaw's Sister was foaled in 1860 (?), sired by Obe Jennings. She was owned by John Adams, of Woodland, California, who bought her in Oregon. She was the dam of the Pilgrim Mare by Pilgrim (1867) and of Nellie by Walnut Bark (1870).

CHRISTABEL, see CHRISTINA.

CHRISTINA (CHRISTABEL). Christina was sired by Little Joe by Old Joe and was born on the Casements' Triangle Bar Ranch, near Whitewater, Colorado. She had been bred by the Springers, of Cimarron, New Mexico. In 1933, while she was owned by Dan D. Casement, she foaled Frosty, one of Balleymooney's last crop of foals.

CHRISTINE C. Christine C was sired by Palm Reader (TB), and she was out of Annie T. Her second dam was Annie May. She was owned by Webb Christian, of Big Spring, Texas. She foaled Lenox by Bobby Lowe, Money Back by Recluse (TB), Sam Sparks by Dr. Austin (TB), and Jackie Boy by Barney Lucas.

CINNABAR. Cinnabar was by Little Joe by Old Joe and out of a Springer Quarter mare. She was bred by Ed Springer, of Cimarron, New Mexico, and sold to Dan D. Casement, of Whitewater, Colorado. She foaled Red Dog by Balleymooney in 1933.

CISS, BIG. Big Ciss was sired by Wawekus (TB), and she was bred by Edwin Blakely, of Kilbourne, Illinois. She was the dam of Vivian B by John Wilkins (1910). See also BIG CESS.

CLARA BERRY. Clara Berry, a sorrel, was foaled in 1902. She was by Rancocas (TB) and out of Dead Cinch. She was bred by C. R. Haley, of Sweetwater, Texas. She was a full sister of Burnie Button.

CLEMENTE GARCIA. Clemente Garcia was sired by Little Joe and was bred by Ott Adams, of Alfred, Texas.

COELIA (CAELIA). Coelia, a Famous Colonial Race Mare, was sired by Goode's Babram and out of a *Fearnought mare. She was foaled in 1768 (?). Coelia was undoubtedly bred by John Goode, Sr. One of her most famous races was against her own daughter, Harlot. She is listed in both Edgar and Bruce.

COLORADO QUEEN. Colorado Queen was by Nick by Old Fred and out of a Quarter mare by Silver Tail. She was a large buckskin that some people called palomino. She was owned by Tom Mills, of Meeker, Colorado, and became the dam of Plaudit when bred to King Plaudit.

COLUMBIA. Columbia was by Sir Archy and was owned by Mark Alexander, of Mecklenburg County, Virginia. She was the dam of Old Veto by Contention in 1827.

CONCHO. Concho was by Harmon Baker. She was owned by J. E. Renfro, of Menard, Texas, and was bred by William

Anson, of Christoval, Texas. She was the dam of Concho Kid by Everett (TB) in 1927.

CONESA. Conesa, foaled in 1917, was by Ace of Hearts. She was bred by Will Copeland, of Pettus, Texas, and later taken to Mexico. Zantanon was one of the few horses that ever bested her in a race.

CORA. Cora was by Blue by Cornstalk. She was foaled in 1910 (?), and she was owned by Gaston Matthis, of Stinnett, Texas. She was the dam of John Brown, Pop Corn, and Stalks, all by John Wilkins.

COTTON TAIL. Little is known about Cotton Tail except that she was sired by a Remount stallion and came into the possession of Albert Harrington, of Correo, New Mexico. For him she produced Navajo by Jack Dempsey.

CRAZY JANE. Crazy Jane was foaled in or near 1818. She was sired by *Merryfield and was out of a sprinting mare. She was bred by Lester Cone, of Ohio, and was the dam of Cone's Bacchus (1825) when bred to Bacchus by Sir Archy.

CRICKET. Cricket was foaled in 1928 (?) and was by Spark Plug by Jack McCue and out of Red Way by Ben. Her second dam was Sash Away. When bred back to Spark Plug, she foaled Fly McCue in 1933.

CROP, OLD. Old Crop was a Kentucky race mare of unknown pedigree. She was raised by Lewis Sanders, Jr., of Kentucky. She foaled Weazle by Kentucky Whip.

CROTON OIL. Croton Oil, a gray, was foaled in 1890 (?) and was sired by Pony Pete and out of Cherokee Maid. She was bred by Mike Smiley, of Sylvan Grove, Kansas, and was later owned by Foxhall Keene, as was her full sister Mountain Maid. She foaled Red Texas by Little Steve in 1902 and

Caw Lady in 1906 (?). Smiley also had a gelding he called Croton Oil.

CRY BABY. Cry Baby was sired by Little Danger by Tom Campbell, and her dam was a fast paint mare named Spot. She was bred by Reed Armstrong, of Foss, Oklahoma.

CUT THROAT (MAY MATTESON). Cut Throat, a sorrel, was foaled in 1889. She was by Gulliver by Missouri Mike and out of Money Spinner by Dan Tucker. Her Thorough-bred pedigree gives Bonnie Joe as her sire and Belle K as her dam, but Ronald Mason, who owned Oklahoma Star, told me that Cut Throat was by Bonnie Joe. Either way she had a good pedigree. She had eight good foals. One was Oklahoma Star, by Dennis Reed, foaled in 1915.

D

DAINTY DANCER. Dainty Dancer was by Young Fred by Old Mick and out of Dulce by Wildcat by Jim Ned. She was bred by Earl Moye, of Arvada, Wyoming. She was the dam of Monty by Red Bird by Buck Thomas.

DAISY DEAN. Daisy Dean was sired by the Thoroughbred Wheatley and bred by J. Leach, of California. She was the dam of Sam Mount, a brown colt foaled in 1889 by Ironclad.

DAISY L. Daisy L, a dun, was foaled in 1882. She was sired by Project (TB) and was out of Mary Lee by Joe Lee. She was bred by W. W. Lock, of Kyle, Texas. Lock wrote to Helen Michaelis in August, 1942, saying that Daisy L was foaled on May 15, 1882, and that she was a dun with a white right hind foot and a snip. He also said that she could run a quarter in 22½ seconds. Daisy L became the dam of Texas Chief by Lock's Rondo in 1890 and of Bonnie Bird II by

Lock's Rondo in 1891. She had two other foals, a colt who was vicious and had to be shot and a sorrel filly who killed herself in a barbed-wire fence.

DAISY LUCAS. Daisy Lucas was sired by Barney Lucas. She was bred by Webb Christian, of Big Spring, Texas. She was the dam of Barney L by Barney Lucas in 1926 and of Turn Back by Set Back (TB) in 1927.

DAISY MILLER. Daisy Miller was sired by Jim Miller, and she was bred by J. King, of California. She was the dam of Joker, a sorrel colt by Joe Hooker foaled in 1886.

DANGER, LITTLE. Little Danger was bred by J. F. Newman, of Sweetwater, Texas, and may have been sired by Danger by Barney Owens. She ran two races in El Paso in 22 seconds flat. Both times were unofficial.

DARE DEVIL MARE. The Dare Devil Mare was sired by *Dare Devil and out of a mare by *Wildair. She was owned by Edmund Irby, of Nottaway County, Virginia. In 1807 she foaled Contention by Sir Archy, in 1808 (?) she foaled Reaphook by the same sire, and in 1809 (?) she foaled Woodpecker by *Dragoon.

DARKEY'S DREAM. Darkey's Dream, a brown, was sired by a Thoroughbred and out of a Watkins Quarter mare. She was bred and owned by Walter Watkins, of Oakford, Illinois. She was the dam of the bay colt Joe Hooker by Peter McCue.

DASH. Dash was a Famous American Quarter Mare of the Revolutionary War era. She was sired by *David and out of a *Janus mare. She was bred by Wyllie Jones, of Halifax County, North Carolina. She is listed both in *The American Stud Book* and in Edgar's studbook.

DAY BREAK. Day Break was by Little Hickory by Hickory Bill and out of Black Bess by Little Joe. She was owned by C. C. Conley, of Raymondville, Texas.

DEAD CINCH. Dead Cinch, a sorrel, was foaled in 1891. She was by Silent Friend, Jr., and out of Mittie Stephens. She was bred by C. R. Haley, of Sweetwater, Texas, and later owned by J. F. Newman, also of Sweetwater. She was the dam of the following horses, all by Rancocas (TB) and all sorrels: Burnie Bunton (1898), Ran After (1899), Clara Berry (1902), and Miss Anxious (1903).

DECK. Deck, a sorrel, was foaled in 1883. She was by Barney Owens by Cold Deck and out of Lucy by Marion. She was bred by James Owen, of Berlin, Illinois, and later purchased by H. A. Trowbridge, of Wellington, Kansas. She is listed in the appendix of *The American Stud Book* (7:1209). She was the dam of Miss Star by Fib (TB), Berda L by Fib (TB), Burnt Foot by Dan Tucker, Judge Rankin by Reputation (TB), and Deck Filly by Blazeaway (TB).

DEER, LITTLE. Little Deer was by Idle Boy (TB) and out of a Kelly Quarter mare. She was owned by Earl Kelly, of Las Vegas, New Mexico. She was the dam of Star Shoot by Hermus by Tom Campbell.

DEER LEGS. Deer Legs, a Famous American Quarter Running Mare, was foaled in 1768. She was sired by Mark Anthony, and her dam was a *Jolly Roger mare. She was bred by Joseph John Alston, of Halifax County, North Carolina. She is listed in Edgar (p. 175) and in Bruce (p. 332).

DELF. Little is known about Delf except that she was a race mare owned by P. D. Bozeman and L. A. Blasingame, of Fresno, California. She became the dam of Old Confidence when bred to John Adams's Walnut Bark.

DELL. Dell was a fast Quarter mare owned by James Owen, of Berlin, Illinois. She was foaled in 1870, sired by Cold Deck. She was the dam of Polly J.

DELLA BEACH. Della, a bay, was foaled in 1885 by Faustus (TB) and out of a mare by Printer. She was owned by J. W.

Lillard, of Richards, Missouri. She foaled Cynthia L by Tehachapi and Marshall Ney by the same sire in 1896.

DELLA MOORE. Della Moore, a sorrel, was foaled in 1915 and died in 1930. She was sired by Dedier and out of Bell by Sam Rock. She was bred by Ludovic Stemmons, of Scott, Louisiana. She was raced extensively in both Louisiana and Texas and passed through several hands. She foaled Joe Reed when owned by Henry Lindsey, of Granger, Texas, and foaled Aloe, Grano de Oro, Joe Moore, and Panzarita when owned by Ott Adams, of Alfred, Texas.

DELPH, see DELF.

DEL VERDE. Del Verde, a bay, was foaled in 1903. She was sired by Gallantry (TB) and out of Pattie by Silent Friend (TB). Her second dam was Betty Bass by Young Socks, and her third dam was by Lunatic. Del Verde was bred and owned by O. G. Park, of Kyle, Texas. She was the dam of Lou Martin by Little Rondo. Del Verde was raced, and she appears in *Goodwin's Annual Turf Guide.* Her dam, Patti, is carried in the appendix of *The American Stud Book.*

DESHA MARTIN. Desha was by Lock's Rondo and out of a Martin short mare. She was bred by Tom Martin, of Kyle, Texas, and was the dam of Rattler by Sam Bass by Steel Dust.

DIAMOND BELL. Diamond Bell was sired by Marcus II, and she was owned by Louis Pacheco, of Santa Monica, California. She was the dam of Pacheco by Silver King by Possum.

DIMPLES. Dimples was by Billy Tom and was bred by J. M. (Monty) Corder, of Sanderson, Texas. She was the dam of Senator by Red Seal in 1925.

DIXIE. Dixie was by Senator, and she was owned by Samuel Russell, Jr., of Middletown, Connecticut. She was the dam of Red Magic by Free Hand (TB).

DIXIE. Dixie was by Rhodes (TB), and she was bred and owned by A. F. Willott, of Des Moines, New Mexico. She produced Red Cedar by Buck McCue in 1928.

DIXIE. Dixie was by Yellow Jacket by Yellow Wolf and out of Mayflower by Nail Driver. She was bred by Guy Troutman, of Tucumcari, New Mexico. She was the dam of Bert Benear, a bay stallion foaled in 1936.

DOGIE. Dogie was sired by Dogie Beasley by Sykes Rondo. She was owned and raced by Jap Holman, of Sonora, Texas. She was the dam of Keggy by Brown Jug by Texas Chief.

DOLLIE. Dollie was by Dennis Reed (TB) and out of Squaw by Moss King. She was owned by the Waddell brothers, of Odessa, Texas. When bred to Captain Costigan (TB), she foaled Powder River.

DOLL PEARSON. Doll Pearson was sired by Old Pearson, but no more is known of her breeding or her owner. She was the dam of Tennessee Brimmer by Club Foot by *Janus. She seems to have been the fountainhead for the Alsups' Brimmers.

DOLLY. Dolly was foaled in 1890 by Red Rover and out of a good McGonigle mare. She was bred by George McGonigle, of Midland, Texas, and later owned by G. Berry Ketchum, who lived near Sheffield, Texas. She was the dam of Damit by Red Rover and of Froggie by Joe Collins.

DOLLY CROKER. Dolly Croker was foaled about 1887 and was by Lock's Rondo by Whalebone. She became the dam of Dolly Tucker by Dan Tucker in 1892.

DOLLY FLAXEN, see POLLY FLAXEN.

DOLLY MACK. Dolly Mack was by Big Jim by Sykes Rondo and out of a Brownfield mare by a son of Old Joe by Whalebone. She was owned by Ott Adams, of Alfred, Texas. She was the dam of Joe Abb by Little Joe in 1923.

DOLLY MILLER (DOLLIE MILLER). Dolly Miller was foaled sometime during the 1880s. She was sired by Jim Miller by Roan Dick. She was owned and raced by John Hancock, of Twisp, Washington. Many of her races can be found in *Goodwin's Annual Turf Guide.* She equaled the world's record in the three-quarter mile, and was never beaten while sound. In 1891 she produced the bay colt Billy Pitman by Sleepy Jim.

DOLLY TUCKER. Dolly Tucker, a brown, was foaled in 1893. She was by Dan Tucker and out of Dolly Croker by Lock's Rondo. She was owned by George Smith in 1896, and she raced three-eighths mile at Butte, Montana, in 36¼ seconds.

DONNA. Donna, a bay, was foaled in 1910 (?). She was by Barney by Danger by Barney Owens and out of Katy Bell by Buckshot by Joe Collins. She was bred by Charles A. Gardner, of Tucson, Arizona, and later owned by Roy Sorrels, of Nogales, Arizona. She foaled Pop Eye by Big Apple by Joe Collins, Little Ben by Ben Hur, and Scooter by Mark by Red Cloud.

DONNA SAPPHO VI. Donna Sappho VI, a palomino, was foaled in 1934. She was sired by Sappho by Brown King and out of a mare by Martin's Traveler. She was bred by W. B. Mitchell, of Marfa, Texas. She was the dam of Sobre by Red Lantados (TB).

DORA. Dora, a gray, was foaled in 1888. She was sired by Bill Garner by Steel Dust and out of Judy by Mount's Steel Dust. She was bred by E. Shelby Stanfield, of Thorp Springs, Texas, and later owned by John Wilkins, of San Antonio, Texas. She was the dam of Joe Howell by Joe Harris in 1894.

DORA. Dora, a sorrel, was foaled in 1882. She was by Billy by Shiloh and out of Paisana by Brown Dick. She was bred by

W. B. Fleming, of Belmont, Texas and later owned by Alex Gardner, of San Angelo, Texas. Alex bought her for $1,500 at the same time he bought Joe Collins and Pancho. Jim Brown bought her from Gardner for a race mare and lost her in a match in the Indian country of Oklahoma.

DORADA, see PITCHIN SIS.

DORA DU MAR. Dora Du Mar was by Little Joe and out of Julia Crowder by John Crowder. She was bred by Ott Adams, of Alfred, Texas. She was the dam of Rialto by Billy Sunday and of Pal-o-Mine by the same sire.

DORA WOOD. Dora Wood, a sorrel, was foaled in 1892. She was sired by Jack Boston by Lexington (TB) and out of Risa K by Harve (TB). She was bred by Fred T. Wood, of Abilene, Texas. She was the dam of Alice Hand by Peter McCue and of two colts by Thoroughbreds Pat Brown and Dr. Hollis.

DOROTHY DUNCAN. Dorothy was sired by Thrive (TB) and out of a Quarter running mare. She was the dam of Nubbin, a bay colt foaled in 1909 by Conjuror (TB).

DOROTHY E. Dorothy E, a sorrel, was sired by Flying Squirrel (TB) and out of a Quarter mare called Kokohi by Celt (TB). She was bred by J. A. Hall, of Stanberry, Missouri, and first run by Bud Hall, of Iowa. Later she was owned and run by W. C. Row, of Wynona, Oklahoma, by Manuel Benevides Volpe, of Laredo, Texas, and finally by Alonzo Taylor, of Hallettsville, Texas.

DOT. Dot was by Traveler; her dam is unknown. She was owned by Alex Garder, of San Angelo, Texas. She was the dam of Billy Bartlett (1902), also by Traveler.

DOTTIE. Dottie was foaled in 1900 (?) by No Good by Barney Owens and out of Birdie (Hopkins) by John Crowder. She was bred by J. J. Kennedy, of Bonita, Arizona. She became the dam of Red Cloud by Possum in 1919 and of Doc by Possum in 1921 (?).

DULCIE. Dulcie was by Sappho by Brown King and was bred by W. B. Mitchell, of Marfa, Texas. She was the dam of Dueno by High Step (TB).

DUMPY. Dumpy was by Little Dick by Sleepy Dick and out of Oklahoma Beauty. She was owned by Preston Johnson, of Rosalia, Texas. She was the dam of Little Joe, Jr.

DUTCH, see DUTCHESS.

DUTCH. Dutch was by Billy Hubbard by Billy Caviness. She was bred by Kirk Williams, of Mancos, Colorado, and later owned by Harry Wommer, of Bayfield, Colorado. She was the dam of Duke by Ignacio Chief (TB) in 1910.

DUTCH. Dutch was foaled about 1880. She was sired by Sykes Rondo and out of a Mangum Quarter mare. She was bred by Joe Mangum, of Nixon, Texas, and later owned by Pleasant Walters, of Oakville, Texas, and still later by Emmet Butler, of Kenedy, Texas. She was quite a race mare, and her race with Eighty Gray in 1898 attracted wide interest. She became the dam of Ben by John Crowder in 1900 (?), Pleasant Walters by John Crowder, and Hondo by John Crowder.

DUTCHESS (DUTCH). Dutchess was foaled in or about 1935 and lived until 1950 (?). She was by Doc by Possum and out of Silver by Blue Eyes by Possum. She was bred by Chester Cooper, of Roosevelt, Arizona. She was the dam of Prissy by Colonel Clyde (1940), Buster by Clabber (1941), Miss Atomic by Red Man, and Betsy Ross by Joe Reed II.

E

EAGLE. Eagle was by Moss King by Big King. She was bred by the Waddell brothers, of Odessa, Texas. She was the dam of Stand Pat by Captain Costigan (TB).

EASTER BELLE. Easter Belle, a Thoroughbred, was sired by Lee Paul by Lexington. She was bred and foaled in Kentucky and in 1886 became the dam of Leadville by Harry O'Fallon.

EDEE REE. Edee Ree was foaled in 1905 (?), sired by Peter McCue and out of Nona P by the Duke of Highlands (TB). Her second dam was Millie D, a half sister of Peter McCue. She was a full sister of Harmon Baker. She was the dam of Mr. Rex Beach (1926) and of Rainy Day by Lone Star (1914). Another source says that Rainy Day was by Lone Star and out of a mare by Old Tom. She was owned by John Wilkins, of San Antonio, Texas, but bred by Sam Watkins, of Petersburg, Illinois.

ELIZA. Eliza, a registered Thoroughbred, was foaled in 1804 and died in 1825 (?). She was sired by *Bedford and out of Mambrina. She was raised by Colonel William Alston, of South Carolina. She was the dam of Bertrand and Pacific, both by Sir Archy.

ELLA MITCHELL. Ella Mitchell, a sorrel, was foaled in 1885. She was sired by Elkhorn by *Australian (TB) and out of Laura Mitchell by Elkhorn. Her second dam was Molly McCreary by Zero by Boston (TB). She was owned by Uriah Eggleston, of Minco, Indian Territory (Oklahoma), and of Garden City, Kansas.

ELLA T. Ella T, a sorrel, was foaled in 1881. She was by Shannon (TB) and out of Bess (Bell) by Uncle Billy. She was bred by John Adams, of Woodland, California. She produced the following foals: Lillie W by Joe Hooker in 1887, Irma by St. Savior (TB) in 1892, Red Iron Miss by Red Iron (TB) in 1893, Soscol by St. Savior in 1895, and El Sabrino by Nephew (TB) in 1898.

ELLEN. Little is known about Ellen's breeding. She was owned by J. Halton, of Oregon, and produced Bill Bingham by Dr. Lindsay (TB) and Al Shaw by Jack Minor.

ELLEN JOURDAN. Ellen Jourdan was sired by Blacknose by Medoc (TB) and out of Emily Jordan. She was the dam of Medoc by Billy Cheatham by Rough and Ready.

ELLOUISE. Ellouise was by Barney Williams by Lexington (TB) and was first owned by James Owen, of Berlin, Illinois. She was the dam of Spinning, the good stallion used by Owen and H. A. Trowbridge, of Wellington, Kansas.

EMELINE. Emeline was by Brown Dick (1860) and owned by W. Cottrill of Alabama. She foaled Chalmette by Daniel Boone in 1866.

EMILY WALKER. Emily Walker was by Moss Brimmer and was raced by the Alsup brothers, of Tennessee and Missouri. She was a very fast mare.

EMMA. Emma was by Bill Worth and raised by C. Cartwright, of Texas. She was the dam of Red Buck (1883) by Wade Hampton (TB).

EMMA HILL. Emma Hill, a bay, was foaled in 1907. She was by Peter McCue and out of Big Cess by Wawekus (TB). She was bred by W. C. Watkins, of Oakford, Illinois. She was also owned by George Newton, of Del Rio, Texas; W. H. Askey, of Sisterdale, Texas; and John Dial, of Goliad, Texas. She was the dam of Janet by Emendorf (TB).

EMORY GOLDMAN. Emory Goldman was by Captain Joe, and her dam has been given as a King (Possum) mare. She was the dam of Golden Wheel and of Blondy S.

ENGLISH, OLD. Old English, a sorrel, was sired by *Uhlan and out of a CS Ranch (New Mexico) Quarter mare, bred by C. S. Springer, of Cimarron, New Mexico. She was the dam of Springer's Little Joe by Old Joe.

ENOUGH, BIG. Big Enough was by Billy Boy by Dominus Arvi (TB). He was bred by Albert Harrington, of Correo, New Mexico. She was the dam of Teddy by Billy Dick.

ENZE. Enze, a bay, was foaled in 1895. She was by Galon (TB) and out of Lemonade by Anthony. She was owned by J. F. Newman, of Sweetwater, Texas. She produced Little Gift by Rancocas (TB) in 1901, Billie Allen by Rancocas in 1903, Stan by Rancocas in 1904, Chuck by Prince Plenty (TB) in 1905, Lee Simple by Prince Plenty in 1906, and Beulah Mac by Abe Frank (TB) in 1910.

EVA NELSON. Eva Nelson, a sorrel, was foaled in 1890. She was by Uncle Tom and out of Mollie McCreary. She was bred and owned by Uriah Eggleston, of Garden City, Kansas, and was later sold to T. E. Archer, of Vesta, Nebraska.

EVE. Eve was by First Chip (TB) and out of Gracie Gould by Master Gould. She was owned by Sam Waring, of Eden, Texas. She is shown as the dam of Red Seal by Seal Skin by Harmon Baker.

EVELYN. Evelyn was by Henry by Sam Watkins and out of a Perez mare by Joe Abb. She was the dam of Clegg's Boy by Jiggs by Uncle Jimmy Gray.

F

FAIR CHANCE, see VERNA GRACE.

FAIR PLAY. Fair Play was foaled in 1923. She was sired by Barney Lucas by Cunningham's Traveler and out of Over-knight (TB). Two other pedigrees are given for Barney Lucas. The Jockey Club says that he was by Dr. Curtis and out of Manacre, while Helen Michaelis said that he was by Traveler and out of Annie May. I am inclined to accept Michaelis's account. Both sources agree that Fair Play was bred by D. W. Christian, of Big Spring, Texas, and later owned by S. L. Morris. She had four foals: Sister Ann by Fleeting Time (TB), Nasty Mess by *Over There (TB), Band Play by Band Time

(TB), and Wayward Boy by Scorcher, perhaps the Thorough-bred Scorcher.

FANCHETTE. Fanchette, a sorrel, was foaled in 1872. She was bred and owned by John M. Mathewson, of Lowell, Michigan. She was sired by Bay Printer by Sweet Owen and out of Wise Mare (Bellona) by Franchi. She had six foals by Morris, Prodigal, Printer, Bertha, Gossip, Fanny, and Sampson; and one by Bangweola, Lottie.

FANCY. Fancy, a black, was foaled in 1932. She was sired by Old Red Bird by Buck Thomas and out of Bonnie by Old Nick, and her second dam was Wild Rose. She was bred by Earl Moye, of Arvada, Wyoming.

FANCY. Fancy was, according to Edgar, a good Quarter race mare, foaled in 1763. Fairfax Harrison, in his *Early American Turf Stock* (2:125), says that her sire did not stand in America until 1765. She was sired by *Bucephalus and out of a mare by Lycurgus. She was bred by C. C. Taylor, of Northampton County, North Carolina, and later owned by Richard C. Taylor. She is listed by Edgar (p. 209) and by Bruce (1:413).

FANCY. Fancy was by John Wilkes by Peter McCue and was bred and owned by J. E. Renfro, of Menard and Sonora, Texas. She was the dam of Tom Polk by Everett (TB).

FANNIE ANDERSON. Fannie Anderson was sired by Billy Caviness and bred by Kirk Williams, of Mancos, Colorado. She was the dam of Columbus by Silver Dick.

FANNIE PACE. Fannie Pace, a sorrel, was foaled about 1890 and died in 1910 (?). She was sired by Gulliver by Missouri Rondo, and her dam was one of "Trump" Pace's good Quarter mares. She was bred by Pace, of Baird, Texas. Later she was owned by C. C. Seale, also of Baird. She was pulling Pace's ice wagon when Seale bought her. She was the dam of Judge Thomas in 1897, Judge Welsh in 1898, and Buster Brown in 1903, all by Traveler.

FANNY. Fanny was by Jack McCue and owned by Charles Francis, of Floyd, New Mexico. She was the dam of Dick Dillon by Jack McCue.

FANNY, LITTLE. Little Fanny was foaled in 1937. She was by Old Joe Reed and out of Fanny Ashwell by Ashwell (TB). Her second dam was Fanny Richardson. She was bred by J. W. House, of Cameron, Texas, and later sold to Bert Wood, of Tucson, Arizona. Her best-known foal was Leo by Joe Reed II. She also produced Bill Reed, Ashwood, Tick Tack, Tucson, Little Sister W, and Sassy Time.

FANNY ASHWELL. Fanny Ashwell was by Ashwell (TB) and out of Fanny Richardson. She was owned by John W. House, of Cameron, Texas. She was the dam of Jonas, Joe Butler, and Little Fanny, all by Joe Reed.

FANNY BRITTON. Fanny Britton's exact pedigree is unknown. She was run by Thomas Atchison, of California, and she was the dam of Marshall MacMahon by Norfolk (TB).

FANNY HARPER (FAY HARPER). Fanny Harper was sired by Gray Eagle by Woodpecker. She was bred in Kentucky. In 1875 she foaled Shiloh by Cosmo, and in 1879 she foaled Lady Norfolk by Shiloh (*The American Stud Book*, 7:525, 1191).

FANNY HOWARD. Fanny Howard was by Illinois Medoc and was owned by J. E. Tyree, of California. She was the dam of Firetail by Norfolk in 1870.

FANNY KING. Fanny King was by *Glencoe and was owned by T. B. Goldsby, of Alabama. She was the dam of Brown Dick by *Margrave and of Billy Cheatham by Cracker in 1853.

FANNY NASH. Fanny Nash, a sorrel, was foaled in the middle or early 1890s. She was by Project and out of Laura T. She was bred by Jack Nash, of Kaufman County, Texas. She was a fast race mare, run by R. Reeves. She lost to Catch Me and Judge Thomas going a quarter in Dallas in 1898. She made Bill Dick run a 21½-second quarter to beat her at Pauls Valley, Oklahoma, in 1902. She was the dam of Jim by Jim Little.

FANNY WHITE. Fanny White was a Quarter mare showing a lot of Thoroughbred. Her breeder and breeding are unknown. She was owned by George White, of Mancos, Colorado. She was the dam of Billy White in 1898 and Silver Dick in 1897, both by Billy Caviness.

FANTAIL. Fantail, a famous early-day running mare, was sired by a son of *Sharke and out of a John Goode mare. She was bred by Goode, of Macklenburg County, Virginia. She is listed in both Edgar and Bruce.

FASHION. Fashion, a brown, was foaled in 1887 or 1888. She was sired by Anthony by Old Billy and was out of Silentina by Silent Friend (TB). Her second dam was Fleecie P by Bulletin. She was bred by Tom King, of Belmont, Texas. Later she was owned by Wade McLemore, of Dallas, and she was raced by T. M. Lipscomb. She was a full sister of Lemonade. She was registered as a Thoroughbred under a different pedigree (*The American Stud Book*, 6:1154). She ran three-eighths in 33 seconds at Helena, Montana, in 1892. She broke the circular-track record at San Angelo, Texas, when she ran three-eighths in 34 seconds. She ran over a fence at New Orleans and had to be destroyed. S. C. Riggs said that he rode her in fifty-six races and won them all.

FAYE. Faye was by Jeff by Printer and out of Lori Trammell by Peter McCue. Her second dam was Ring Tail. She was bred by Clyde McClain, of Leedey, Oklahoma. She was a full sister of Joy (1912). It is claimed that she ran a quarter in 22 flat three weeks after being gentled. She was later matched against Tucumcari in a race in Cheyenne, Oklahoma. They started scoring at 2:00 P.M., but the moon was up before they were off. She was ridden by Cliff Carl of Cheyenne, and she won the race.

FAY HARPER, see FANNY HARPER.

FAY LARKIN. Fay Larkin was sired by Barney Lucas by Traveler and out of a Christian short mare. She was bred by Webb Christian, of Big Spring, Texas. She had the following foals: Mud Lark by Set Back (TB) in 1928, Sealark by White Seal (TB) in 1932, and Wandering Jew by Set Back (TB) in 1927.

FILLY, BYNUM'S BIG. Bynum's Big Filly was foaled in 1773 by *Janus and out of a *Jolly Roger mare. She got her name from her breeder, Turner Bynum, of Northampton County, North Carolina. She was raced mostly by Bynum's father-in-law, Colonel Jeptha Atherton. She was very large for her breed, 15 hands and heavily built. Her most famous race was against Wyllie Jones's double *Janus colt Paoli. Her name is found in Edgar (p. 133) and in Bruce (1:267).

FILLY, MANCOS' BIG. Mancos' Big Filly was sired by Little Bert and out of Old Mancos. She was the dam of Lady Gladys in 1885.

FIVE DOLLARS, OLD. Old Five Dollars was extremely fast and is said to have won nineteen successive starts as a two-year-old. Her pedigree is confusing, but she appears to have been by Barney Owens, or by a son of his, and out of New Money. She had only one foal, a filly called Five Dollars II. Old Five Dollars died of blood poisoning.

FIVE DOLLARS II. Five Dollars II was sired by Jim Trammell by Barney Owens. She was 14-3 hands and weighed 1,150 pounds. She was bred by Thomas Trammell, of Sweetwater, Texas, and later owned by J. Frank Norfleet, of Hale Center, Texas. She had a full brother named Bartender. She was the dam of Norfleet by *Brettenham (TB) and of Panzarita (1931).

FLASHLIGHT. Flashlight was sired by Sam King by Hondo and out of a Harmon Baker mare. She was bred by O. W. Cardwell, of Junction, Texas. She was known as Sam King's fastest daughter and was a remarkable polo mare, ridden by both Cardwell and Jim Chittem. She was the dam of Dutch by Little Joe.

FLAXIE B. Flaxie B was sired by Tubal Cain by Berry's Cold Deck and out of a Gray Wolf mare. She was bred by Coke Blake, of Pryor, Oklahoma. She was the dam of Blake's Traveler by Gold Button.

FLEET. Fleet, a sorrel, was foaled in 1922. She was sired by Bob H by Old Fred and out of Lady Eckstine by Big Black. She was bred by Marshall Peavy, of Clark, Colorado, and was the dam of Saladin by Ding Bob.

FLEET. Fleet was sired by Duke by Ed Howell and out of Wildcat, and she was the dam of Skeet, a sorrel mare foaled in 1935 by Interrogator.

FLEETFOOT. Little is known about Fleetfoot, who was foaled about 1880. She was raised on the Morris Ranch in Texas and was the dam of Lone Man (1889) by Lock's Rondo. She was owned by Santana Cruz, of Driftwood, Hays County, Texas.

FLEXY. Flexy was a fast short mare owned by Elias Watkins, of Petersburg, Illinois. She was sired by Voltigeur (TB) and out of a mare by Barney Owens, raised by Sam Watkins. She was the dam of one of the last foals the Watkinses bred by Dan Tucker before they sold him into Texas in 1898. The colt was Coal Oil Johnny, foaled in 1899.

FLORA. Flora was sired by Pilgrim (TB) and out of a Sulden Quarter mare. She was bred by Wilson Sulden, of Hallettsville, Texas. She was the dam of Little Dick by Sleepy Dick in 1911.

FLORA V. Flora V was sired by Voltigeur (TB) and out of a good Quarter running mare. She was bred by Samuel Watkins, of Petersburg, Illinois, and was the dam of Ramsey by Peter McCue and of Hazel Hughlett by Dan Tucker.

FLOSSIE. Flossie was sired by Sheik by Peter McCue and out of a blue mare by Bob H by Old Fred. She was bred and owned by Marshall Peavy, of Clark, Colorado. She had four foals: Si Ding by Ding Bob by Brown Dick, Red Sage by Saladin by Ding Bob, Panther by Ding Bob, and Little Buck by Ding Bob.

FLY. Fly was sired by Little Steve and out of a mare by Comet. She was owned by Charley Walker, of Kiowa, Colorado. She was the dam of Sweet and Sweetheart, both by Johnny Corbett.

FLYING MARY. Flying Mary was foaled in 1924. She was 14-2 hands and weighed 1,050 pounds. Joe Herridge, of Fairfax, Oklahoma, bought her from Rowe Morgan, of Fort Worth, Texas. She was an outstanding race mare at any distance from 220 to 440 yards. She was raced for several years before she was bred. She was the dam of Bear Cat.

FLY McCUE. Fly McCue, a sorrel, was foaled in 1933. She was sired by Spark Plug by Jack McCue and out of Cricket by Spark Plug. She was bred by Donald King, of Alton, Texas.

FOURTH OF JULY. Fourth of July was by Bobby Lowe by Eureka and out of Old Mary by Old Joe Bailey. She was probably bred by Webb Christian, of Big Spring, Texas. She was the dam of Chubby in 1924 and of Bill Thomas in 1929.

FOXY. Foxy was by Peter McCue and was bred by M. B. Huggins, of Clinton, Oklahoma. She was the dam of Ranger II by Eagle Chief (TB) in 1925.

FREE GOLD. Free Gold, a sorrel, was foaled in 1932. She was sired by Mark by Red Cloud and out of Betsy by Red Cloud. Her second dam was Brown Bit.

FREE SILVER. Free Silver was foaled in 1902 and died of colic in 1908. Her dam was by John Crowder, according to Tito Harper. She was owned by Cornelius H. Bess, of Eagle Pass, Texas, and Piedras Negras, Coahuila, Mexico. She was branded 7V connected. Her picture hangs in Sanbourne's in Mexico City. She was trained by "Crook Neck" Johnson, and she could run 220 yards in 10½ seconds carrying 114 pounds. She also ran three-eighths in Juárez in 33 seconds, said to be the world's record at the time.

FREE SILVER. Free Silver, a sorrel, was foaled in 1942. She was sired by My Texas Dandy and was out of Knee Action by Uncle Jimmy Gray (TB). She was bred by Willie Myers, of Sonora, Texas. In 1944 she ran a 220-yard race in 12.7 at Eagle Pass, Texas, and at the same meet a 440-yard race in 22.8.

FRESNO FIFTY. Fresno Fifty was by Fresno (TB) and out of a Matador mare of good but uncertain breeding. She was bred by the Matador Land and Cattle Company, of Channing, Texas. She was the dam of Frank Gray by Sheik.

FROG, see FROGGY.

FROGEYES. Frogeyes was by Frogtown by *Bonnie Scotland (TB) and out of a good short mare. She was bred by Roy Kimble, of Clayton, New Mexico, and she was the dam of Raincocas by Mose by Old Mose by Traveler.

FROGGY (FROG). Froggy was foaled in 1908 and was sired by Joe Collins by Billy and out of Dolly by Red Rover by Old Billy. She was bred by Berry Ketchum, of Sheffield, Texas, and then owned by Jim Harkey, of Fort Stockton, Texas. She was the dam of Miss Harkey (1923) and Dodger (1924), both by Harmon Baker.

FURY. Fury was a fast Quarter mare that did not come with a pedigree. Those who saw her run thought that her breeding must be the best. She was owned by Robert Wade, of

Plymouth, Illinois. She became the dam of Silver Dick by Roan Dick in 1892.

FUZZY. Fuzzy was by Three Finger Jack by Traveler, and she was owned by J. M. Brister, of Lordsburg, New Mexico. She was the sire of Pankey's Lucky by Apache Kid.

G

GALLANT MAID. This brown mare was foaled in 1939. She was sired by Major Speck by Uncle Jimmy Gray and out of Edna Truesdale by Prince Pal.

GARDNER MARE, see MAUD.

GAZETTE. Gazette was sired by Cid Campeador, a French Thoroughbred, and she was out of Grazzer by Lou Farina.

GENERAL HOOD MARE. The General Hood Mare was sired by General Hood and out of a mare by Shiloh. She was bred by J. R. Nasworthy, of Bridgeview Stud, San Angelo, Texas. She foaled Little Sister (1887) and Mabel Scott (1892), both by Buck Walton.

GENEVIEVE. Genevieve, a bay, was sired either by John Crowder or by Blue Eyes out of a Rondo mare. She was owned first by Dow Shely and then by Ott Adams. She was the dam of Bonnie Joe (Dr. Rose) by Little Joe.

GEORGIA LANE. Georgia Lane, a brown, was foaled in 1893. She was by Short Bob by Bill Garner and out of Silkie by Cunningham's Rondo. She was bred by Gus Lane, of Comanche, Texas, and raised by a relative of Gus, E. Lane, of Sunray, Texas. She was a 22-second mare. She was raced in Kansas, Nebraska, and Oklahoma, as well as in Texas. She was defeated only once, according to available records.

GEORGIE. Georgie was by Pancho and out of Maud. She was owned by the Gardner family, of San Angelo, Texas.

She was the dam of Chief Wilkins by John Wilkins and of Chulo Mundo by Traveler.

GERTRUDE W. Gertrude W, a bay, was foaled in 1892. She was sired by Fib (TB) and out of Vologne by Voltigeur (TB). Her second dam was a Quarter mare.

GIFT, LITTLE. Little Gift was by the Thoroughbred Rancocas and out of a Trammell Quarter mare. She was raised by Thomas Trammell, of Sweetwater, Texas, and was the dam of Hanks by Prince Plenty (TB).

GINGER. Ginger was sired by Will Stead by Billy McCue, and she was out of Snowfly by Will Stead. She was bred by Roy McMurty, of Silverton, Texas.

GINGER ROGERS. Ginger Rogers, a sorrel, was foaled in 1932. She was sired by My Texas Dandy and out of Mañosa by Uncle Jimmy Gray. Her second dam was Meanie by Possum. She was bred by Jim and Lucy Roach, of Big Foot, Texas, who sold her to Carroll Thompson of Devine, Texas. She was raced throughout Texas, Louisiana, and neighboring states. In 1937 she was taken to Oklahoma by E. F. Lovelace, of Seguin, Texas, and she won seventeen consecutive races. In 1939 she was owned by J. D. Raines, of Mexico City. In Mexico, Raines had her open to the world. One of the few reliable times we have for her was 22.2 seconds in a race at Junction, Texas, in 1939. She was a full sister of Chain Lay.

GLADIOLA. Gladiola, a bay, was sired by Norfolk. She was owned by T. M. Riggs, of Oregon, and was raced extensively on the Pacific Coast. She became the dam of Jack Sheppard, a brown colt foaled in 1885 by Nathan Combs by Lodi.

GLADYS. Gladys was sired by a Paul L colt and out of an O'Connor Quarter mare. She was the dam of Spring Steel, a bay colt foaled in 1937, sired by Red Joe.

GODIVA. Godiva was sired by Senator. She spent most of her life in Colorado. She was the dam of Tom Roy by Free Hand.

GOLD DUST. Gold Dust, a sorrel, was sired by Cold Deck and foaled in 1890 (?). She was a fast mare owned by Tom Cook, of Amarillo, Texas. She lost a close race to Nellie Miller in Kansas City. *Goodwin's Turf Guide* lists various races she ran between 1892 and 1896 at distances from 3½ furlongs to a half mile. Her fastest listed time was 44 seconds for 3½ furlongs and 51½ seconds for a half mile.

GOLDEN GIRL. Golden Girl was by Uncle Jimmy Gray and out of Blondie S by Lone Star. Melville Haskell listed her as out of Suzie by Possum. Her second dam was Emory Goldman by Captain Joe. According to A. A. Nichols, she was unbeaten at three-eighths mile.

GOLDEN SLIPPERS. Golden Slippers was sired by Lone Star and out of Lilly White by A. M. White (TB). She became the dam of Bonnie High, a brown mare foaled in 1928, sired by Uncle Jimmy Gray.

GOLDEN SLIPPERS. Golden Slippers, a palomino, was foaled in 1940. She was sired by My Texas Dandy and out of Grandma by the Tampsky Horse. She was owned and probably bred by J. N. Davis, of Leakey, Texas.

GOLDEN WHEEL. Golden Wheel was sired by Uncle Jimmy Gray and out of Emory Goldman by Captain Joe. She was owned by Frank Smith, of Big Foot, Texas. She became the dam of Clabber when bred to My Texas Dandy in 1935.

GOLDIE. Goldie was by Big Jim, and she was owned by George Doty, of Afton, Oklahoma. She was the dam of Chicken Smart.

GOLDIE. Goldie was by Fred S (TB) and out of Stockings by Old Fred. She was bred by Marshall Peavy, of Clark, Colorado. She was the dam of Tim by Saladin.

GOLDIE. Goldie was by Madder Music (TB) and out of Ruby by Tango Kelly. She was owned by Elmer Helper, of Carlsbad, New Mexico, and became the dam of Little Joe the Wrangler, a bay colt foaled in 1935, sired by Joe Hancock.

GOLD MEDAL. Gold Medal, a sorrel, was by Little Joe and out of an Anson Quarter mare. She was bred and raised by Jim A. Winn, of Uvalde, Texas.

GOLD NUGGET. Gold Nugget was by Lucky by Possum and out of Katy Belle by Big Dutch.

GOLD SOPHIE. Gold Sophie was sired by Brass Button by Gonzalo, and she was bred by Roy Davis, of Big Spring, Texas. She was the dam of Don Topaz by Golden Dan.

GOOD ENOUGH. Good Enough was by Tom Campbell by Bob Peters and out of Lizzie, a mare bred by Smith Kellam, of Cheyenne, Oklahoma. She was bred by E. A. Meek, of Foss, Oklahoma, and later purchased by A. D. Hurley, of Canute, Oklahoma. She was the dam of A. D. Reed by Peter McCue, foaled in 1916.

GOOD LUCK. Good Luck was sired by Booger Red by Rancocas (TB). She was owned by Robert Land, of Southhold, Long Island, New York. She was the dam of Vito by Gold Bug (TB) in 1933.

GRACIE GOULD. Gracie Gould, a bay, was foaled in 1903. She was sired by Register (TB). She was bred by Charles Ferguson, of Ballinger, Texas, and later owned by Sam Waring, of Eden, Texas. She was listed in both *The American Stud Book* and in *The Half Breed Stud Book*. Dick Stanton, of Menard, Texas, claims that she was falsely registered and that she was a sprinting Quarter mare. *The Half Breed Stud Book* gives her breeding as unknown. Among her produce were Operator and Gracie Chip by First Chip (TB), as well as Beloved and Nancy Gould.

GRASSHOPPER. Grasshopper was foaled in 1874 (?). She was sired by Cold Deck and out of Alice by Harry Bluff (a full sister of June Bug). She was bred and raised by Joe Lewis, of Hunnewell, Kansas. She was one of the all-time great Quarter mares. She got Sykes Rondo when bred to McCoy Billy, and Doe Belly, Rolling Deck, and Joe Lewis when bred to Bobby Cromwell.

GRAY ALICE. Gray Alice was by One-Eyed Joe, and her dam was a Kentucky Thoroughbred. She was bred by Ove Oldham, of Buda, Texas. She stood a scant 14-3 hands and weighed almost 1,100 pounds. She could run a consistent 23-second quarter mile and a half mile in a shade under 47 seconds. She was foaled in Bear Creek, a few miles west of Buda. When she was three years old, Oldham sold her to Al Robinson, of Austin, Texas. Robinson entered her in a race a few days later, and she ran for a new local track record of 46½ seconds for the half mile. Jim Brown, of Giddings, who had a mare in the same race, bought Gray Alice after the race.

GRAY ALICE. Gray Alice, a gray, was foaled in 1868 (?) and died in 1895 (?). She was sired by Steel Dust and was out of Cora by Blue Dick. She was bred by Shelby Stanfield, of Thorp Springs, Texas. She was raced by Jim Brown, of Giddings, Texas. At one time or another she was also owned or handled by Will Jenkins, of Menard, Texas; Colonel Gay, of the same city; and Ruff Winn, of Rock Springs, Texas. She was a truly great dam, and her best-known colts were Dunman's Billy Fleming by Old Billy (1884), June Gray by Old Billy (1885), Jim Reed by Rebel Morgan (1886), Sis by Joe Collins (1887), Blue Gown by Joe Collins (1888), Black Beauty by Joe Collins (1890), Eighty Gray by Bill Fleming (1891), and Gray Alice by Harvester (1892).

GRAY JENNIE (JENNY). Gray Jennie, a gray, was foaled about 1886. She was by Alsup's Cold Deck or by Berry's Cold

Deck, and her dam was a Lightning mare. She was bred by Foss Barker, of Van Buren, Arkansas, and later owned and raced by M. S. ("Small") Baker, of Beggs, Oklahoma. She was raced in Saint Louis in 1894, according to *Goodwin's Turf Guide*. Herb McSpadden said: "They never knew Jenny could run until one day she got a fright and ran off with a double shovel, and that shovel never hit the ground for the first quarter of a mile. Mr. Small's daughter took her back East [to Saint Louis] and won lots of races with her."

GRAY MAE. Gray Mae was by Possum by Young White Lightning. She was bred by Coke Blake, of Pryor, Oklahoma. She was the dam of Gray Wolf by Young Cold Deck.

GRAY MARE, OLD, see CHEROKEE MAID.

GRAY NELLIE. Gray Nellie, a gray, was foaled in 1890. She was by Buck Walton and out of a mare by Shiloh. She was bred and raised at the Bridge View Stud, of San Angelo, Texas, owned by J. R. Nasworthy.

GRAY PLANTER. Gray Planter was sired by Planter (TB) and out of a short mare. She was owned by H. L. Forker, of Nara Visa, New Mexico. She was the dam of Swanky, a sorrel colt by Brown Smoot by Billy Smoot.

GRECIAN PRINCESS. Grecian Princess, an outstanding mare, was foaled in 1816. She was a smooth bay and was sired by Kentucky Whip and out of the famous Jane Hunt. She was bred and owned by William Buford, of Woodford County, Kentucky.

GUN, BIG (KATE GEORGE). Big Gun, a sorrel, was foaled in 1869 (?), sired by Old George. She was bred by Theodore Winters, of Sacramento and Woodland, California. She was the dam of Bay Kate (1874), Chestnut Belle (1877), Jim Renwick (1878), and Gwen Kapiolani (1882), all by Joe Hooker.

GYPSY QUEEN. Gypsy Queen was a Quarter mare of unreported breeding owned by J. R. Nasworthy, of San Angelo, Texas. She was the dam of Wall Paper by Buck Walton in 1981.

H

HABY MARE. The Haby Mare was foaled in 1918 (?) and was sired by Lone Star. She was bred by Nick Haby, of Riomedina, Texas. She was the dam of three well-known colts, all sired by Uncle Jimmy Gray: Golden Amel, Golden Streak, and Tom Mix.

HALLETTSVILLE MARE. The Hallettsville Mare was sired by a son of Rondo, and she was owned by Dow and Will Shely, of Alfred, Texas. She became the dam of Texas Chief, a sorrel colt foaled in 1905 by Traveler, and of Ann, a sorrel filly by Traveler.

HALLIE, CHICARO'S. Chicaro's Hallie was by Chicaro (TB) and out of Ada Jones. She was bred by John Dial, of Goliad, Texas, and later purchased by Bob Kleberg, of the King Ranch. Chicaro's Hallie's daughters founded a dynasty of sprinters. Hallie won her first race as a two-year-old, as did her daughter Bruja and her granddaughter Miss Princess (Woven Webb). Bruja had four fabulous daughters. As a two-year-old Encantadora set a world's record for 5 furlongs in 57 seconds flat. Haunted, also a stake winner, set a world's record for 4½ furlongs in 52 seconds flat. Mickie (Witch Brew) ran 350 yards in 18 seconds flat. Miss Princess tied the world's record for 2½ furlongs in 27 1/5 seconds and set the world's record for a standing-start quarter in 22 seconds flat.

HARLOT. Harlot was a famous colonial running mare, sired by Goode's Bacchus and out of Coelia by Goode's Babram.

She was foaled in 1770 (?). She was bred by either John Goode, Sr., of Mecklenburg County, Virginia, or Charles R. Eaton, of North Carolina. Later she was raced by Hugh Snelling, of Granville County, North Carolina. One of her most famous races was with her dam, Coelia. This race was run at Oxford, North Carolina, for $10,000 a side. Harlot was the dam of Black Snake by *Obscurity.

HARMLESS, OLD. Old Harmless was foaled probably in or about 1779. She was sired by *Fearnought and out of a *Jolly Roger mare. Her second dam was by *Monkey. She was owned by Henry Deloney, of Mecklenburg County, Virginia. Edgar lists her as an American quarter running mare.

HATTIE TROWBRIDGE. Hattie was by Little Danger by Cold Deck and out of Miss Murphy by Grand River Chief. She was raised and raced by Mrs. H. A. Trowbridge, of Wellington, Kansas.

HATTIE JACKSON. Hattie Jackson was foaled in 1908 (?), and she was sired by Peter McCue and out of Nona P by Dan Tucker. She was bred by Samuel Watkins, of Petersburg, Illinois.

HATTIE SHIPLEY. Hattie Shipley, a gray, was foaled in 1892. She was sired by Dan Tucker and was out of Miss Buckler. She was owned and raised by Oliver and Barnes, who later sold her to J. H. Smith.

HATTIE W. Hattie W was foaled in 1894 (?) and died in 1914 (?). She was sired by either Hi Henry or the Duke of Highlands (TB). Hi Henry's dam was Lady Bug, and the dam of the Duke of Highlands was a daughter of *Bonnie Scotland, so both had a strong infusion of sprinting blood. Hattie W was out of Katie Wawekus. She was one of the last brood mares that Samuel Watkins owned. She was purchased by George Clegg, of Alice, Texas, after Watkins died. She was the dam of Never Fret, Sillex, Kendricks, and Hi Knocker, all by Hero (TB). When bred to Peter McCue, she foaled Cotton Eyed Joe. By the Thoroughbred Nimrod she produced Miss Pace, Erline, Edith A, and Hunter. By Hickory Bill she foaled Basil Prince and Sam Watkins in Texas.

HAZEL. Hazel was sired by Pid Hart by Shelby, and she was out of an Armstrong running mare. She was bred by Dan Armstrong, of Doxey, Oklahoma. She was the dam of Library (1909) by Tom Campbell.

HEADLIGHT. Headlight, a bay, was sired by Daylight by Meady, and she was out of Little Pet by Traveler. She was owned by L. A. Kirk, of Farmington, New Mexico.

HEELEY. Heeley, a sorrel, was foaled in 1889 and died in 1910 (?). Her sire was Blue Dick by Wade Hampton (TB), and her dam was the great Mittie Stephens by Shiloh, Jr. Heeley was bred and raised by C. R. Haley, of Sweetwater, Texas, and later owned by his friend J. F. Newman, of the same town. She can be found in *The American Stud Book.* Her foals include Aunt Joe by Sol Cleveland, Red Nellie by Boston, and Minyon, Sad Sam, Red Sam, I Must, Black Sam, and Kid Weller, all by Rancocas (TB).

HENNIE FARROW (BETTY MANEY). Hennie Farrow, a bay, was foaled in 1853. She was sired by *Shamrock (TB) and was out of Ida. She was the dam of Shannon (Tuesday) by Monday, a bay colt foaled in 1872.

HEREFORD. Hereford was by Black George by Morland, and she was bred by Thomas Trammell, of Sweetwater, Texas. She was the dam of Easter by Barney Owens.

HETTA BELL. Hetta Bell, a brown, was foaled in 1934. She was sired by Jack McCue, and her dam was Dolly by Prince. She was bred by M. E. Andres, of Portales, New Mexico.

HETTIE HUMPHRIES. Hettie Humphries was sired by Joe Hooker by Monday (TB). She was owned by Theodore Winters, of Woodland, California, and she was the dam of Winter's Telegraph.

HIGHLAND G. Highland G was by Little Joe by Traveler, and she was out of Julia Crowder by John Crowder. She was bred by John Dial, of Goliad, Texas. She was the dam of Maurine, a sorrel mare foaled in 1933 by Pride of India (TB).

HINDOO ROSE. Hindoo Rose was foaled in 1900 (?). Her breeding is unknown. She was owned by one "Hogmouth" Phillips. John Armstrong said that she was a real race mare up to a half mile. She was stabled at Denton, Texas.

HIPPIE. Hippie was sired by John Wilkins by Peter McCue and was owned by J. Erwin Renfro, of Mineral, Texas. She was the dam of Glad One by Prepare Away (TB) in 1928.

HOLLY HOCK. Holly Hock was sired by No Good by Barney Owens and was owned by Mark Dubois, of Bonita, Arizona. She was the dam of Chris Linda by Red Cloud.

HUNTSINGER MARE (SPANISH DUN MARE). The following record of the Huntsinger Mare was given to Helen Michaelis by Ove Oldham, of Buda, Texas, in 1940. The mare was bred by Indians in Oklahoma. She was bought—or just brought to the Pedernales River area by a man named Huntsinger. The mare was an outlaw and unbroken. When Oldham was fencing his land in the 1870s, he threatened to kill the mare if Huntsinger did not get her off his pastures. Huntsinger asked Oldham what he would give for her. Oldham offered $5.50, if he could catch her without crippling her. Oldham did, and he bought her. She became the dam of Lizzie when bred to Old Kingfisher.

I

IDA. Ida, a sorrel, was foaled in 1870. She was by Dr. Lindsey by Lexington and out of a Red Buck mare. She was bred by W. H. Musgrove, of Oregon.

IDA OSA. Ida Osa, a bay, was foaled in 1867. She was by *Bonnie Scotland and out of Red Kitty by Woodpecker. She was bred by a man named Hogge, of Ohio.

IMA CARWAY. Ima Carway was sired by Handy Shot and bred by Henry Talley, of Nixon, Texas. She was the dam of Rex, Jr., by Rex Beach by Conjuror (TB) in 1926.

INDIAN MAID. Not much is known about Indian Maid except that she was sired by Moss King. She was owned by the Waddell brothers, of Odessa, Texas. She was the dam of Waddell's Rondo (1927) and of Johnnie Reed (1928), both by Dennis Reed (TB).

INKY. Inky was by a Joe Bailey horse usually called Costello's Joe Bailey, after his owner and breeder, C. E. Costello, of Woodson, Texas. She was the dam of Sammy by Yellow Wolf.

ISLA SUNSHINE. Isla Sunshine was by Frank Norfleet by Joe Rutledge. She was owned by J. Frank Norfleet, of Hale Center, Texas. She was the dam of Texas Reynolds by Norfleet by *Brettenham.

ITA. Ita, a sorrel, was foaled in 1879, sired by Brick by Oregon Charlie and out of Jennie Gipson by Walnut Bark. Her second dam was Big Kate by Old Dan. She was bred and owned by John Adams, of Woodland, California. She became the dam of Lori B by Jim Douglas in 1885.

IVY'S GLORY. Ivy's Glory was sired by Cymon. She was bred in Virginia and taken into Texas, where she became the dam of Tar River by Nicholas in 1935.

J

JABALINA. Jabalina was sired by the Strait Horse by Yellow Jacket and was owned by C. Manuel Benevides Volpe, of

Laredo, Texas. She was the dam of King by Zantanon and of Queen by Valentino.

JACK MARE, LITTLE. The Little Jack Mare, a bay, was foaled in 1908. She was by Little Jack by Anthony and out of a William Fleming mare. She was bred by Fred Matthies, of Seguin, Texas. She was a very fast 300-yard mare. Willie Anderson, who lived near Belmont, Texas, trained and ran her, according to O. N. Crawford, of Seguin.

JAMIE JIMINY. Jamie Jiminy, a gray, was foaled in 1920. She was sired by Concho Colonel by Jim Ned and out of Rooka, who is referred to as a Spanish mare. Jamie was owned by Dan D. Casement, of Whitewater, Colorado.

JANE BAKER (ROAN JANE). Jane Baker, a roan, was foaled in 1884 (?), sired by Berry's Cold Deck. Her dam was a half-Thoroughbred mare owned by Tom Latham, of Missouri. She was taken from Missouri into Texas to run against Nellie Miller. The race was held at either Canadian or Mobeetie, and run for $500 a side. Nellie won the race. They also met in Kansas City, Missouri, with similar results.

JANE HUNT (PARAGON MARE). Jane Hunt, a bay, was foaled in 1796. She was sired by General Wade Hampton's Paragon and out of Moll by Figure. Jane was bred by Daniel Hunt, of New Jersey, and given to his son-in-law, John Harris, of Kentucky. According to an article in the *Franklin Farmer* (April 21, 1838), Harris sold Jane Hunt to a Judge Todd after breeding her for a number of years. Jane was raced until she was six and then bred. She had several fillies, and in 1812 she foaled a bay colt, Tiger, by Kentucky Whip. In 1816 she had a filly, and in 1818 she had another foal by Kentucky Whip, Little Tiger. Both Tiger and Little Tiger were fine Quarter Horse sires.

JANET V. Janet V was foaled in 1920 (?) and was sired by Elmendorf (TB) and out of Emma Hill by Peter McCue.

She was owned by Ed and Henry Pfefferling, of San Antonio, Texas. She became the dam of Tommie Gray by Uncle Jimmy Gray in 1928.

JACQUETTE. Jacquette was a Traveler mare owned by Webb Christian, of Big Spring, Texas. She was the dam of Palmistry by Palm Reader (TB) in 1907 and of Smitty by Dr. Curtis (TB) in 1910.

JANA LADY. Jana Lady was by Beggar Boy by Black Tony (TB) and out of Star Bird by Oklahoma Star. She was bred and owned by Ronald Mason, of Nowata, Oklahoma.

JEANETTE. Jeanette was foaled in 1920 (?) and was by Billy by Big Jim and out of a Sykes Rondo mare. She was bred by Ott Adams, of Alfred, Texas. She was bred to Little Joe four times and foaled Pancho Villa, Zantanon, Little Sister, and Black Annie.

JEANETTE (JENNY). Jeanette was by Harmon Baker and was bred by William Anson, of Christoval, Texas. She was later owned by C. Manuel Benevides Volpe, of Laredo, Texas. She became the dam of Valentino by Camaron by Texas Chief and of Zaino by the same stallion.

JENNY, OLD. Old Jenny, a brown, was foaled in 1891 (?) and died in 1905 (?). She was sired by Sykes Rondo and out of May Mangum. She was bred by Dow and Will Shely, of Alfred, Texas, and later owned by Ott Adams, of the same town. In 1903 she foaled Black Bess by Captain Sykes; in 1904, Little Joe by Traveler; and in 1905, King (Possum) by Traveler. She established two important Quarter Horse families through Little Joe and King (Possum), one in south Texas and one in Arizona.

JENNY, see JEANETTE.

JENNY, see GRAY JENNY.

JENNY (DENTON MARE). Jenny, the Denton Mare, was foaled in 1872. According to Wayne Gard, she was of Steel Dust blood. Sam Bass bought her in the fall of 1874. She lost only one race around Denton, and that one to Rattler. Soon thereafter Bass ran afoul of the law and rode Jenny to get away. We lose track of her after this time, though some of the McGonigal horses in the Midland, Texas, area are said to trace to this mare. It is certain that she never left Texas.

*JENNY CAMERON. *Jenny Cameron was sired by Cuddly by Fox and out of Cabbagewise. She was imported before the Revolutionary War by John Tayloe II. In England she was bred to Blaze and foaled *Betty Blazella, who was also imported into America. Jenny also foaled Silver Legs, Lloyd's Traveler, Smiling Tom, Little David, and several fillies.

JENNY CAPPS. Jenny Capps was foaled in 1882 (?) and died in 1898 (?). She was sired by Dash (or Black Dash) by Little Jeff Davis, and she was out of Bay Puss by Mounts by Steel Dust. Her second dam was Old Lit by Methodist Bull. She was bred by Shelby Stanfield, of Thorp Springs, Texas. She was the dam of Ned Wilson by Red Seal in 1924 and of Stepping on It by Hadrian (TB) in 1930.

JENNY CRASSOM. Jenny Crassom was sired by Ackley's Boanerges by Boanerges, and her dam was Fenton's Weasel. She was bred by Edward Lowrey, of Norwich, New York. She became the dam of Lowrey's Boanerges.

JENNY GIPSON. Jenny, a sorrel, was foaled in 1870 and died in 1897. She was bred and owned by John Adams, of Woodland, California. She was by Walnut Bark and out of Big Kate by Old Dan. She was the dam of Berryessa by Oregon Charlie; Tom, Ita, and Liza by Brick; Mart Gipson by Joe Hooker; and Jenny Shannon by Shannon.

JENNY JOHNSON. Jenny Johnson, a bay, was foaled in 1857. She was sired by Sweet Owen by Gray Eagle, and she was out of Lux by Wagner. Sweet Owen was out of Blinkey (Mary Porter), and Lux was out of Butterfly. She was bred by V. M. Flournoy, of Kentucky.

JENNY OLIVER. Jenny Oliver, a black, was foaled in 1881. She was by Billy by Shiloh and out of Paisana by Brown Dick. She was bred by Bill Fleming, of Belmont, Texas. She was a very fast mare and ran one quarter-mile race in 22 seconds. Jim Brown, of Giddings, Texas, also owned her for a while. She produced Brown Alice by Whalebone and Mamie B, Little Joe, and Blue Eyes by Sykes Rondo. She is listed in the appendix of *The American Stud Book.* Jenny Oliver and her Little Joe are found in *Goodwin's Turf Guide.*

JET GAL. Jet Gal was by Jet Sam (TB) and out of a Corder Quarter mare. She was bred and owned by Monty Corder, of Sanderson, Texas. She was the dam of Ned Wilson by Red Seal in 1924 and of Stepping on It by Hadrian (TB) in 1930.

JIMINY, see JAMIE.

JOANNE. Joanne was sired by Old Joe by Harmon Baker, and she was out of a Springer Quarter mare. She was owned and bred by the CS Ranch of Cimarron, New Mexico. She was the dam of Pat (or Padriac) by Mustard Seed (TB) in 1934.

JOAN OF ARC. Joan of Arc was by Candy Man by Kipskin (TB) and out of Quail by Possum. She was owned and bred by Melville H. Haskell, of Tucson, Arizona. She was the dam of Misty Toy by Red Racer in 1939.

JOE MARE, BIG. The Big Joe Mare was sired by Chrisman's Swayback, and she was out of Alsup's Steel Dust. She was bred by Ben Alsup, of Bald Knob, Missouri. She was the dam of Alsup's Red Buck by Grinder.

JOE MARE, OLD. The Old Joe Mare was by Harmon Baker by Peter McCue and out of a Minnick polo mare. She was bred by Jim Minnick, of Crowell, Texas, and was the dam of Young Eagle by Gray Eagle by Beetch's Yellow Jacket.

JOHNNIE. Johnnie was sired by John Wilkins by Peter McCue, and she was out of a good Quarter mare. She was bred by J. Renfro, of Sonora, Texas, and became the dam of Helter, a sorrel colt foaled in 1927, sired by Everett (TB).

JOHNNY WILKINS. Johnny Wilkins was sired by Horace H (TB) and out of a Wilkins Quarter mare. She was the dam of Verna Grace (Fair Chance) by Little Joe. She was bred by John Wilkins, of San Antonio, Texas.

JUANITA. Juanita, a bay, was foaled in 1912 and died in 1942. She was sired by the Barefield Horse by Little Joe and out of a Cuadro mare by Cuadro. Although she was a "catch colt," she proved to be a great race mare. Her best race was run at Houston, Texas, where she beat D. J. by 10 feet, running a quarter mile in 21 2/5 seconds. When I saw her in Richmond, Texas, in 1939, she was a long-bodied bay with short legs, standing 14-1 hands. She was owned for most of her life by Ed Fields, of Richmond, Texas. She was the dam of Red Joe by Grano de Oro in 1931 and of Tanglefoot by Rialto in 1937, both registered by the AQHA.

JUANITA ARMSTRONG. Juanita Armstrong was by Peter McCue and out of a running mare. She was owned in California by John J. Armstrong, and she was the dam of Moore by Dominus Arvi (TB) in 1918.

JUDGE, LITTLE. Little Judge was foaled in 1889. She was sired by Little Steve and was out of Sal by Gray Joe. She was bred by Mike Smiley, of Sylvan Grove, Kansas, and later purchased by Dan D. Casement, of Whitewater, Colorado, from Charles Walker, of Kiowa, Colorado. She was the dam of Olivia by Senator in 1911 and of Balleymooney by Concho Colonel in 1914.

JUDY. Judy was sired by Old Joe Bailey by Eureka and owned by Jack Joyce, of Graham, Texas. She was the dam of Prince Charming by Lion D'Or (TB).

JULIA CROWDER. Julia Crowder was sired by John Crowder by Old Billy and out of a Shely Quarter mare. She was bred by Dow and Will Shely, of Alfred, Texas, and purchased from them by Ott Adams when they had their dispersal sale. She was the dam of Dora Du Mar, a bay mare sired by Little Joe.

JUNE. June was sired by Captain Daugherty (TB) and was out of a Renfro running mare. She was bred by Matt Renfro, of Fort Sumner, New Mexico. She was the dam of Pecos Pete by Prepare Away (TB) in 1923.

JUNE BUG. June Bug, a bay, was foaled in 1859. She was by Harry Bluff (sire of Steel Dust) and out of Munch Meg by Alford (Snow Ball). Her second dam was Monkey by Boanerges. She was probably bred by Joe Lewis, of Hunnewell, Kansas, but Sam Watkins bought her in Greene County, Illinois. Her produce include (Nannie) Reap by Dr. Cash in 1870, Honest Abe by Voltigeur (TB) in 1874, Cricket by Voltigeur (TB) in 1875, and Lady Bug (Butt Cut) by Jack Traveler in 1876.

JUNE BUG. June Bug was sired by Harvester (TB) and bred by James Allred, of Mineral Wells, Texas. She became the dam of Dan by Joe Bailey in 1920.

JUNE BUG'S SISTER, see ALICE.

JUNE GRAY. June Gray, a gray, was foaled in 1885, sired by Old Billy and out of Gray Alice. She was bred by E. Shelby Stanfield, of Thorp Springs, Texas. According to George Clegg, she produced Ace of Hearts by Cuadro. Another equally reliable source, Helen Michaelis, said that Ace of Hearts was by the Dunderstadt Horse.

JUNE SUNDAY. June Sunday was by Tom Sunday (TB) and out of a polo mare sired by Senator. She was owned by the 7-11 Ranch, of Hot Springs, South Dakota. She became the dam of July by Mentor (TB) in 1925.

K

KANACK. Kanack was a good Quarter mare, though her breeding is not as easy to find as her running record. There is some evidence that she was out of Kitty Menard. She was owned by S. E. Lawrence, of Maple City, Kansas, and Smithtown, New York. The Lawrences were friends of the Trowbridges, of Wellington, Kansas, and Belle Mead Farm, in New Jersey. Kanack eventually wound up in the hands of Dan D. Casement, of Manhattan, Kansas, and Whitewater, Colorado. All three of these families were wealthy and influential Quarter Horse breeders before the association was formed. Kanack was the dam of Young Pawhuska.

KATE. Kate, a brown, was foaled in 1820. She was sired by Printer by Atkinson's Janus by *Janus. She was bred by a man named Thompson and owned by John A. Scott, of Woodville, Mississippi. She was the dam of a bay mare by Lord Byron and of Caldwell's Whip by Kentucky Whip (1824).

KATE, BIG. Big Kate was foaled in 1865. She was sired by Old Dan by Selim and out of an Ariel mare by Casper's Ariel. She was owned by John Adams, of Woodland, California, and was the dam of the sorrel race mare Jenny Gibson by Walnut Bark.

KATE BERNARD. Kate Bernard, a sorrel, was foaled in 1910. She was sired by Santa Claus by Red Buck and out of a Meek running mare. Jim Caldwell told me that she was big and powerful and was raced by Jim and Ralph Avant, of Clinton, Oklahoma. Probably the Avants were her breeders.

In 1918 she foaled Kate Blair by Joe Blair, and in 1919, Katy Jones by Casey Jones.

KATE BLAIR. Kate Blair was sired by Joe Blair (TB) and out of Kate Bernard. George Clegg bought her from Ronald Mason, of Nowata, Oklahoma, when she was in foal to Oklahoma Star. She had a filly foal that was sold to the King Ranch, of Kingsville, Texas.

KATE GEORGE, see BIG GUN.

KATIE BAR THE DOOR. Katie Bar the Door was sired by the Duke of Highlands and out of a mare bred by Sam Watkins, of Petersburg, Illinois, who also bred Katie. She was the dam of Wake Up Jake by Peter McCue.

KATIE (KATY) FLANGER. Katie, a bay, was foaled in 1895, sired by Fib (TB) and out of Puss B by Tom Flood. She was bred, owned, and raced by James Owen, of Berlin, Illinois.

KATIE M. Katie M was sired by Big Jim by Sykes Rondo, and she was bred by Ott Adams, of Alfred, Texas. She was the dam of Jim Wells by Little Joe in 1910 (?).

KATIE WADDEL, see KITTIE WATKINS.

KATIE WAWEKUS. Katie Wawekus was a Thoroughbred. Bred to Peter McCue, she foaled John Wilkins. She also foaled Hattie W by Hi Henry.

KATY BELL. Katy Bell, a black, was foaled in the early 1900s. She was sired by Buckshot by Joe Collins and out of Sir by Joe Collins. She was owned in Arizona by Joe McKinney, of Wilcox, but was undoubtedly bred by the McGonigals, of Midland, Texas. She was the dam of Katy Bell II.

KATY BELL II. Katy Bell II was sired by Red Cloud and out of Katy Bell by Buckshot. She was foaled in 1930 (?) and was owned and bred by Charles A. Gardner, of Elgin, Arizona.

KATY FLYER (KATY FLY). Katy Flyer was foaled in 1914, sired by Paul Murray and out of a Sleepy Joe mare. Her second dam was by Tom Gray, and her third dam was by John Crowder. She was bred by F. G. Senne, of Hondo, Texas. She was used for farm work and plowed until she was eleven, when it was discovered that she could run. In 1926 she was sold to George Miller for a polo pony. She was also owned by a Judge Staddler of Brackettville, Texas. When bred to Uncle Jimmy Gray, she produced Black Streak 1924).

KIDDO. Kiddo was sired by John Wilkes by Peter McCue, and she was bred and owned by Matt Renfro, of Sonora, Texas. She was the dam of Moon Mullins, a sorrel colt foaled in 1926, sired by Everett (TB).

KIRKINDALL. Kirkindall, a Famous American Quarter Running Mare, was foaled sometime between 1756 and 1758. She was a gray, sired by *Janus and out of a *Silver Eye mare. She was bred by George Kirkindall, of Virginia, from whom she got her name. She is listed in Edgar (p. 287) and Bruce (1:584).

KITTIE WADDELL, see KITTIE WATKINS.

KITTIE WATKINS (KITTIE WADDELL). Kittie Watkins, a bay, was foaled in 1877, sired by Jack Traveler and out of the great Kitty Clyde, who was by Star Davis. She was bred by C. B. Carpenter, of Tolona, Illinois. *The American Stud Book* also shows that she was owned by B. C. Watkins and by Samuel Watkins, of Petersburg, Illinois. She was a full sister of Bird. She had nine outstanding offspring for Watkins between 1888 and 1897, including two by Famous (TB), Dobbins and Sealum; two by the Duke of Highlands (TB), Tom D and the Duke of Little Grove; and two by Hero (TB), Kitty Hero and Dry Camp.

KITTY. Kitty was sired by a son of Kentucky Whip and out of Lady Williams by Gray Eagle. Her second dam was Brick by Pilgrim. She was probably bred by John Adams, of Woodland, California. She was the dam of John A, a bay colt foaled in 1889, sired by Gabriel (TB).

KITTY. Kitty was foaled in 1900 (?). She was sired by Blue Eyes by Sykes Rondo and out of a Crockett mare. She was bred and raised by Will Shely, of Alfred, Texas. She was also the dam of Whalebone by Texas Chief.

KITTY. Kitty was foaled in 1932 (?). She was sired by Tony by Guinea Pig and bred by John E. Kane, of Douglas, Arizona. She was the dam of Sonny Boy by Mack.

KITTY. Kitty was by Mineral and out of a Berry Ketchum mare. Little is known about the breeding of the Ketchum horse stock, except that they could all fly. Ketchum lived at Sheffield, Texas. Kitty was the dam of Harkey's King, a sorrel colt by Dodger, foaled in 1930.

KITTY CLYDE. Kitty Clyde, a bay, was foaled in 1860 and died in 1888 (?). She was sired by Star Davis (TB) and out of Margravine by *Margrave (TB). This pedigree is given by Bruce (2:22). She was bred by Thomas Bryon, of Fayette County, Kentucky. She was later sold to C. V. Carpenter, of Talona, Illinois, and she was given to Samuel Watkins, of Petersburg, Illinois, in 1882. Sometime before that, Tom A. Gay, of Menard, Texas, either owned her or had her during the years 1870 and 1871. While she was in Texas, she was bred to Marion and produced Kitty Menard. It appears that James Owen had her in the spring of 1882, when Bird was foaled. She is supposed to have run a quarter mile in 21½ in 1892, not bad time for a thirty-two-year-old mare. Another, more likely, race was held in 1864 in New Philadelphia, Ohio (*Wilkes' Spirit of the Times* 9 [1864]:290). Among her produce were the great mares Kitty Menard, Kittie Watkins, Nora M, and Bird. She may well have been the greatest producer of Quarter Horse dams.

KITTY DEAN. Kitty Dean was foaled in 1882, and she was owned by T. C. Dean, of Merced, California. She was the dam of three well-known Pacific Coast racing mares, Iodine (1887), Lottie (1888), and Daisy (1891), all by Little Alp.

KITTY FISHER. *Kitty Fisher, a gray colonial mare, was sired by Cade, and her dam was by the Cullen Arabian. She was bred by the Marquis of Granby and imported by Carter Braxton, of Virginia, in 1759. Several of her foals, such as Crippled Fearnought, Virginia, Forest Garrick, Gallatin, and Pilot made contributions to the colonial Quarter Horses.

KITTY MENARD (KITTY MAYNARD). Kitty Menard, a sorrel, was foaled in 1872 and bred by Tom A. Gray, of Menard, Texas. She was sired by Marion by Lexington (TB) and out of the great Kitty Clyde. She is found in both the appendix and the main sections of Bruce. She is transformed from an unknown mare in volume 3 to a pedigreed mare in volume 6. She was later owned by S. E. Lawrence, of Maple City, Kansas, who bred her several times to Mrs. H. A. Trowbridge's Kiro. Among her foals were Peter L, Tatnai, Lon Welch, Spectre, Kitty Lawrence, and Little Kit. See KANACK.

KITTY PEASE. Kitty Pease, a sorrel, was foaled in 1882, by Jack Hardy (TB) and out of Mollie by Tar River. She was bred by H. T. Batchler, of Dallas, Texas.

KNEE (BIG KNEE). Knee was sired by John Wilkes by Peter McCue, and she was bred by J. E. Renfro, of Menard, Texas. She was the dam of Tinkertoy by Toyland (TB).

L

LADY. Lady was foaled about 1910, sired by Little Joe. She was owned by Jim Adams, of Alfred, Texas. She was the dam of J. D. by Paul El and of Annie L by Billy Sunday.

LADY. Lady was sired by Ben Hur by Rainy Day and out of a Thoroughbred mare. She was owned by Roy Smith, of Patagonia, Arizona, and became the dam of Donna Rica in 1937.

LADY. Lady was by Spark Plug by Jack McCue and out of Mamie by Old Joe Bailey. She was owned by T. J. Bridges, of Olton, Texas. She was the dam of Dutch McCue, foaled in 1934.

LADY BEATRICE. Lady Beatrice, a sorrel, was foaled in 1882. She was bred by Uriah Eggleston, of Garden City, Kansas. She was sired by Uncle Tom, and her dam was Mollie McCreary, who was by Zero (TB).

LADY BLACKBURN. Lady Blackburn was foaled in 1920 (?) and was sired by Barney Lucas by Traveler. She was owned by Dick Gray, of Gorman, Texas. She foaled Will Run when bred to Rummore (TB).

LADY BLAKE. Lady Blake was foaled in 1920 (?). She was sired by Young Cold Deck by Berry's Cold Deck, and she was out of Gray Meg by Possum by Young White Lightning. She was bred and owned by Coke Blake, of Pryor, Oklahoma.

LADY BUG (BUTT CUT). Lady Bug, a sorrel, was foaled in 1876 or soon after and died in 1900. She was often called

Butt Cut because she had a wire cut on her left hip. Her sire was Jack Traveler by Steel Dust, and her dam was June Bug by Harry Bluff. She was owned and bred by Samuel Watkins, of Petersburg, Illinois. She was the dam of both Dan Tucker and Hi Henry. When Lady Bug was twenty-five years old, Watkins was dared to match her against the Thoroughbred Famous, a grandson of *Bonnie Scotland. She won the match on a circular track. Elias Watkins, who rode Barney Owens, Peter McCue, and Dan Tucker in races, said that Butt Cut was the fastest horse he ever rode.

LADY BUNBURY. Lady Bunbury was sired by Trumpator and bred by John Randolph, of Roanoke, Virginia. She was the dam of Roanoke by Sir Archy in 1817.

LADY C. Lady C was by Guinea Pig by Possum and out of a mare by Bulger. She was bred by Chester Cooper, of Roosevelt, Arizona, and later owned by A. A. Nichols, of Gilbert, Arizona. According to Jo Flieger, she was never beaten between one-eighth and one-quarter mile in Arizona or California. In 1941 she became the dam of the good sorrel colt Chester C by Clabber.

LADY DAVIS. Lady Davis, a sorrel, was foaled in 1846. She was by Red Bill by Medoc. Her breeder was Theodore Winters, of Woodland, California. She was the dam of Ramrod by Rifleman in 1866.

LADY FOSTER. Lady Foster was sired by Foster by Lexington and out of Jenny Hull by Belmont. She was first owned by Andrew Wackman, of Elk Grove, California. She was the dam of Kiro by Joe Hooker in 1887. Kiro was registered Thoroughbred but bred a large number of excellent sprinters for Mrs. H. A. Trowbridge, of Wellington, Kansas, who bought him and took him to Kansas.

LADY FOX. Lady Fox was sired by Gray Wolf by Young Cold Deck, and she was bred by Coke Blake, of Pryor,

Oklahoma. She became the dam of Smuggler by Tubal Cain by Berry's Cold Deck in 1916 (?).

LADY GLADYS. Lady Gladys, a sorrel, was foaled in 1885 (?) and died in 1900. She was sired by Bill Garner by Steel Dust, and she was out of Mancos' Big Filly. While racing in Idaho and Montana Lady Gladys was accidentally bred to another racehorse, Pid Hart. When she was too far along to run, Shelby Stanfield had her taken home to Thorp Springs, Texas, where in 1890 she foaled Rocky Mountain Tom, named for a Stanfield employee and the area in which she was bred.

LADY KINNEY. Lady Kinney was sired by A. D. Reed by Peter McCue and out of Joy Lady by Joy by Jeff. She was bred by A. D. Hurley, of Canute, Oklahoma.

LADY LAWRENCE (POLLY). Lady Lawrence, a sorrel, was foaled in 1877. She was sired by Wisconsin Harry and out of Fairy. She was owned and bred by S. E. Lawrence, of Maple City, Kansas. She foaled Level Lady by Leveller (TB) in 1888, Jack the Ripper by Eph Gray (TB) in 1890, Lady Boston by Tom Boston in 1892, and Pawhuska by Okema (TB) in 1893.

LADY LUCK. Lady Luck, a bay, was foaled in 1930 (?), sired by Booger Red by Rancocas (TB) and out of a Thoroughbred mare raised by Jim Newman, of Sweetwater, Texas. In 1936 she was owned by Floyd Miller, of Chamita, New Mexico, and in 1938 by Warren Shoemaker, of Watrous, New Mexico.

LADY LYON II (TB). Lady Lyon II, a registered Thoroughbred, was raised by Maggie Watkins, of Oakford, Illinois, a niece of Samuel Watkins. She was bred to Peter McCue in 1906, and in the spring of 1907 foaled Tucker Miller.

LADY McCUE. Lady McCue was sired by Peter McCue and was owned by J. M. Leavitt, of San Jose, Illinois. She was the dam of Nelson by Thicket (TB). She was probably foaled about 1900.

LADY MACK. Lady Mack was sired by Joe Bailey, of Weatherford, Texas, and she became the dam of Do Go by Slipalong (TB) in 1928.

LADY S. Lady S, a bay, was foaled in 1911 (?) and was sired by Jess Parsons by Traveler and out of Mamie Echols by Brown Billy by Pancho. She was bred by Art Echols, of San Antonio, Texas, and owned by Will Wingate, of Devine, Texas. She was the dam of Magician, a black colt sired by Rainy Day by Lone Star. She was occasionally referred to as the Cut Foot Mare, because of a wire cut on her left-rear pastern.

LADY S. Lady S was sired by John Crowder, and she was bred and owned by Will Shely, of Alfred, Texas. She outran Texas Chief at 300 yards but he outran her at 400 yards. Ott Adams said that Little Joe beat her by eight feet, though no distance was mentioned.

LADY SPECK. Lady Speck, a sorrel mare, was foaled in 1935 (?). She was sired by Major Speck by Uncle Jimmy Gray and out of Water Lily by Yellow Jacket. She was bred by John Kenedy, of Sarita, Texas. She was later owned by Estevan Garcia, of McAllen, Texas, and raced by Sheriff Cardway, of Kenedy County. She beat the good King Ranch racehorse Don Manners by a nose at Kingsville in 1940 in 22.6 seconds for the quarter. She beat Cyclone going 350 yards in 18½ seconds. In 1943 she was owned by Ed Rachal.

LADY TOWNSEND. Lady Townsend, a sorrel, was foaled in 1844, sired by Robert Bruce and out of a Tiger mare. Tiger was by Kentucky Whip and out of Jane Hunt by Paragon.

LADY WINSTON. Little is known about Lady Winston. She was owned by Theodore Winters, of Woodland, California, and she was the dam of Broncho, a sorrel colt foaled in 1886.

LARKSPUR. Larkspur was by Concho Colonel by Jim Ned and out of Lark by Ban (TB). She was owned by Jack Casement, of Whitewater, Colorado. She was bred to Deuce three times and foaled Ready Fox in 1937, Lapwing in 1938, and Annette in 1940, all three registered AQHA.

LAURA LEE. Laura Lee, a bay, was foaled in 1885. She was sired by Jack Boston and out of Mischief by Keene Richards. She was bred and owned by J. R. Nasworthy, of Bridge View Stud, in San Angelo, Texas. She was the dam of the bay filly Zuleta by Judge Kirk, the bay colt Get There by Get Away (TB), the brown colt Judge Cook by Ferg Kyle (TB), and the bay filly Georgia (1892) by Buck Walton.

LAURA MITCHELL. Laura Mitchell, a sorrel, was foaled in 1885. She was bred and owned by Uriah Eggleston, of Garden City, Kansas. She was sired by Elkhorn (TB) and out of Molly McCreary by Zero.

LEMONADE. Lemonade, a brown, was foaled in 1888. She was sired by Anthony by Old Billy and out of Silentina by Silent Friend (TB). She was bred by Tom King, of Belmont, Texas, and later owned by Wade McLemore, also of Belmont. According to *Goodwin's Turf Guide* (1894), she was run as a Thoroughbred showing Whalebone as her sire and Silver Beam her dam. In Bruce's appendix to *The American Stud Book* (6:1156) she is shown as by Whalebone and out of Silverscreen. In the main text of Bruce (6:551) she appears as Lemonade II. She was a full sister of Fashion. She, Fashion, and Yellow Wolf were all raced by McLemore. She had a bay filly, Enze, by Galen (TB) in 1895; a brown colt, S. B. Cooper, by Rebel in 1898; a brown colt, Lucky John, by Play in 1901; Little Gift by Rancocas (TB) in 1901; and Phil King by *Gallantry in 1902.

LENA G. Lena G, a bay, was foaled in 1891. She was sired by Jack Hardy (TB) and out of Miss Cleveland by Rebel Morgan. She was owned by H. T. Batchler, of Lancaster and Dallas, Texas.

LEONA. Leona was by Cirildo (the Canales Horse) by Leonell and out of Vensidora by Joe Shely by Traveler. She was owned by Luis Reuteria, of Edenburg, Texas. She was the dam of Turco by Grano de Oro.

LEVEL LADY. Level Lady, a sorrel, was foaled in 1888. She was sired by Leveller (TB) and out of Lady Lawrence by Wisconsin Harry. She was bred and owned by S. E. Lawrence, of Maple City, Kansas. She was bred to Kiro, H. A. Trowbridge's stallion, four times and produced Busby, Ida Rogers, In-to-Rah, and Zillah. She also had Joe Welsh by Eph Gray and W. H. Ashland by Ashland II.

LIGHT FOOT. Light Foot was by June Bug by Captain Daughtery. She was raised by A. J. Beck, of Brownwood, Texas. She was the dam of Sun Man, a sorrel colt by Leonard B (TB) foaled in 1935.

LIGHTFOOT. Lightfoot was foaled in 1905 (?). She was by Traveler, and she was owned by J. M. Corder, of Sanderson, Texas. She was the dam of Select by Esquire (TB).

LILLIE. Lillie was foaled in 1880 (?), sired by California and out of a Norfolk (TB) mare. She was bred and owned by W. P. Diggs, of Woodland, California. She was the dam of Red Iron.

LILLIE W. Lillie W, a sorrel, was foaled in 1887. She was sired by Joe Hooker (TB) and out of Ella T by Shannon. She was bred by John W. Adams, of Woodland, California. She foaled Lomo by Red Iron in 1894, Loconomo by St. Savior in 1895, and Mozita by Mosby in 1896.

LILLY WHITE. Lilly White was by Horace H (TB) and out of Carrie Nation by Peter McCue. She was bred by Eugene J. Schott, of Riomedina, Texas. She was the dam of Twin City by A. M. White, foaled in 1924.

LINNET. Linnet was sired by Baldwin's Friday and out of Pumpkin Filly by Blue Boar. She was bred by Thomas Goode, of Chesterfield County, Virginia, and later owned by Wyllie Jones, of Halifax County, North Carolina. According to Edgar, she was a Celebrated American Quarter Running Mare. She was also the dam of Edmunton's Janus, a bay colt foaled in 1760 (?) by Bellair.

LIZ, BIG. Big Liz was foaled in 1920. She was sired by Paul El and out of Nettie Harrison. She was bred by Ott Adams, of Alfred, Texas, and later owned by John Dial, of Goliad, Texas. She was also owned and handled by Bill Nack, of Cuero, Texas; George Groll, of Berclair, Texas; Tom Burns, of Yoakum, Texas; and Robert J. Kleberg, of the King Ranch, Kingsville, Texas. She was raced primarily by George Groll. Kleberg bought all her daughters that were available: Bill's Liz, Roan Liz, and Little Liz. The first two were by Lion D'Or (TB), and the last was by Chicaro (TB).

LIZA GRAY. Liza Gray was by Uncle Jimmy Gray by Bonnie Joe and out of a mare by Jim Wells. She was bred by John Dial, of Goliad, Texas. She was the dam of Mary Dee, a bay mare foaled in 1938 by Universe (TB).

LIZZIE. Lizzie was foaled in 1890 (?) and was sired by Old King Fisher. Most agree that her dam was the Huntsinger Mare (sometimes called the Spanish Dun Mare). This mare was a mustang, and she was raised by Indians in Oklahoma. Her daughter Lizzie was bred either by Ove Oldham, of Buda, Texas, or by J. N. Brazier, of Willow Creek, Texas. Lizzie outran Blue Jacket at Kyle, Texas. She could run a quarter in 22½ seconds. She was the dam of Doc Oldham by *Gallantry (TB).

LIZZIE. Lizzie was foaled in 1900 and was sired by Doc Oldham, her half brother, and was out of the Huntsinger Mare. She was bred by Ove Oldham, of Buda, Texas. She was the dam of Ben Bolt by Aguinaldo.

LIZZIE PARKS. Lizzie Parks, a sorrel, was sired by General Hood (TB) and out of a Shiloh mare. She was foaled around 1880 and was bred by J. R. Nasworthy, of the Bridge View

Stud, San Angelo, Texas. She foaled Little Sister (1887), Mable Scott (1892), and Lizzie Walton (1893), all three sired by Buck Walton (TB).

LIZZIE WALTON. Lizzie Walton, a brown, was foaled in 1893, sired by Buck Walton (TB) and out of Lizzie Parks. Her second dam was by Shiloh. She was bred by J. R. Nasworthy, of San Angelo, Texas.

LOLA MONTEZ. Lola Montez, a gray, was foaled in 1846. She was sired by Gray Eagle by Woodpecker and out of a Duncan mare. She was bred by Major H. T. Duncan, of Kentucky, and was later owned by James Moore, of Yolo County, California. She was the dam of Odd Fellow by Jack Hawkins and of Harkaway by Bill Cheatham.

LOMA. Loma was sired by Sam King by Hondo and was owned by O. W. Cardwell, of Junction, Texas. She was the dam of Hill Top, foaled in 1925.

LONE DOVE. Lone Dove, a gray, was foaled in 1931. She was sired by Big Heart Joe by Joe Blair and out of Old Robinson by Danger.

LONE STAR MARE. The Lone Star Mare was sired by Lone Star by Gold Enamel (TB), and she was out of a good Schott Quarter mare. She was bred and owned by Eugene Schott of Riomedina, Texas. She was the dam of Little Fox by Uncle Jimmy Gray.

LORETTA. Loretta was a short-race mare bought without a pedigree by J. J. Kennedy, of Bonita, Arizona. When bred to Baby King by Possum, she foaled Monte Cross.

LOTTERY. Lottery, a sorrel, was foaled in 1803. She was sired by *Bedford, and her dam was *Anvilina by Anvil. She was the dam of Kosciusko by Sir Archy, foaled in 1815.

LOU B. Lou B, a bay, was foaled in 1885. She was sired by Jim Douglas and out of Ita by Brick. Her second dam was Jennie Gipson by Walnut Bark. After being raced, she was bred and foaled Zora B by Shannon. She was probably bred by John Adams of Woodland, California.

LOUISE. Louise was a mare of unknown breeding but very fast for under three-eighths mile. She was owned by Tom Stogdon, of Alba, Missouri. She was bred to Cold Deck by Steel Dust and became the dam of Brown Dick in 1887.

LOU TRAMMELL. Lou Trammell was sired by Peter McCue and bred by Clyde McClain, of Leedey, Oklahoma. She was the dam of Joy by Jeff, foaled in 1912.

LUCILE. Lucile was sired by Rob Roy by Chulo Mundo and out of Nigger by Chulo Mundo. She was bred and owned by Homer Runnels, of Fort Worth, Texas. She became the dam of Sun Flower Lady, a dun mare foaled in 1938 by Tom C.

LUCINDA. Lucinda was sired by a son of Kid Weller. She was bred by P. L. Fuller, of Snyder, Texas. She was the dam of Little Fort (Little Fort Worth) in 1929 by Black Bob by Bob Carraway.

LUCRETIA M. Lucretia M, a sorrel, was foaled on March 17, 1901. She was sired by Hero (TB) and out of Bird by Jack Traveler. Her second dam was Kitty Clyde. She was bred by Sam Watkins, of Petersburg, Illinois. When Watkins died, his wife sold several horses to George Clegg, of Alice, Texas, including Lucretia M and her offspring Hickory Bill, foaled in 1907. She was also the dam of Jodie by Little Joe.

LUCY. Lucy, a bay, was foaled in 1871. She was sired by Marion by Lexington and owned by James Owen, of Berlin, Illinois. She was the dam of Deck by Barney Owens.

LUCY. Lucy, a gray, was sired by Tom Campbell and out of Bear Paws by Tom Campbell. She was bred by E. A. Meek, of Foss, Oklahoma. She was a first-class race mare.

LUCY CHERRY. Lucy Cherry was owned by Walter Priestly Dickson, of Flatonia, Texas. She was the dam of Sam Harper,

Jr., by Sam Harper. I could not determine a pedigree for her that made sense.

LUCY MAXWELL (BRIMMER MARE). Lucy Maxwell, a sorrel, was sired by Alsup's Red Buck by Grinder and out of a line-bred Brimmer mare. She was 14 hands and weighed 1,200 pounds. She was bred by Napoleon Maxwell, of Wendell, Tennessee, and later sold to Coke Blake, of Pryor, Oklahoma. In 1902 she foaled Big Danger by Berry's Cold Deck, and the following year she foaled Tubal Cain by the same stallion. Coke Blake claimed that she was the fastest mare he ever saw run.

LULU. Lulu was by Rex Beach II by Rex Beach (TB) and out of Lady Lu by Big Jim. She became the dam of Betty Scruggs in 1933, sired by a Little Joe colt.

LULU B. Lulu B, a brown, was sired by Indicator and out of Nettie Moore.

LULU MAC. Lulu Mac was a Blue Eyes mare owned by Will Shely, of Alfred, Texas. In 1900 she became the dam of Buster by Little Rondo by Locks Rondo.

LULU RIGGS. Lulu Riggs was sired by Humbolt, and she was out of Crooked River. She was owned by A. J. Foster, of Paisley, Oregon. She had three foals: in 1880 Amy B, by Ballot Box; in 1886 Hercules, by Joe Hooker; and in 1887 Oregon Eclipse, by Joe Hooker.

M

MABEL. Mabel was sired by Ben Bolt by Aguinaldo, and she was raised and owned by Corinne Huetlig, of Kyle, Texas. She was the dam of Rex by Ben Bolt in 1929.

McKINNEY BLACK. McKinney Black was sired by Bill Garner and owned by J. T. McKinney, of Wilcox, Arizona.

She was the dam of Garner's Barney by Danger by Barney Owens, foaled in 1900 (?).

MacMURRAY MARE. The MacMurray Mare was by Doc Oldham by *Gallantry (TB) and out of an Arab mare. She was owned by Bob MacMurray, of Hebbronville, Texas. She was the dam of Sam C by Texas Chief and of Ordeon by the same stallion in 1912.

MADAM MURRAY. Madam Murray, a sorrel, was foaled in 1910. She was by Cotton Eyed Joe by Peter McCue and out of Babe Ruth by Sykes Rondo. She was bred by Bill Nack, of Cuero, Texas. George Clegg said that she beat Ace of Hearts at the Alice fair in 1912. He also said that she had been falsely registered as a Thoroughbred.

MAG. Mag was a fast mare of Printer breeding owned by the Keeney brothers, of Long Creek, Oregon. She was the dam of Simtuck by Oregon Dick in 1860 (?).

MAGGIE (B. B.). Maggie, a sorrel, was foaled in 1867 by *Australian (TB) and out of Madelene by Boston. According to Bruce, she was said to be the dam of Okema by Reform (Okema was the good stallion used by Mrs. H. A. Trowbridge, of Wellington, Kansas). There are strong indications, however, that Okema was out of Cherokee Belle, a mare bred by Joe Lewis, of Hunnewell, Kansas.

MAGGIE GALE. Maggie Gale (TB) was owned by Webb Christian, of Big Spring, Texas. She was the dam of Merle Lee by Barney Lucas in 1913.

MAGGIE KING. Maggie King was sired by Peter McCue, and she was owned by George Newton, of Del Rio, Texas. She was the dam of Tormentor by Barnsdale (TB) in 1914.

MAID OF OATS, YOUNG. Young Maid of Oats, a sorrel, was foaled in 1817. She was sired by *Expedition and out of Maid of Oats by *Spread. She was the dam of Medoc by American Eclipse in 1829.

MAID OF THE MILL. Maid of the Mill, a bay, was foaled in the 1870s. Her sire was Censor. She was the dam of Uncle Tom by Uncle Vic by Lexington.

MAJESTY. Majesty was sired by Dalston (TB), and she was owned by Ben Savage, of Steamboat Springs, Colorado. She was the dam of Chocolate Soldier by Ding Bob, foaled in 1932.

MALBROOK. Malbrook was sired by *Mexican, and she was bred by John R. Eaton, of Granville County, North Carolina. She was the dam of Eaton's Van Tromp by Ball's Florizel by *Diomed, foaled in 1809.

MALEY. Maley was by Tar River and owned by Henry T. Batchler, of Lancaster, Texas. She was the dam of Tom Gay by Jack Hardy (TB), foaled in the 1890s.

MAMIE. Mamie was sired by No Good by Barney Owen, and she was out of Birdie by John Crowder. She was owned by Jim Kennedy, of Bonita, Arizona. She was the dam of Guinea Pig by Possum (King), foaled in 1922.

MAMIE B. Mamie B, a brown, was foaled in 1890. She was sired by Sykes Rondo and out of Jenny Oliver. She was bred by W. B. Fleming, of Belmont, Texas, and raced by J. O. Blades. She was a half sister of Blue Eyes and of Mamie Sykes. She was registered by Bruce and appears in *Goodwin's Turf Guide.*

MAMIE CROWDER. Mamie Crowder was foaled in 1900 (?) and died in 1920 (?). She was sired by John Crowder by Old Billy and out of a mare by Blue Eyes by Sykes Rondo. She was bred by Will and Dow Shely, of Alfred, Texas, and was purchased by Ott Adams at the Shely dispersal sale. She was a noted race mare in the early 1900s. She outran Pleas Walters, her half brother, at the Dallas fair, and when she was rematched at Kerrville, running three-eighths instead of a quarter mile, she won again. She was the dam of Captain

Joe by Traveler (1910?), Mamie Jay by Little Joe (1916?), and Ada Jones by Little Joe (1918?).

MAMIE ECHOLS. Mamie Echols was sired by Brown Billy by Pancho and out of a cold-blooded gray mare owned by Art Echols, of San Antonio, Texas. She was bred by J. B. Echols, of Big Foot,Texas. She was a fast mare. She ran a race against Blue Jacket at Kyle and beat him. She was the dam of Lady S by Jess Parsons, foaled probably in 1911.

MAMIE HOGETT. Mamie Hogett was sired by Captain Joe by Traveler and bred by Del Wingate, of Devine, Texas. She was the dam of Lone Star by Uncle Jimmy Gray, foaled in 1927.

MAMIE J, see MAMIE JAY.

MAMIE JAY (MAMIE J). Mamie Jay was sired by Little Joe by Traveler and out of Mamie Crowder by John Crowder. She was bred by Ott Adams, of Alice, Texas, and owned by John Dial, of Goliad, Texas. She was the dam of Little Rex by Rex Beach and of Sunol by Paul El, foaled in 1934.

MAMIE ROBERTS. Mamie Roberts was by Ace of Hearts and out of a Captain Sykes mare. She was owned by Ott Adams, of Alfred, Texas. He bought her from a man he could remember only as a Mr. Roberts. She was a race mare before he bought her. She became the dam of Gray Buck in 1925, of Old Gray in 1926, and of Plain Jane by Little Joe in 1927.

MAMIE SYKES (MINNIE SYKES). Mamie Sykes was foaled in 1894 (?) and was sired by Sykes Rondo and out of May Mangum. Some reports say that she was May's last foal. She was owned by W. A. Wright of Kingsbury, Texas. Truston Polk and Bill Nack took her to Louisiana for a race. She pulled a leader and was sold around Abbeville, Louisiana. Earlier she lost a race to Judge Thomas at Sonora but turned around and beat him in a rematch, running the quarter in 22 seconds. Mamie was a full sister of Dogie Beasley. Her best-known foal was Major Gray by Uncle Jimmy Gray, foaled when she was returned to Texas by W. A. Wright, sometime before 1920.

MAMIE TAYLOR. Mamie Taylor, a sorrel, was foaled in 1934. She was sired by Jack Dempsey by Big Boy and out of Red Cloud by Tex. She was owned by L. A. Kirk, of Farmington, New Mexico. She was the dam of Hardtwist by Cowboy in 1943.

MAMMOTH (MONMOUTH). Mammoth was sired by Shiloh by Van Tromp, and she was bred by Harrison Stiff, of McKinney, Texas. Her dam is reported to have been sired by Stiff's stallion Monmouth, who had a famous race with Steel Dust. Later Mammoth was owned by Henry T. Batchler, of Lancaster, Texas. She became the dam of Tom Driver by Steel Dust.

MANDY. Mandy was sired by the Old Dutchman by Lock's Rondo and out of Het by Bill Gregory by Steel Dust. In 1908 she foaled the dun mare Old Mary by Ben Burton.

MAÑOSA. Mañosa, a sorrel, was foaled in 1925. Her sire was Uncle Jimmy Gray, and her dam was Meanie by Possum. Her second dam was Billy May. She was bred by Carroll Thompson, of Devine, Texas, or perhaps by Jim Roach, of Big Foot, Texas. Thompson had her after 1936. She was a great producer of sprinters. She had one foal, Cyclone by Alamo; one foal, Jimmy King, by Captain White Sox; and five foals by My Texas Dandy: Ginger Rogers, Chain Lay, Carol Dandy, Jack Mystery, and Tommy's Pride.

MARCHEE A. Marchee A, a bay, was foaled in 1891. Her sire was Fib by Storey (TB), and she was out of Vologne by Voltigeur (TB). She was owned by James Owen, of Berlin, Illinois.

MARE, BROWN'S. Brown's Mare was foaled in 1840 (?). She was of Brimmer and Printer stock and was bred in Missouri, probably by Ben Alsup. She was the dam of Old Dan by Selim in 1846 (?) and of Comet by Selim in 1847 (?).

MARE, CLAY'S. Clay's Mare was a well-known Quarter running mare. She was foaled soon after the Revolutionary War. She was sired by *Speculator and out of the Celebrated American Quarter Running Mare Blue Sow. She was the dam of Alasco by Tiger by Kentucky Whip.

MARGARET CARTER. Margaret Carter, a bay, was foaled in 1835. She was sired by Medoc (TB) and out of Lady Whip by Kentucky Whip. She was bred by Charles Webb, of Kentucky.

MARGARET W. Margaret W, a bay, was foaled in 1890. She was sired by Jack McDonald, and Fly, her dam, traced to Copperbottom by Sir Archy. She was bred by George H. Williams, of Paris, Texas. Copperbottom died in Sulphur Springs, a few miles east of Paris, in 1860.

MARGUERITE. Marguerite, a sorrel, was sired by Barlow by Lock's Rondo, and she was out of Daisy by Rail. She was bred by J. W. Francis, of Floyd, New Mexico. She was very fast. She was the dam of Jack McCue by Peter McCue, a sorrel colt foaled in 1914.

MARIA (HAYNIE'S MARIA). Maria was foaled in 1802. She was sired by *Diomed and was his last offspring. Her dam was by Tayloe's Bellair. She was a dark chestnut, 15 hands, with great stamina, muscular power, and symmetry. She was bred in Virginia by Bennett Goodman, who soon moved to North Carolina. Not finding what he wanted there, he moved on to Tennessee, again taking Maria with him. There he sold her to Captain Jesse Haynie, of Sumner County. She began running as a three-year-old and won consistently at all distances from 220 yards to 4 miles. For more on this remarkable mare see J. D. Anderson, *Making of the American Thoroughbred* (Nashville, Tenn., 1946).

MARY. Mary was a good mare owned by Thomas Trammell in the 1880s. Her pedigree has not come down to us. Trammell worked closely with Jim Newman, his brother-in-law. Both owned some of the best horses in Sweetwater, Texas. She was the dam of Blind Barney by Steel Dust. Barney was used on both Trammell and Newman mares.

MARY. Mary was sired by Blue Eyes by Possum and was bred by the Goodyear Farms, of Litchfield Park, Arizona. She was said to be the dam of Rowdy by Cheppy (TB), foaled in 1920. This pedigree seems somewhat doubtful, however, for Cheppy (TB) was foaled in 1918.

MARY, OLD. Old Mary, a dun, was one of the great Texas Quarter mares. She was foaled in 1908 and died in 1925 (?). She was sired by Ben Burton by Blind Barney, and she was out of Mandy by the Old Dutchman. Her second dam was Het by Bill Gregory by Steel Dust. She was bred by Dick Baker, of Weatherford, Texas. Later she was purchased by Parker, who sold her to W. T. Waggoner, of Fort Worth, in 1912. She foaled Yellow Wolf by Old Joe Bailey the first year Waggoner had her. In 1913, the following year, she had Yellow Bear by Joe Bailey, and in 1920 she foaled Yellow Boy by Yellow Jacket. Jim McFarlane, a Weatherford rancher who was acquainted with Mary, said that she was by Ben Burton and out of Mandy by Eureka.

MARY BAKER. Mary Baker was sired by Harmon Baker. She was owned by Jim Harkey, of Fort Stockton, Texas. She was the dam of Four Flush by Damit, foaled in 1922.

MARY BILL. Mary Bill was by John Gardner by Traveler and out of a Blue Eyes mare. She was owned by George Clegg, of Alice, Texas. She was the dam of Albert by Hickory Bill, foaled in 1918.

MARY BROWN. Mary Brown was sired by Paul Murray and was out of Little Nellie. Mary Brown was primarily a rodeo mare, used in roping and dogging. She was matched many times, however, and could run one-eighth in 11 1/5 seconds from a flat-footed start. "She was seldom beaten when we wanted her to win," wrote George Schneider to Helen Michaelis in 1945.

MARY BROWN. Mary Brown was sired by Hondo by John Crowder, and she was owned by Ott Adams, of Alfred, Texas. When bred to Paul El, she foaled Jim Brown.

MARY COOK. Mary Cook was by Printer, and she was owned by Tom Haley, of Sweetwater, Texas. She was the dam of Little Jeff Davis by Shiloh, Jr., and of Dan Secres by Joe Chalmers, Jr.

MARY DAWSON. Mary Dawson was of Coke Roberds breeding, and she was owned by Earl Moye, of Arvada, Wyoming. She was the dam of Dutch Martin by Old Nick.

MARY GRAY. Mary Gray, a gray, was sired by Tippoo Saib, and her dam was by Goode's Brimmer. In 1800 she foaled Wonder by *Diomed; in 1805, Palafox by *Diomed; and in 1806, Pocolet by *Citizen.

*MARY GRAY. *Mary Gray, a gray, was foaled in 1742. She was sired by Roundhead and out of Ringbone by Croft's Partner. She was imported into America in 1746 by Ralph Wormeley, of Middlesex County, Virginia. No other imported mare had as much influence on the colonial Quarter Horse as Mary Gray. Her descendants include Blue Boar, Club Foot, Poll Smiling, Polly Williams, Polly Flaxen, and Red Bacchus.

MARY KEITH (THIRD PARTY). Mary Keith, a sorrel, was foaled in 1890. She was by Tom Campbell by Bob Peters, and she was raised by C. B. Campbell, of Minco, Oklahoma. A Mr. Brumley, of Clarendon, Texas, told Helen Michaelis that he rode Mary Keith in a race in Stephensville about 1895. She was matched against Black Reb by Rebel by Steel Dust. She was then running under the name Third Party. She was the dam of Chickasha Bob, probably by Pid Hart or Rocky Mountain Tom.

MARY LEE. Mary Lee, a dun, was foaled in 1877. She was sired by Joe Lee and out of a dun Lock mare named Nellie. She was bred by W. W. Lock, of Kyle, Texas. She had the following foals: Barbee Dun by Lock's Rondo in 1881, Daisy L by Project in 1882, and Blue Jacket in 1888, Barney in 1889, Bonny Bird in 1890, and Minnie Lee in 1892, all by Lock's Rondo.

MARY LOU. Mary Lou was sired by Pride of India (TB) and raised by John Cowey, of Dewville, Gonzales County, Texas. She was the dam of Rambling Jack by Major Speck.

MARY McCUE. Mary McCue was sired by Peter McCue, and she was raised by Si Dawson, of Hayden, Colorado. She was bought by Marshall Peavy, of Clark, Colorado, who raced her for a number of years and then bred her. She became the dam of Ding Bob, registered 269 by the AQHA.

MARY P. Mary P was by Gilroy by Lexington, and she was owned by J. R. Nasworthy, of the Bridgeview Stud, San Angelo, Texas. She was the dam of Buck Walton, a bay foaled in 1882 by Post Guard by Silent Friend. Post Guard's dam was also by the great Lexington.

MARY PORTER, see BLINKEY.

MARY S. Mary S was a good race mare owned by Robert T. Wade, of Plymouth, Illinois, who bought her without learning her pedigree. He bred her to Silver Dick in 1908, and she foaled Sirock.

MARY T. Mary T was sired by Traveler, and she was out of a part-Thoroughbred mare. She was bred by D. W. Christian, of Big Spring, Texas, and was later owned by W. E. Moody, of Toyah, Texas. She was the dam of Frank Allen, Rigsby, and Lonnie Gray, all by Thoroughbred stallions. Lonnie Gray was foaled in 1913, the other two earlier.

MATCHLESS. Matchless was foaled in 1778 (?). She was sired by *Janus and out of a *Fearnought mare. She was bred by Wyllie Jones, of Halifax County, North Carolina. She was owned by Governor Williams, of Craven County, North Carolina. She was a full sister of Blue Boar. She was the dam of Comet by Lee's Mark Anthony. Edgar says that Comet was a skewbald, which would indicate that he was a pinto.

MATTIE LUCK. Mattie Luck, a sorrel, was foaled in 1887. She was sired by Billy Melbourne by Marion and out of Nellie Bly by New York. Her second dam was Crazy Jane by Harry Bluff. She was the dam of Josephus, Min Rhodes, Mary Fern, Dinah Wat, and Inlook. Her breeder-owner was Thomas Watkins, of Petersburg, Illinois.

MAUD. Maud was sired by Little Billy, and she was bred by A. H. Bodie, of Pontotoc, Texas. She was the dam of Pablo by Pablo (TB).

MAUD. Maud, a Quarter mare, was bred by William Sumners, of Lineville, Iowa. She was the dam of Dr. Glendening by Tubal Cain in 1895.

MAUD. Maud, a bay, was foaled in 1880. She was sired by Jack Hardy (TB), and according to the appendix of *The American Stud Book*, her dam was by Mike Clusky. More likely, however, she was out of Alice by Billy. Four of her foals were Alliance, Whizzer, Maud M, and Hardy Baltic. She was bred and owned by Marion Martin, of Corsicana, Texas.

MAUD. Maud was sired by Arch Oldham and was owned by Columbus Sykes, of Stockdale, Texas. She was the dam of Spokane by Paul El.

MAUD. Maud, a bay, was foaled in 1885. She was bred and owned by John Adams, of Woodland, California. She was sired by Uncle Billy, and her dam was by Jenkin's Charlie. Her second dam was by Oregon Dan.

MAUD (ALLEN BORDEN MARE). Maud, a sorrel, was sired by Billy by Shiloh and out of Old Alice. She was owned by Cliff Neafus, of Newkirk, New Mexico, but bred by Jim Garrett and raced by Bob Wise. She was the dam of Little Buck by Buck Walton and of Young Chickasha Bob, Bob the Neafus Horse, Sorrel Alice, Carrie, and Silver, all by Chickasha Bob.

MAUD (GARDNER MARE). Maud, a brown, was foaled in the 1880s and died about 1900. She had excellent conformation. She was sired by Traveler, but her dam has not been identified. She was bred and owned by Alex Gardner, of San Angelo, Texas, and was later owned and used by Charles Gardner. She was the dam of Brown Billy and Jim Ned, both by Pancho. It would seem that Traveler began siring colts too late to have been Maud's sire, but there is no way to be sure today. She is also supposed to be the dam of Georgie.

MAUDY. Maudy was by Old Joe Bailey by Eureka and out of Opal Smith (TB). She was bred by E. A. Whiteside, Sipe Springs, Texas, and later became the dam of Buckskin Joe by Fred Bailey.

MAY, OLD, see MAY MANGUM.

MAY BAKER. May Baker was by Harmon Baker and was bred by Jim Harkey, of Fort Stockton, Texas. She was the dam of Four Flush by Damit in 1922.

MAYFLOWER. Mayflower, a sorrel, was foaled in 1867. She was sired by *Eclipse (TB) and out of Hennie Farrow (Betty Maney). In 1872 she foaled Joe Hooker by Monday (TB). She was owned by Theodore Winters, of Woodland, California.

MAYFLOWER. Mayflower was foaled in 1880 or soon thereafter. She was sired by Bill Garner and out of a Stanfield running mare. She was bred by Shelby Stanfield, of Thorp Springs, Texas, and owned by Lee McCameron, of Baird, Texas. She was the dam of Archie by Pid Hart in 1894 (?). Archie's racing record is in *Goodwin's Turf Guide.*

MAYFLOWER. Mayflower was by Nail Driver, and she was owned by Mike Beetch, of Lawton, Oklahoma. She was the dam of Beetch's Smokey by Beetch's Yellow Jacket in 1929.

MAYFLOWER. Mayflower, a black, was foaled in 1927. She was sired by Uncle Jimmy Gray, and she was out of a mare by Possum (King). She had a streaked face, stood 15-2 hands high, and weighed 1,100 pounds. She was bred by John Buss, of Hondo, Texas; sold to Templo Adams, of Devine, Texas; and then sold to J. J. Kennedy, of Bonita, Arizona. She had a famous race against Big Liz in Houston. She fell, got up, and won the race.

MAY GIRL. May Girl was foaled in 1925. She was sired by Filemaker (TB) and out of Lady C by Guinea Pig. She was owned by Chester Cooper, of Tonto County, Arizona. She was a successful race mare. She became the dam of Star Dust by Speedy, Victory by Red Man, and Tonto Boy by Joe Reed II.

MAY KENNEDY. May Kennedy, a black, was foaled in 1882. She was sired by Faustus (TB) and out of a mare by Printer by Gray Eagle by Woodpecker. She was bred by Mrs. B. J. Treacy, of Lexington, Kentucky, and owned by J. W. Lillard, of Richards, Missouri. She was a registered Thoroughbred, but several of her colts, such as Mahogany, a grandson of *Bonnie Scotland, bred short speed.

MAY KETCHUM. May Ketchum, a gray, was foaled in 1924. She was by Captain by Harmon Baker and out of a Berry

Ketchum mare. She was raised by Berry Ketchum, of Sheffield, Texas.

MAY MANGUM. May Mangum, a bay, was foaled in 1882 and died in 1904 (?). She was sired by Anthony by Old Billy, and she was out of Belle Nellie by Fanning's Tiger. Anthony must have been twenty-five when he sired May. She was probably bred by William Fleming, of Belmont, Texas, though she spent many productive years in the ownership of Dow and Will Shely, of Alfred, Texas. She had six fillies by Sykes Rondo: Nellie, Jenny, Mamie Sykes, Nettie Harrison, Kitty, and Baby Ruth. She also had four colts by Sykes Rondo: Little Joe (the gelding), Blue Eyes, Dogie Beasley, and Blazer. There have been few mares greater than May Mangum.

MAY MATTERSON, see CUT THROAT.

MAY NEWMAN. May Newman was sired by the Thoroughbred Portland and bred by T. O. Atwell, of Miles, Texas. She was the dam of Saltosh, a brown colt by Walking John, foaled in 1922.

MAY SENATOR. May was sired by Senator by Leadville (TB), and she was bred by R. J. Kurruish, of Littleton, Colorado. She was the dam of Senator Don by Beauty Boy (TB) in 1930.

MAZIE. Mazie was sired by Sappho by Brown King, and she was bred by W. B. Mitchell, of Marfa, Texas, and owned by Thomas B. Dibbs, of Santa Barbara, California. She was the dam of Golden Maize, a palomino colt foaled in 1933.

MAZIE MARIE (POWELL MARE). Mazie Marie, a brown, was foaled in 1908 (?), sired by Tom Campbell. She was bred by John Parvell, of Elk City, Oklahoma. She was the dam of Badger by Peter McCue in 1912.

MEANIE. Meanie was sired by Possum and out of Billy May. She was owned by Carrol Thompson, of Devine, Texas. She was the dam of Mañosa by Uncle Jimmy Gray.

MEDINA BELLE. Medina Belle was sired by Uncle Jimmy Gray and was raised by Eugene Schott, of Riomedina, Texas. She was the dam of Handsome Hiram by Hiram Kelly (TB) in 1935.

MEDINA DOLL. Medina Doll was sired by A. M. White by Everett (TB), and she was raised by Eugene Schott, of Riomedina, Texas. She was the dam of Red Wing Sir by Chicaro (TB) in 1934.

MEDOC MARE. The Medoc Mare, a sorrel, was foaled in 1837. She was sired by Medoc and out of Morocco by Tiger. She was bred by William Buford, Jr., of Woodford County, Kentucky, and she was later owned by J. Wilcox.

MERINO EWE. Merino Ewe was by *Jack Andrews (TB), and she was the dam of Johanna by Sir Archy in 1822.

METHODIST FILLY. Methodist Filly was sired by *Whip, and she was owned by J. W. McIntosh, of Kentucky. She was the dam of Severe by Kosciusko in 1831.

METROPOLIS. Metropolis was sired by Peter McCue and bred and owned by W. C. Watkins, of Oakford, Illinois. She was the dam of Walking John by Nimrod (TB) in 1909.

MIDNIGHT. Midnight, a black, was foaled in 1923. She was sired by Uncle Jimmy Gray and out of a Little Tom mare. She was bred by Henry Ferricks, of Hondo, Texas, and raced by "Red" Hysaw, of Luling, Texas.

MILDRED JUHL. Mildred Juhl was sired by Peter McCue and bred by J. F. Newman, of Sweetwater, Texas. She was the dam of Reno Rebel by Rancocas (TB) in 1905.

MILLIE D. Millie D was by Tennyson (TB) and out of Nora M by Voltigeur (TB). She was bred and owned by Sam Watkins, of Petersburg, Illinois. She was the dam of Running Mallard by Peter McCue and of Nona P by Dan Tucker. Nona P was registered as by the Duke of the Highlands (TB).

MILLE DENISE, see ALICE.

MINNIE. Minnie, a bay, was foaled in 1871. She was by Dr. Lindsey by Lexington (TB). Her dam was by Rifleman.

MINNIE FRANKS. Minnie Franks, a bay, was foaled in 1882. She was sired by Project and out of a Franks mare. She was bred by Louis Franks, of Kyle, Texas, and later owned by O. G. Parks, also of Kyle, who later sold her to a man named Peevy, of Bastrop, Texas. Parks bred her to Lock's Rondo and got Little Rondo in 1895. Minnie was raced all over Texas.

MINNIE LEE. Minnie, a dun, was foaled in 1892. She was sired by Lock's Rondo, and she was out of Mary Lee by Joe Lee. She was a small mare and weighed 900 pounds. She had the scar of a bad wire cut and a black stripe down her back. She was bred by W. W. Lock, of Kyle, Texas. She was a full sister of Blue Jacket. She was widely raced and ran a quarter mile in 22 seconds and a three-eighths mile in 35½ seconds. She was sold in Roswell, New Mexico, along with Bonnie Bird II.

MINNIE S. Minnie S was by Raymond M and out of Nellie B. She was bred by Cash Spencer, of Peyton, Colorado. She was the dam of Woodrow Wilson, a sorrel colt foaled in 1916 by Senator.

MINNIE SYKES, see MAMIE SYKES.

MINYON. Minyon, a sorrel, was foaled in 1897. She was sired by Rancocas (TB), and her dam was Heeley by Blue Dick. She was bred by J. F. Newman, of Sweetwater, Texas, and later owned by the Morris Ranch, of San Antonio, Texas. In a letter to me dated December 20, 1937, Walter Trammell said that she was the dam of Pan Zarita. Walter's father, Thomas Trammell, had been an associate of Newman in his horse operations; however, this claim hardly seems likely. She was the dam of Callise by Abe Frank (TB) in 1908 (?) and of Prince by Billy Bartlett in 1912.

MISS ALSUP. Miss Alsup, a famous running mare, was foaled in 1772, sired by *Janus and out of a mare by *Fearnought. She was bred by Thomas Field, of Mecklenburg County, Virginia, and later sold to John Goode, Sr. Both Edgar and Bruce list her in their studbooks.

MISS ANXIOUS. Miss Anxious, a sorrel, was foaled in 1903. She was sired by Rancocas (TB) and was out of Dead Cinch. She was bred by C. R. Haley, of Sweetwater, Texas.

MISS BROWN. Miss Brown was sired by Albert by Hickory Bill, and she was out of Brownie by Rexall by Rex Beach (TB). She was bred and owned by Frank Rooke, of Woodsboro, Texas. She was the dam of Little Bootlegger, a black colt foaled in 1939 by Bootlegger by Red Bug.

MISS HACKNEY. Miss Hackney, a sorrel, was foaled in 1881. She was sired by Engraver by Enquirer (TB). Her dam was a Quarter mare. She foaled No Remarks in 1887, Captain Trumbell in 1893, and Marathon in 1895. Marathon was sired by Okema. She was bred and owned by Mrs. H. A. Trowbridge, of Wellington, Kansas.

MISS HARVEY. Miss Harvey was by Rex by Billy and out of Lady Nichols by Ashwell (TB). She was owned by Hershel Harvey, of Willow, Oklahoma. She was the dam of Blue Bell, a roan mare foaled in 1937 by Waggoner by Midnight.

MISS MITFORD. Miss Mitford, a sorrel, was foaled in 1885. She was sired by Joe Hooker and was out of Pearl by Brick. She was bred and owned by John Adams, of Woodland, California. She was the dam of Adell by Uncle Billy, Minnie by Red Iron, Milford by Shannon (TB), and Mefford, also by Shannon (TB).

MISS MURPHY. Miss Murphy, a sorrel, was foaled in 1882. She was sired by Grand River Chief by Satanta and out of a Harry Bluff mare. She was bred and owned by Mrs. H. A. Trowbridge, of Wellington, Kansas.

MISS PASSMORE. Miss Passmore was by Lightning by Joy and out of a mare by Archie H, who was by Tom Campbell. She was bred and owned by Jack Passmore, of Sayre, Oklahoma. She was the dam of Mickey McQuay, a sorrel mare foaled in 1936.

MISS PATTON. Miss Patton was sired by Joy by Jeff and out of a Tom Campbell mare. She was bred by C. B. Campbell, of Minco, Oklahoma, and owned by Bill Patton, of Leedey, Oklahoma. She was the dam of Red Lightning by Joy.

MISS PRINCESS (WOVEN WEB), see BRUJA.

MISS RHODES. Miss Rhodes, a bay, was foaled in 1884. She was sired by Willie Renfro by Therit and out of Mattie Luck by Billie Melbourne. She was bred by Thomas Watkins, of Petersburg, Illinois. She foaled Billy Mason by Oliver Twist (TB) in 1895, Barney Seal by Don H. in 1896, Outline by Outlook (TB) in 1897, Agnes Mack by Hero (TB) in 1900, and Lady Deer by Deering in 1903.

MISS SLEEPY. Miss Sleepy was sired by Star Shoot (TB) and out of a good Zurick mare. She was bred by John W. Zurick, of Stead, New Mexico. She was the dam of Pancho by Peace Buddy, foaled in 1930 (?).

MISS TEXAS. Miss Texas was sired by Rocky Mountain Tom and out of Betty. Betty was raised by Shelby Stanfield, of Thorp Springs, Texas. It is believed that Miss Texas was bred by J. H. Helm, of Newark, Texas. Betty had been shipped in foal to Albuquerque, where Miss Texas was foaled. Albert Harrington, of Correo, New Mexico, then purchased the filly. In 1917, Miss Texas foaled Red Harrington by Jack Harrington by Grover Cleveland.

MISS VASSAR (TB). Miss Vassar was a Thoroughbred, according to reports. She was sold to Henry Pfefferling, of San Antonio, Texas, who kept Remount stallions. He bred

Miss Vassar to Uncle Jimmy Gray, and the resulting foal was Eddie Gray, dropped in 1928.

MITTIE STEPHENS. Mittie Stephens, a sorrel, was foaled in 1869 and died in 1892 (?). She was sired by Shiloh, Jr., by Shiloh and out of Nellie Gray by Dan Secres. Her second dam was Mary Cook by Printer. She can be found in the appendix of *The American Stud Book*. She produced Shelby by Tom Driver in 1878, Lock's Rondo by Whalebone in 1880, Governor Roberts by Jack Boston in 1882, General Ross by Havre (TB) in 1888, Heeley by Blue Dick in 1889, Sally Johnson by Blue Dick in 1890, and Dead Cinch by Silent Friend in 1891. She is one of the top four or five Quarter mares foaled since the Civil War.

MLLE DENISE, see ALICE.

MOANA. Moana was sired by the Thoroughbred Wernberg, and she was out of Marie by Old Confidence by Walnut Bark. She was bred by John Adams, of Woodland, California, and owned by Byran Jennings, of Visalia, California. She produced Orphan's Pride in 1921 by Wernberg (TB).

MOLLIE. Mollie is recorded as sired by Steel Dust. She was owned by Charles Haley, of Sweetwater, Texas. She was the dam of Old Dutchman by Lock's Rondo, Barney by the same sire, and One-Eyed Kingfisher by Old Kingfisher. She was a great foundation mare.

MOLLIE. Mollie, a sorrel, was foaled in 1874. She was sired by Tar River. Her dam was a race mare owned by Batchler. She was bred by H. T. Batchler, of Lancaster, Texas. She had five offspring by Jack Hardy: Kitty Pease, Molly Hardy, Winnie Davis, Tom Gray, and Emma Lee.

MOLLIE. Mollie, a brown, was foaled in 1881. She was sired by Rebel by Socks and out of Flora by Bulletin. She was bred and owned by John Hancock, of Austin, Texas.

MOLLIE H. Mollie H was by Bob H by Old Fred and out of Ribbon by Mike by Silvertail. She was owned by Ben Anderson, of Craig, Colorado. She became the dam of John H, a brown colt foaled in 1938 by Fred by Brown Dick.

MOLLIE McCREARY. Mollie McCreary, a sorrel, was foaled in 1875. She was sired by Zero by Boston (TB). Her dam was Lucy by Humbolt. She was bred by Albert Snapp, of Illinois, and then sold to Uriah Eggleston, of Garden City, Kansas. Later she was owned by T. A. Cook, of Oklahoma City. She foaled Eve Nelson by Uncle Tom, Lady Beatrice by Uncle Tom, Newby by Elkhorn, Laura Mitchell by Uncle Tom, Chat by Mexique, Tim McCarthy by B. G. Bruce, and Miss Byron, also by B. G. Bruce.

MOLLY MOORE. Molly Moore, a brown, was foaled in 1870. She was by Rebel by Socks and out of a mare by Albert Gallatin. She was bred by R. W. Crawford, of Texas.

MONICA (TB). Monica, a Thoroughbred, was sired by *Sovereign and out of Dust by Highlander. She was owned by General W. G. Harding, of Nashville, Tennessee, whose Belle Meade Stud was responsible for many sprinting racehorses. Monica is listed for checking purposes only. She was the dam of Tom Watkin's Voltigeur, a bay colt foaled in 1871 by Yandal by *Glencoe. *Bonnie Scotland was at the Belle Meade Stud.

MONKEY. Monkey was foaled about 1836. She was sired by Boanerges by Printer by *Janus. She was the dam of Munch Meg by Alford.

MONMOUTH, see MAMMOTH.

MOTHER SNOOKS. Mother Snooks was by Yellow Boy by Yellow Belly, out of Pansy by Young Dr. Mac. She was bred by W. T. Waggoner, of Fort Worth, Texas.

MOROCCO. Morocco, a sorrel, was foaled in 1823. She was by Tiger and out of a mare by *Archer. Her second dam was by *Dare Devil. She was bred and owned by Colonel William Buford, of Tree Hill Stud, Woodford County, Kentucky. She was the dam of the sorrel filly Ellen Tree by Medoc, foaled in 1835, and of the sorrel filly Red Morocco by Medoc, foaled in 1836.

MOUNTAIN MAID. Mountain Maid, a bay, was foaled in 1889. She was by Pony Pete and out of Cherokee Maid. She was bred by Mike Smiley, of Sylvan Grove, Kansas, and she was a full sister of Little Steve and Croton Oil. She was a well-known race mare. While she was running, she was owned by C. A. Underwood, who sold her to Foxhall Keene.

MOZETTE (TB). Mozette, a Thoroughbred, was owned by D. W. Christian, of Big Spring, Texas. She was the dam of Rock and Rye, a brown colt foaled in 1913 by Bobby Lowe.

MUNCH MEG. Munch Meg was foaled around 1850. She was by Alford (Snow Ball) and out of Monkey by Boanerges by Printer. She was the dam of Alice and June Bug, both by Harry Bluff. Alice was foaled in 1858, and June Bug was foaled in 1859.

MY JANE. My Jane was by King of Hearts by Ace of Hearts and out of Top Dancer by Grano de Oro. She was bred by Will Northington, of Egypt, Texas, and became the dam of the sorrel filly Center Fire by Lucky Strike in 1940.

MYRTLE HUNTER. Myrtle Hunter, a bay, was foaled in 1887. She was sired by Jack Hardy and was out of a mare of Printer breeding. She was bred by H. T. Batchler, of Lancaster, Texas. She was the dam of Myrtle Sawyer and of Lilly B by the same stallion.

N

NAN. Nan had a Standardbred background. Alex Chote, of Lockwood, Missouri, bred her to a good Quarter stallion,

Missouri Rondo by Missouri Mike, and got Black Ball in 1888.

NANCE, BIG (TB). Big Nance was a Thoroughbred whose exact breeding is difficult to determine. Bruce (7:1223) indicates that she was by Timoleon. When Thomas Trammell owned Dan Tucker, he had a broadside printed advertising the stallion. In the broadside he said that Big Nance was of Timoleon stock. It would seem that, if Big Nance had been directly by Timoleon, Trammell would have said so, for the rest of the broadside was explicit. She could easily have been a granddaughter, since Timoleon was foaled in 1813. Big Nance was probably owned by Middleton Perry, in Kentucky, and she became the dam of Harry Bluff by Short Whip in 1860 (?). Perry moved first to Illinois, then to Texas.

NANCY. Nancy was by Honest Jim, and she was owned by Arthur Young, of Moorcroft, Wyoming. In 1928 she foaled Wyoming Clown by Historicus (TB).

NANCY BROWN. Nancy Brown was by Nixon's Joe Bailey and out of a Quarter mare. She was owned by Bert Bendele, of Riomedina, Texas. It is believed that her dam either was raised by Eugene Schott, also of Riomedina, or was out of a Schott mare. Nancy was the dam of Little Boy by Uncle Jimmy Gray in 1923.

NANCY OWEN. Nancy Owen was by Barney Owens by Cold Deck and out of a Watkins mare. She was owned by Thomas Watkins, of Petersburg, Illinois. In 1883 she foaled Weaver by Big Henry (TB).

NANCY WAKE. Nancy Wake was a Famous American Quarter Running Mare, bred in Wake County, North Carolina. She was owned by L. Higgs, of that county. She was sired by John Goode's Babram, and her dam was by *Selim. Edgar says that she was taken by the British during the Revolutionary War and, along with Little Bacchus, Red Bacchus, and several other horses, purposely drowned in the York River. Her name can be found in Edgar and in Bruce.

NANCY WILLIS. Nancy Willis was a famous racing mare of colonial days. She was foaled in 1758, sired by *Janus and out of a mare by Morton's *Traveler. She was bred by Joseph John Alston, of Halifax, North Carolina. She is listed in both Bruce and Edgar.

NANNIE REAP, see REAP.

NANNY GUM. Nanny Gum was sired by Nimrod (TB) and out of Pansy H by Hero (TB). She was owned by J. W. Moore, of Mobeetie, Texas. She was the dam of Judge Wilkins by John Wilkins in 1914 and of Sam Watkins by John Wilkins in 1911.

NAPANEE. Napanee was by Barney. She was bred by the Waddell brothers, of Odessa and Kermit, Texas, and she was the dam of Dinero by Moss King by Big King and of Napanee II by the same sire in 1928 (?).

NAPANEE II. Napanee II was sired by Moss King and out of Napanee. She was bred and raised by the Waddell brothers of Odessa and Kermit, Texas. She was the dam of Nigger Baby, a black colt foaled in 1934, sired by Dennis Reed.

NATALIE. Natalie was foaled in 1920 (?), sired by Frank and Charles Springer's Old Joe and out of a CS Ranch (New Mexico) mare. She became the dam of Billy Byrne by Balleymooney when Dan Casement moved a group of CS mares to his Colorado ranch.

NELL. Nell was sired by Ben Burton, and she was owned by Dick Baker, of Weatherford, Texas. In 1920 she foaled Little Ben by Old Joe Bailey.

NELL, OLD. Old Nell was sired by Printer and owned by John Hamilton, of Flint, Michigan. She foaled Telegraph in 1830 (?) and John Bacchus in 1835 (?).

NELLIE. Nellie was sired by Ace of Diamonds and out of Lady Bright by Sykes Rondo. She was the dam of Doodlum, a gray mare foaled in 1936 by Little Dick by Sleepy Dick.

NELLIE. Nellie was sired by Arch Oldham and was owned by W. S. Hall, of Boerne, Texas. She was the dam of June Bug, foaled in 1924 (?).

NELLIE. Nellie was by Doc Link and was owned by Roy C. Davis, of Sterling City, Texas. She was the dam of Concho by Ketchum by Captain.

NELLIE. Nellie was sired by Old Joe by Whalebone, and she was owned by Jim Morris, of Devine, Texas. She was the dam of Little King by King (Possum) in 1910.

NELLIE. Nellie was sired by Panmure (TB) and was owned by C. F. Meyer, of Ellinger, Texas. She was the dam of Sleepy Dick by Little Dick, foaled sometime in the early 1920s.

NELLIE. Nellie was by Pat Garrett, and she was owned by Oliver Lee, of Alamogordo, New Mexico. She was the dam of Little Trouble by Trouble by Dan Tucker.

NELLIE. Nellie, a bay, was foaled in 1870. She was a California mare sired by Walnut Bark and out of Choctaw's Sister by Obe Jennings. She was bred and owned by John Adams, of Woodland, California. She was the dam of Lela B by Jenkins Charley (Oregon Charlie) in 1875 and Pearl by Brick in 1879.

NELLIE BLY. Nellie was foaled in 1873, and she was sired by New York and was out of Crazy Jane. She was owned by Thomas Watkins, of Petersburg, Illinois. She was the dam of Mattie Luck by Billy Melbourne (1877), Kate Shelby by Renfro (1884), Tony Pastor by Billy Melbourne (1888), Joe

Menard by Black Oak (1889), and Tommy Tucker by Dan Tucker (1891).

NELLIE GRAY, see NELLY GRAY.

NELLIE HART. Nellie Hart, a bay, was foaled in 1887. She was sired by Pid Hart and was out of Queen Victoria by Lock's Rondo. She was bred by C. B. Campbell, of Minco, Oklahoma, and was given to the Armstrong brothers when they left his employ and moved to Elk City, Oklahoma. She foaled Catch Me by Bob Peters in 1905 and Hermus by Tom Campbell in 1910. Catch Me had hardly any legs yet consistently ran a chained quarter mile in 21½ seconds.

NELLIE HARVE. Nellie Harve, a bay, was foaled in 1888. She was sired by Harve (TB) and out of Brownlow by Lunatic, Jr. Her second dam was Fanny Heath by Shiloh, Jr. Nellie was bred by G. B. Harms, of Colorado, Texas, and later used as a brood mare by Charles R. Haley, of Sweetwater, Texas. Her offspring between 1893 and 1906 were as follows: Black Gal by Blue Dick, Star Opal by Boston Boy, Ranco by Rancocas (TB), Wolverine by Rancocas, White Heel by Rancocas, Come to Bed by Rancocas, Fairness by Rancocas, Mae Geogan by Rancocas, Avela by Prince Plenty (TB), and Charlie Felt by Prince Plenty (TB).

NELLIE MIER. Nellie Mier was sired by Peter McCue and was owned by George Newton, of Del Rio, Texas. She was the dam of Marion Wilson (1914) and Little Menard (1915), both by Barnsdale (TB).

NELLIE MILLER. Nellie Miller, a gray, was foaled in the late 1880s. She was sired by Gray Cold Deck by Cold Deck, and her dam was part Thoroughbred. Milo Burlingame rode Nellie in many of her races. Nellie outran Gold Dust in Kansas City and Jane Baker in Mobeetie, Texas. One of her most famous races was against Roan Jane, whom she beat going a quarter mile for $5,000 a side. She was a 22-second mare. Bill Miller, an early settler in the Texas Panhandle, is supposed to have purchased her after seeing her pulling a milk-delivery wagon in Kansas City. She can be found in *Goodwin's Turf Guide.*

NELLIE REED. Nellie Reed was sired by Dennis Reed (TB), and her dam was Pocahantas by Moss King. She was bred by the Waddell brothers, of Odessa, Texas. In 1930 she foaled Oddfellow II by Captain Costigan (TB).

NELLIE TAMSIT. Nellie Tamsit was sired by the Thoroughbred Palm Reader, and her dam was a Christian race mare. She was bred by Webb Christian, of Big Spring, Texas. She foaled Earl Ederis by Bobby Lowe in 1912 and Burton Brown by Barney Lucas in 1926.

NELLIE TRAMMELL. Nellie Trammell a sorrel, was foaled just before 1900. She was by Pid Hart and had a club foot. She was owned by John Parvell, of Elk City. She was bought by Jess Cooper, of Roosevelt, Oklahoma. In 1916 she foaled Midnight by Badger.

NELLIE TRAMMELL. Nellie Trammell was sired by Ace by Peter McCue. She was foaled several years after the Nellie Trammell listed above. She was owned by Bill Patton, of Leedey, Oklahoma, and she became the dam of Little Red by Joy in 1920 (?).

NELLIE W. Nellie W, a sorrel, was foaled in 1863. She was by Billy Cheatham and out of Lady Davis by Red Ball. She was owned by Theodore Winter, of Woodland, California.

NELLINE. Nelline was by Fleeting Time (TB) and out of Little Red Nell by Brown Billy by Pancho. She was owned by J. W. House, of Cameron, Texas. She was the dam of Joe Reed II, a sorrel colt foaled in 1936, sired by Joe Reed.

NELLY. Nelly, a bay, was foaled in the 1890s. She was by Sykes' Rondo and out of May Mangum. She was bred by

William Fleming, of Belmont, Texas, and later was owned by W. A. Cameron. Her races are recorded in *Goodwin's Turf Guide.*

NELLY GRAY. Nelly Gray was by Dan Secres by Joe Chalmers, and she was out of Mary Cook by Printer. She was owned by Charles R. Haley, of Sweetwater, Texas. She was the dam of Mittie Stephens by Shiloh, Jr.

NETTIE HARRISON. Nettie Harrison was sired by Sykes Rondo and was out of May Mangum. She was bred by Crawford Sykes or by Joe M. Mangum, of Nixon, Texas, and later came into the ownership of Bill Nack, of Cuero, Texas. There is considerable confusion about the ownership and moves of this mare, though her breeding and produce are not questioned. She was the dam of Big Liz by Paul El in 1930 (?) and Big Blaze in 1920 (?). She also foaled Pitchin Sis sometime between these dates.

NETTIE JACKET. Nettie Jacket was sired by Yellow Jacket, and she was bred by Eugene Schott, of Riomedina, Texas. She produced Ben Hur by Rainy Day by Lone Star in 1921.

NETTIE OVERTON. Nettie Overton has been recorded in a number of places, so her existence cannot be doubted; however, those same records and documents defy rationalization. If they are to be believed, she was foaled in the late 1860s. She was bred by John Hedgepeff, of Joplin, Missouri. Later she was owned by Robert T. Wade, of Plymouth, Illinois, and by Grant Rea, of Carthage, Illinois. She was the dam of Barney Owen by Cold Deck in 1870 (?) and of Bob Wade by Roan Dick in 1886. Roan Dick (foaled in 1877) has been recorded as her sire, a feat somewhat difficult to believe. For a longer discussion of this mare see chapter III of this book.

NETTIE S. Nettie S, a gray, was sired by Roan Dick. She was probably bred by Robert T. Wade, of Plymouth, Illinois, but she was raised by Mose Toland, of Hancock County, Illinois. Later she was raced by J. P. Sutton, who took her to

Montana, where two men named Barker and Parrott, of Anaconda, bought her. She ran a world's-record 600 yards in 30¼ seconds. She ran second to her half brother Bob Wade when he set the world's-record 440-yard race in 21¼ seconds. Later, when she retired from the tracks, she foaled Bay Billy by her sire Roan Dick in 1889 and Baby P by Eolian (TB) in 1892.

NEVADA (TB). Nevada, a registered Thoroughbred, was by Lexington. Her principal claim to fame was made when she was bred to *Bonnie Scotland and she foaled Luke Blackburn, a bay colt, in 1877. He later became an important name in short-horse pedigrees.

NEWBY. Newby, a sorrel, was foaled in 1883. She was sired by Elkhorn and out of Molly McCreary. She was bred and owned by Uriah Eggleston, of Garden City, Kansas.

NEW MOORE. New Moore was sired by Brettenham (TB), and she was out of Flugget by Jim Trammell by Barney Owen. She was owned by W. R. Norfleet, of Kress, Texas. In 1928 (?) she foaled Kayo by Spark Plug by Peter McCue.

NINA T. Nina T was foaled in 1890 (?) by Barney Owen. She was bred by J. F. Newman, of Sweetwater, Texas. She was the dam of Dr. All Good by Charley Wilson.

NIXON MARE. The Nixon Mare was sired by Rebel by Nixon's Joe Bailey and was bred by J. W. Nixon, of Hondo, Texas. She was the dam of Nixon's Billy by Little Ring in 1921.

NONA P. Nona P, a sorrel, was foaled in 1895. She was registered as sired by the Duke of Highlands, but her sire was Dan Tucker. She was a half sister of Peter McCue. She was out of Millie D, who was by Tennyson (TB) and out of Nora M by Voltigeur (TB). Nora M was Peter McCue's dam. Nona P was bred and owned by Hugh Watkins, of Petersburg, Illinois, and later purchased by John Wilkins, of San Antonio, Texas. She was one of the greatest producers of short horses. Among her produce were Little G, Jennie Jackson, Hattie Jackson, Uncle A, Tot Lee, Buck Thomas, Harmon Baker, Edee Ree, and San Antonio. Most were by her half brother Peter McCue.

NOO. Noo was sired by Barney Lucas by Traveler and was owned by H. R. Saunders, of Roswell, New Mexico. She was the dam of Nooblis by *Batchlors Bliss (TB) and of Robert A by Setback (TB), foaled in 1928.

NORA M. Nora M, a bay, was foaled in 1880 and died in 1897 (?). She was sired by the Thoroughbred Voltigeur, and her dam was Kitty Clyde by Star Davis. She was bred by James Owen, of Berlin, Illinois. She was raised an orphan after her dam died. She ran on the short track for three years, trained by Hap Mitchell, of Ashland, Illinois. She was named for Hap's daughter. Her best distance was a half mile, which she ran regularly in 49 seconds. When she was fourteen, she was bred to Dan Tucker and foaled her most famous colt, Peter McCue. Her other offspring were Millie D by Tennyson (TB), Briggs by Dan Tucker, Nola D by Pantaloon, Mollie D by Tennyson, John J by Lycurgus, Kate Hamilton by Duke of Highlands, Minnie Hero by Hero, and Hannah D by Hero.

NORMA. Norma, a bay, was foaled in 1870. Her sire was Norwich (TB), and her dam was a mare by Oregon Charlie. She was bred by a man named Crabtree, of Oregon, and raced by R. H. Baker, of Helena, Montana. Among her offspring were Formosa by Sun Dance (TB), Queen Prewitt by Red Boy, Red Buck by Red Boy, Bonnieville by Sun Dance and Annie Moore by Regent (TB).

O

ODETTE. Odette, a sorrel, was said to have been foaled in 1886. She is entered here only because of the interesting statement that she was by Shiloh but foaled in California.

She is listed in the appendix of *The American Stud Book.* It shows her ownership as J. C. Ghio, of Saint Louis, Missouri. Since Shiloh went to Texas in 1849 and died in 1874, Odette must have been bred to Shiloh in Texas and then taken to California. There is no record of her produce. Also, she must have been foaled before 1886.

OKLAHOMA QUEEN. Oklahoma Queen, a sorrel, was foaled in 1910 (?). She was sired by Tom Campbell by Bob Peters, and her dam was Brunk's Queen by Quartermaster (TB). She was probably bred by John Harrel, of Canute, Oklahoma. She was the dam of Jack Dempsey by Big Boy by Dominus Arvi (TB) and of Queen (Oklahoma) by A. D. Reed in 1920 (?).

OKLAHOMA QUEEN. Oklahoma Queen was foaled in or about 1920. She was sired by A. D. Reed and was out of Oklahoma Queen by Tom Campbell. She was the dam of Duck Hunter in 1924 and of Scarecow in 1925.

OLIVIA. Olivia was by Senator by Leadville (TB), and her dam was Little Judge by Little Steve. She was bred and owned by J. S. and D. D. Casement, of Whitewater, Colorado. She was bred to the Thoroughbred Ganadore, and the resulting foal was Zaal (1927).

OLNA. Olna was sired by Traveler and bred by Webb Christian, of Big Spring, Texas. She foaled Step Back by Step Back (TB) in 1924.

ORPHA. Orpha was by Senator and out of a Charles Walker mare. She was bred by Charles Walker, of Kiowa, Colorado, and owned by J. H. Deboard, of Gillette, Wyoming. She was the dam of Senator Elect by Election (TB) in 1926 and of Senator West by Dr. West.

OVERKNIGHT. Overknight was sired by Benighted (TB) and out of a Quarter mare. She was owned by Webb Christian, of Big Spring, Texas. She was the dam of Eddie Earl (1919) and Webbs Choice (1922), both by Barney Lucas.

OVER THERE. Over There was by Possum (King) and out of Katy Bell by Necktie by Fuzzy. She was the dam of Hard Tack by Apache Kid in 1930.

P

PAISANA. Paisana was one of the truly great Quarter mares of all time. She was a small seal-brown mare. She was foaled in 1854 (?) and died in 1888 (?). Paisana's sire was Brown Dick, and her dam was Belton Queen. She was probably bred by Webb Ross, of Scott County, Kentucky, and sold to Frank Lilly, of Thorp Springs, Texas. Sometime later Oliver and Bailes, of Seguin, Texas, had her, and she ended in the ownership of Bill Fleming, of Belmont, Texas. Although it seems incredible, authorities and records agree that she had twenty foals between 1856 and 1886, most of whom were sired by Old Billy. They were Anthony, Jenny Oliver, Red Rover, Artie, Dora, Old Joe, Cuadro, Chunky Bill, John Crowder, Alice, Sweet Lip, Little Brown Dick, Pancho, Joe Collins, Pine Knot, Whalebone, Yellow Wolf, Blaze, Kitty, and Big Mare.

PANSY. Pansy was sired by Dave Waldo (TB), and her dam was Silvie T. She was bred by Bryant Turner, of Colorado Springs, Colorado. She was the dam of Red Vigil, a brown colt by Booger Red, sired in 1923.

PAN ZARITA. Pan Zarita, a sorrel, was foaled in 1910. When mature she stood 15-2 hands and weighed 1,000 pounds. She was sired by Abe Frank (TB), and her dam was Caddie Griffith by Rancocas (TB). Her second dam was Sally Johnson by Blue Dick. Both Abe Frank and Rancocas had *Bonnie Scotland blood on their distaff side. She was bred by J. F. Newman, of Sweetwater, Texas. She held the world's record for five-eights on a circular track, a mark of 57 1/5. Her match races with Joe Blair in Juárez, Mexico, are still discussed. She died before she could be bred and was buried in the center of the old fairground track in New Orleans. Beside her is Black Gold. Perhaps it is fitting that both had Quarter Horse blood in their veins.

PAPOOSE. Papoose was sired by Bob H by Old Fred, and she was out of the Blue Mare by Bob H. She was bred by Marshall Peavy, of Clark, Colorado. She was the dam of Sue Peavy by Ding Bob in 1937 and of Chipeta by Ding Bob in 1940.

PARAGON MARE. General Wade Hampton, of Kentucky, owned the stallion Paragon. There were several mares who were referred to simply as the Paragon Mare. One was Jane Hunt. Another was a bay, foaled in 1808 by Buzzard. She was bred by Jack Harris, of Franklin County, Kentucky. Still another Paragon Mare, also a bay, was foaled in 1833. She was by Harris's Paragon and out of Cherokee by Cherokee. Her second dam was by Kentucky Whip. Several of the offspring of these mares produced good sprinters.

PATH TENNYSON (TB). Path Tennyson, a Thoroughbred, is mentioned here because her owner, Walter Watkins, of Oakford, Illinois, bred her to Peter McCue, and she foaled Jessie Hoover.

PATSIE. Patsie, a sorrel, was sired by Paul Murray and out of Patsie Keith by Billy Dibrell. In 1930 she foaled Bill Fleming (Bouldin's) by a son of Jimmy Elder.

PATTIE BILLET. Pattie Billet was sired by Volturno (TB), and her dam was Billeta by Billet (TB). Her second dam was Etta by Bill Alexander. She was owned by Edwin Blakeley, of Kilbourne, Illinois. She was the dam of Menzo Shurtz by Peter McCue in 1906 and of Kilbourne by Peter McCue in 1908.

PATTY TENNYSON (TB). Patty Tennyson, a Thoroughbred, was owned by B. C. Watkins, of Oakford, Illinois.

When bred to Peter McCue, she foaled Oakford and, in 1904, Peter's Cue.

PEACHIE. Peachie was sired by Joy by Jeff, and she was out of Perfect Doll by Pid Hart. She was bred by C. B. Campbell, of Minco, Oklahoma.

PEACHUM. Peachum was sired by Peter McCue, and she was owned by T. V. Cunningham, of Lanesboro, Iowa. She was the dam of Lanesboro by Jim Dunn (TB).

PEARL. Pearl, a bay, was foaled in 1879. She was sired by Brick by Oregon Charlie, and her dam was Nellie by Walnut Bark. Her second dam was a full sister of Choctaw by Obe Jennings. She was owned by John Adams, of Woodland, California. She foaled Miss Mitford by Joe Hooker, Steam Beer by Uncle Billy, and Ben Martin, also by Uncle Billy. She was the dam of Mable T and Birdie C by Red Iron (TB) and of Zem Zem and Electra C by Shannon.

PEARL BARNES. Pearl Barnes, a bay, was foaled in 1896. Her sire was Barnes by Billet (TB), and her dam was Betty W. Pearl was bred and raced by O. G. Parke, of Kyle, Texas. She ran a half mile in 50 seconds in New Orleans in 1898. She produced three well-known foals by *Gallantry (TB): Arch Oldham, Buster Jones, and Kerrville. She also foaled Buncom by First Mate (TB), El Pato by Conjuror (TB), and Call Shot by Malik. It might be pointed out that the record shows Call Shot foaled in 1912 and Malik foaled in 1911.

PEARL, MANCOS'. Mancos' Pearl was by Charles Sumner, and she was bred by the Brown brothers, of Farmington, New Mexico. She was the dam of Tex by Cowboy by Yellow Jacket in 1927.

PEARLY C. Pearly C was sired by Senator. She was bred by C. A. Allison, of Weston, Wyoming. She was the dam of Pearly Belle by Election (TB) and of Pearly C II by Senator.

Both were foaled around 1930 or before. Pearly C herself was foaled around 1915.

PEARLY C II. Pearly C II was sired by Senator and out of Pearly C. She was bred by C. A. Allison, of Weston, Wyoming. She was the dam of Picarella II by Election (TB) in 1927.

PEGGY. Peggy was foaled in the early 1930s. She was sired by Traveler, and she was out of an old Cunningham racing mare. She was bred by Jack Cunningham, of Comanche, Texas. She was the dam of Little Dusty by Dusty Brown by Barney Owens.

PEGGY C. Peggy C was foaled in 1933. She was sired by Doc by Possum, and her dam was Silver by Blue Eyes. She was a great race and roping mare, and she was owned by Chester Cooper, of Roosevelt, Arizona. She and her family could run. She was the dam of Sleepy Dick by Colonel Clyde, Tonta Gal by Clabber, Little Wolf by Clabber, and Wac Chaser by Red Man.

PEGGY MORGAN (TB). Peggy Morgan was by Asteroid by Lexington and was owned by James Owen, of Berlin, Illinois. She was the dam of Fib by Story (TB) in 1887.

PEPITA. Pepita, a sorrel, was foaled in 1925. She was sired by Kenward (TB), and she was out of Phyllis F. Her second dam was Burnie Bunton by Rancocas (TB). Her third dam was Dead Cinch by Silent Friend. Ed Springer told me that she was purchased for Waite Phillips at Caliente and that she was a crack short-distance mare. She was registered in the Jockey Club for racing purposes only. Springer leased her from Phillips and bred her. She has been listed as the dam of Springer's Little Joe, foaled in 1916, though more reliable information has Little Joe's dam as a mare by Uhlan.

PET. Pet was sired by Old Fred, and she was out of a mare named Primera sired by Primero (TB). She was bred and owned by Coke Roberds, of Hayden, Colorado. She was the dam of Sheik, a grulla colt foaled in 1918, sired by Peter McCue.

PET. Pet was by Ned Oak by Peter McCue. She was owned by Harry Clark, of Boise City, Oklahoma. She foaled Taffy by Joe T in 1927.

PET DAWSON. Pet Dawson was by Jeff by Printer by Cold Deck and out of Old Babe by Little Earl. She was the dam of Red Buck by Red Man by Tubal Cain.

PET KID. Pet Kid was sired by Serf Savin (TB) and was bred by M. E. Andes, of Portales, New Mexico. She was the dam of the sorrel colt Jack of Diamonds by Jack McCue in 1934.

PILGRIM MARE. The Pilgrim Mare was sired by Pilgrim and was out of Choctaw's Sister by Obe Jennings. She was owned by John Adams, of Woodland, California. She produced Brick (1871) and Bell (1872) by Oregon Charlie.

PINK BLOOMERS. Pink Bloomers, a bay, was foaled in 1892. She was sired by Big Henry and was owned by A. J. Jones. She ran five-eighths in 1.08¼ at Roadhouse, Illinois, in 1895. Her name is more unusual than her time for five-eighths.

PINK CHEEK (TB). Pink Cheek was a Thoroughbred that Henry Pfefferling, of San Antonio, Texas, bred to his Remount stallion Uncle Jimmy Gray. The resulting foal was Major Speck, foaled in 1926.

PITCHIN SIS (DORADA). Pitchin Sis was foaled in 1930 (?). She was sired by Paul El and out of Big Liz. Paul El was by Spokane, and Big Liz was by Paul El. She was bred by George Groll, of Berclair, Texas. She was a good race mare.

PLOW MARE. The Plow Mare was foaled around 1890; her pedigree has not been traced. Helen Michaelis found some indication that she may have been sired by Confidence.

195

It was reported that she did farm work all week and then raced on Sunday (it sounds as though she and the Arizona Clabber would have made a pair). She was being raced in Fresno, California, in 1896 by S. W. Kane, of that city. She eventually became the dam of Orphan Boy by Wineburg (TB).

POCAHONTAS. There were two mares named Pocahontas in Texas. One was sired by Sumpter, and the other by Moss King. The Sumpter Pocahontas was the dam of Big Wash and was owned by G. P. Theobald, of McKinney, Texas. The Moss King Pocahontas was bred by Bill Moss, of Marble Falls, Texas.

POLL. Poll was a Celebrated American Quarter Running Mare. She was sired by Skipwith's Black-and-All-Black, and she was out of Figure by *Janus. She was foaled in the early 1790s and was bred by Henry Delony, of Mecklenburg County, Virginia. Later she was owned by John Goode, Sr.

POLL FLAXEN, see POLLY FLAXEN.

POLL PITCHER. Poll Pitcher was a Famous American Quarter Running Mare, foaled in the 1770s. She was sired by *Janus and out of a Mark Anthony mare. She was bred by Joseph John Alston, of Halifax, North Carolina. She later became the dam of two other Celebrated American Running Mares, both by *Janus: Broomtail and Sweeping Tail.

POLL SMILING. Poll Smiling was one of two *Janus mares with similar names (see POLL) owned by John Goode, Sr., of Mecklenburg County, Virginia. She was by *Janus and out of a *Janus mare. She was a Celebrated American Quarter Running Mare, foaled in 1774. She was a red sorrel with a blaze and two white hind feet. She stood 13-2 hands. Her breeder was John Goode, Sr. Her dam was probably Sweepstakes, a mare bred by Wyllie Jones, of Halifax, North Carolina.

POLLY, see LADY LAWRENCE.

POLLY. Polly was by Tom Campbell by Bob Peters. She was owned by Alden Meek, of Foss, Oklahoma. She was the dam of Santa Claus by Red Buck.

POLLY FLAXEN (POLL FLAXEN OR DOLLY FLAXEN). Polly Flaxen was foaled in the late 1760s. She was sired by *Jolly Roger and out of *Mary Gray. She was bred by Captain Thomas Turpin, of Powhatan County, Virginia. She was the dam of Camden by *Janus, Fleetwood by the same sire, and most important for the Quarter Horse, Goode's Brimmer by Harris' Eclipse.

POLLY J. Polly J, a bay, was foaled in 1887 and died in 1897. She was bred and owned by James Owen, of Berlin, Illinois. She was sired by Spinning by Voltigeur (TB) and out of Dell by Cold Deck. She was the dam of the sorrel colt Gabe by Billy Sherman in 1895 and of Reputation, Jr., by Reputation (TB). She also had several fillies whose names have not come down to us.

POLLY WILLIAMS. Polly Williams, a sorrel, was one of the most famous of the colonial running mares. She was foaled in 1774, sired by Lee's Old Mark Anthony and out of a *Janus mare. She was bred by Peter Williams, of Dinwiddie County, Virginia. Later she was owned and run by William Davis, of North Carolina. She appeared rather grotesque: she had a high goose rump, ragged hips, and a narrow behind, but she could fly. A blaze and four white feet also made her conspicuous. She was shot to save a forefeit.

POLLY WILLIAMS. Polly Williams, a gray, was foaled about 1780. She was sired by Flag of Truce and out of a mare by Twigg. She was probably bred by John Goode, and she was later owned by a Mrs. Edwards, of Granville County, North Carolina. She is supposed to have been the fastest mare of her time. She ran against Twigg nine times and beat him once. Her owner lost 200,000 pounds of tobacco in those races.

POLLY WILLIAMS, JOHNSON'S. Johnson's Polly Williams was a Famous American Quarter Running Mare. She was sired by *Janus and was out of a *Janus mare. She was bred by Marmaduke Johnson, of Warren County, North Carolina. Edgar says that from this mare descended Johnson's Medley Mare, Roanoke, Variety, Reality, Carolinian, Slender, Medley, and the unequaled mare Bonnets-o-Blue.

POOR MAMA. Poor Mama was sired by Joy by Jeff and was owned by Aubra Bowers, of Allison, Texas. She was the dam of Cimarron by Jeff Self by A. D. Reed in 1930.

PRIDES ELLA. Prides Ella was sired by Pride of India (TB) and out of Emma Hall by Peter McCue. She was bred by John Dial, of Goliad, Texas, and was the dam of Sudden Change by Chicaro (TB) in 1933.

PRINCESS PEEP. Princess Peep was sired by Walking John, and she was out of Madame Peep by Bo Peep, a Quarter Horse. She was owned by Arch Wilkinson, of Menard, Texas, and she was the dam of Walking Prince by Hendricks (TB) in 1928.

PRINTER. Printer was sired by Gray Eagle, and she was out of a Quarter mare. She was bred by Mrs. B. J. Treacy, of Lexington, Kentucky. She was also the dam of May Kennedy. Mrs. Treacy was one of the two greatest women breeders of short horses. The other was Mrs. H. A. Trowbridge, of Wellington, Kansas.

PRINTER MARE. The Printer Mare, a black, was foaled in 1874. She was sired by Printer by Cold Deck and was bred by Bill Owen, of Smithville, Missouri. Later she was owned by the notorious Jesse James. In 1881 she produced Bay Cold Deck by Hamburg Dick.

PRISSY. Prissy, a sorrel, was foaled in 1939. She was sired by Colonel Clyde by My Texas Dandy and out of Phoebe C by Blue Eyes. She was bred and owned by Chester Cooper, of Roosevelt, Arizona. She was a fast mare, and in one match race she beat Painted Joe, going 300 yards for $3,000. Painted Joe had run a 300-yard race in 16.2, so she beat a racehorse.

PUG, LITTLE. Little Pug, a sorrel, was foaled in 1897. She was sired by Bobby Beach and was out of Vashti by Tom Sawyer. Her second dam was a Quarter mare of Steel Dust breeding. She was bred by H. T. Batchler, of Lancaster and Dallas, Texas. Later she was owned and raced by D. C. Armstrong, of Doxey, Oklahoma. She was registered in *The American Stud Book.* In 1944, Earl Kelly said that Little Pug could outrun all her competition going three-eighths and most all going a quarter. Her progeny include Little Danger by Tom Campbell; Oklahoma Deck and Speedy Ball, both by Joe Brocked (TB); Anna Armstrong, Dick Cato, Bud Armstrong, and Fanny A, all by Bob O; and Nada H, by Peter McCue.

PUMPKIN FILLY. Pumpkin Filly was a Celebrated American Quarter Running Mare. She was foaled in 1766 (?) and died in 1778. She was sired by Wyllie Jones's Blue Boar by *Janus and out of a *Janus mare. She was bred by Thomas Goode, of Chesterfield County, Virginia, and later owned by John Goode, Sr., Henry Delony, Shippey Allen Puckett, and Wyllie Jones. During her racing years she defeated most of her competitors. Later she became the dam of Linnet. She is listed in both Edgar and Bruce. There is some confusion in the records, for there are indications that Blue Boar was not foaled until 1774.

PUSS. Puss was by Red Bird by Jim Trammell by Barney Owens and out of Gypsy Maid by Jim Trammell. She was undoubtedly bred by Jim Trammell, of Sweetwater, Texas.

PUSS. Puss was by Norfolk (TB) and out of a short-race mare of Thoroughbred breeding owned by Theodore Winters, of Wahoe, Nevada, and Woodland, California. She was bred by Winters. She was the dam of Johnny Hooker by Joe Hooker in 1887.

PUSS, OLD. Old Puss was sired by Freedom by *Emancipation. She was owned by Charles Haley, of Sweetwater, Texas. She was the dam of Shiloh Jr. by Shiloh by Van Tromp in 1863.

PUSS B. Puss B, a bay, was foaled in 1882. She was sired by Tom Flood by Voltigeur (TB), and she was out of Reap by Dr. Cash. Her second dam was June Bug by Harry Bluff. She was bred by W. C. (Bill) Owen, of Smithville, Missouri. Later she was owned by Bill's relative James Owen, of Berlin, Illinois. Her produce include Flush and Katie Flanger by Fib and Katie G. by Reputation. The Owens and the Watkinses bred to each others' stallions.

Q

QUAIL. Quail was by Tanglefoot by Young Cold Deck and she was out of Gray Kate by Young White Lightning. She was bred by Coke Blake, of Pryor, Oklahoma. She foaled Rambler by Tubal Cain in 1920.

QUEEN. Queen was sired by Ashton (TB) and out of a fast polo mare. She was owned by the Lindauer brothers, of Grand Valley, Colorado. She was the dam of Bumble Bee by King Plaudit in 1934.

QUEEN. Queen was sired by Dedier and owned by Lake Neal, of Gillett, Texas. She was the dam of Ace of Hearts by the Dunderstadt Horse in 1904.

QUEEN. Queen was sired by a grandson of Peter McCue, and she was owned by B. G. Anderson, of Craig, Colorado. She was the dam of Fred by Brown Dick.

QUEEN. Queen was sired by Pilgrim by Lexington. She was owned by Jack A. Batchler, of Lancaster and Dallas,Texas. She was the dam of Jack Traveler, a bay colt foaled in 1875, sired by Steel Dust. She also may have been the dam of Louise (the dam of Brown Dick), for she was also owned by Alfred Bailes, of Hopkins County, Texas, and by Sam Watkins, of Illinois.

QUEEN. Queen was sired by Lynx, a Thoroughbred owned by H. Kirkendall, of Helena, Montana. She was the dam of Panama, a sorrel colt foaled in 1891 by Glen Elm (TB).

QUEEN. Queen was sired by Traveler's Boy by Traveler, and she was owned by J. M. Corder, of Sanderson, Texas. She was the dam of Robin Hood, a sorrel colt foaled in 1926, sired by Esquire (TB).

QUEEN. Queen was sired by Valentino by Cameron Shrimp and was out of Jabalina by the Strait Horse by Yellow Jacket. She was bred by Manuel Benevides Volpe, of Laredo, Texas. She was the dam of Sonny Kimble by Zantanon, a sorrel colt foaled in 1936.

QUEEN. Queen was sired by Yellow Jacket by Little Rondo and was owned by J. A. Laning, of Rocksprings, Texas. She was the dam of Jimmie by Runflor (TB).

QUEEN, see OKLAHOMA QUEEN.

QUEEN KAPIOLANI. Queen Kapiolani, a sorrel, was foaled in 1883. She was by Joe Hooker and out of Big Gun (Kate George) by Old George. She was bred by Theodore Winters, of Wahoe, Nevada, and Woodland, California. Later she was owned by M. Cunningham, of Sacramento. She was the dam of Claudie and Pansie by Three Cheers (TB) and of the sorrel colt Dun Boy by *Loyalist (TB).

QUEEN LITZE. Queen Litze (TB) was owned by Si Dawson, of Hayden, Colorado. She was the dam of Fred Litze (1915) and Bob H (1916), both by Old Fred.

QUEEN OF HEARTS. Queen of Hearts was foaled in 1920 (?). She was sired by (who else?) Ace of Hearts by the Dunderstadt Horse. She was bred by Bill Copeland, of Pettus, Texas, and later owned by George Clegg, of Alice, Texas. She was the dam of Siminoff's Uncle Jimmy Gray by Bull Dog by Uncle Jimmy Gray.

QUEEN VICTORIA. Queen Victoria was sired by Lock's Rondo, and she was out of Margie by Old Cold Deck. She was bred by C. B. Campbell, of Minco, Oklahoma, and run by John Armstrong, of Sayre, Oklahoma. She was later owned by C. L. Franics, of Floyd, New Mexico. She was the dam of Nellie Hart by Pid Hart.

R

RAINBOW. Rainbow was foaled in 1920 (?), and she was sired by Senator by Leadville (TB). She was owned by Henry Leonard, of Colorado Springs, Colorado. She could run a quarter in 22+ seconds. She foaled Leinster by Helmet (TB) in 1928, Rainmaker by Senator in 1929, St. Damian by Dark Friar (TB) in 1923, and Just Right by Just David (TB) in 1930. It has also been said that Just Right was out of Rain No More.

RAIN NO MORE. Rain No More was sired by Rainy Day by Lone Star. She was bred by Martin Haby, of Riomedina, Texas. One source says that she was the dam of Just Right by Just David (TB), but another says that Just Right's dam was Rainbow.

RAINY HANCOCK. Rainy Hancock was by Rainy Day by Midnight and out of Triangle Lady by Joe Hancock. She was bred by the Tom L. Burnett estate, of Fort Worth, Texas.

RAM CAT. Ram Cat was foaled in 1855 (?) and died in 1870 (?). She was sired by Steel Dust and was out of Fanny

Wolf. She foaled Old Billy in 1860 (?), Ribbon by Yellow Horse in 1866, and Martin's Cold Deck by Billy in 1868.

RAMONA. Ramona, a black, was foaled in 1924 (?). She was sired by Tom Glover by Sykes' Rondo, and she was out of a Jim Rogers mare. She was a small, heavy-muscled mare, bred by Jim Rogers and later owned by Merlin Rogers, of McKavett, Texas.

RASKA. Raska was a range mare of undetermined breeding but a good, straight-legged individual. She was bought by Dan D. Casement, of Whitewater, Colorado, as a riding horse. When bred to Concho Colonel, she produced Starlight, foaled in 1918 (?).

RAYMOND MARE. The Raymond Mare was a Little Joe mare out of Lucretia M. She was owned by Fred Raymond, of Raymondsville, Texas, but was never named. She was the dam of Tuerto by Hickory Bill in 1913.

READY. Ready, a sorrel, was sired by Red Joe of Arizona, and she was out of Ruby by Red Cloud. She was owned by Melville H. Haskell, of Tucson, Arizona.

REAP (NANNIE). Nannie Reap was sired by Dr. Cash and out of June Bug by Harry Bluff. She was bred by James Owen, of Berlin, Illinois. She was the dam of Puss B by Tom Flood in 1882 (?).

RED, OLD. Old Red was sired by Red by Possum (King) and was owned by Clyde Smith, of Big Foot, Texas. She was the dam of Colonel Clyde by My Texas Dandy and of Little Shadow.

RED BIRD. Red Bird, a sorrel, was foaled in 1885 (?). She was sired by Bill Garner, and she was probably bred by E. Shelby Stanfield, of Thorp Springs, Texas. Later she was bought by C. A. Lane, of Dumas, Texas, and later by Bill Miller, of Mobeetie, Texas. She was the dam of Idle Boy by

Long Tom in 1891. Milo Burlingame trained and raced her for a time.

RED BIRD. Red Bird, a sorrel, was foaled in 1880 (?). Her sire was Lock's Rondo. She was a race mare, and she won perhaps her most famous race against one of Sheriff Jim Brown's mares called Blue Bird. The race was run in Fort Worth in 1885.

RED LADY. Red Lady was sired by John Wilkins by Peter McCue and out of a Quarter mare named Dusty Ann. Red Lady was owned by G. B. Mathis, of Stinnett, Texas. She was the dam of Dusty Wilkins, a palomino horse foaled in 1939.

RED MOROCCO. Red Morocco, a sorrel, was foaled in 1836. She was sired by Medoc and out of a Tiger mare named Morocco. She was bred, owned, and raced by William Buford, of Tree Hill Stud, Woodford County, Kentucky.

RED MOROCCO. Red Morocco, a sorrel, was of Thoroughbred and short-horse breeding. In the late 1870s or early 1880s, Vincent Hildreth, of Cunningham, Missouri, took her to Texas in an attempt to beat Jim Brown's Gray Alice. When Red Morocco lost the race, Hildreth had to sell her to Brown to get enough money to go home.

RED NELL. Red Nell was foaled around 1910. She was by Texas Chief by Traveler. She was owned by J. W. Horn, of Cameron, Texas. She was the dam of Little Red Nell.

RED NELL, LITTLE. Little Red Nell, a sorrel, was foaled about 1928. She was sired by Brown Billy by Pancho, and she was out of Red Nell by Texas Chief. She was bred by Henry Lindsey, of Granger, Texas, and later owned by John W. House, of Cameron, Texas. She was the dam of Nelline by Fleeting Time (TB) and of Red Joe of Arizona by Joe Reed.

RED NELLIE. Red Nellie was sired by Boston Boy and out of Heely by Blue Dick. She was bred and owned by Jim

Newman, of Sweetwater, Texas. She produced Tex Anna by Rancocas (TB) in 1900, Smithy Kane by the same sire in 1902, Red Ray by Lord Dalmeny (TB) in 1903, Alonza by the same sire in 1904, and Simple Sam by Prince Plenty (TB) in 1905.

RED WING. Red Wing was by Moss King by Big King and was bred by the Waddell brothers, of Odessa, Texas. She was the dam of Red Dennis by Dennis Reed (TB), Samoset by Captain Costigan, and Woodpecker (1927) by Dennis Reed.

RED WINGS. Red Wings was sired by Reincocas by Mose. She was owned by Joan Williams, of Stead, New Mexico. She was the dam of Speedy by Kelly by Star Shoot (TB).

RIX. Rix was by Senator and was owned by C. A. Allison, of Weston, Wyoming. She was the sire of Polo King by Election (TB) in 1929 and of Jim Rix by Election in 1927.

ROAN BEAUTY. Roan Beauty, a roan, was by Jim Miller by Roan Dick. She ran races throughout the West.

ROAN JANE, see JANE BAKER.

ROSE BRADWARDINE. Rose Bradwardine, a bay, was foaled in 1869. She was by Rupee by Rebel (?) and out of Glenda Fly (TB) by Union. She was the dam of Mark Tapley by Silent Friend (TB).

ROSETTA. Rosetta was foaled around 1800, sired by *Obscurity and out of a mare by Lee's Mark Anthony. She was bred by Hugh Norrell, of Mecklenburg County, Virginia, and sold as a filly to Samuel Puryear and later to Henry Carlton. She is listed in both *The American Stud Book* and Edgar's studbook.

ROSY CLARK. Rosy Clark was by *Saltram (TB). She was the dam of Tennessee Oscar, a bay colt foaled in 1815 by Wilkes' Wonder.

ROXANA. Roxana was probably foaled in or near 1815. She was sired by Hephestion by *Buzzard, and she was out of a

*Marplot mare. She was owned and probably bred by a Dr. Hayward and later purchased by Colonel Singleton, of South Carolina. She was the dam of the Cherokee sired by Sir Archy in 1824 (?).

RUBY. Ruby was foaled in 1928 (?), sired by Red Cloud by Possum (King) and out of a mare by John Crowder. She was the dam of Pay Dirt, Baby Bunting, Ready, and of Red Racer, all of whom could run.

RUBY. Ruby was by Wildcat by Jim Ned, and she was owned by Earl Moye, of Arvada, Wyoming. She was the dam of Starlight by Young Fred by Old Nick.

RUPEE GIRL. Rupee Girl was by Rupee. She was owned by Sam Harper, of Texas. She was the dam of Texas Ranger by Rebel, foaled in 1869, and of Austin by the same stallion, foaled in 1870.

RUTH. Ruth was sired by Brettenham (TB), and she was out of the Norfleet mare by Ed Withers (TB). She was the dam of Manitobian, a sorrel stallion foaled in 1935 by Chubby.

S

SADIE M. Sadie M was born in the mid-1920s. She was sired by Little Dick by Sleepy Dick, and she was out of Nellie by Panmure (TB). She was bred by Charles Meyer, of Ellinger, Texas, and later owned by Albert Mays, of Wharton, Texas. She was a full brother of Sleepy Dick by Little Dick, and she was the dam of My Texas Dandy, foaled in 1927 by Porte Drapeau (TB).

SALLY FRANKLIN. Sally Franklin was sired by Illinois Medoc and was owned by A. Musick, of California. She was the dam of Johnny Moore by George Moore in 1867 and of Vanderbilt by Norfolk in 1872.

SALLY JOHNSON. Sally, a bay, was foaled in 1870. She was sired by Blue Dick, and she was out of Mittie Stephens. She was bred by C. R. Haley, of Sweetwater, Texas, and later owned by Jim Newman, also of Sweetwater. She foaled Boston Girl by Boston Boy in 1896 and Add Ran by Rancocas in 1897.

SALLY JOHNSON. Sally, a brown, was foaled in 1850. She was sired by Blue Dick by Wade Hampton and out of Mittie Stephens by Shiloh, Jr. She was bred and owned by C. R. Haley, of Sweetwater, Texas.

SALLY POLK. Sally Polk was sired by Brown Dick, and she was owned by W. W. McClunne, of Batesville, Virginia. In 1875 she foaled Shiloh by Watson by Lexington.

SALTRAM MARE. The Saltram Mare was by *Saltram, and her dam was a mare sired by Symme's Wildair. She was bred and owned by Major Thomas Gibbon, of North Carolina. In 1814 she foaled Timoleon by Sir Archy, one of the greatest sires of short horses.

SALTY. Salty was by Billy the Tough by A. D. Reed and out of Peachie by Joy by Jeff. She was owned by Kenneth Montgomery, of Reydon, Oklahoma. In 1939 she foaled Salty Chief by Chief by Peter McCue.

SAM JONES MARE. The Sam Jones Mare was sired by Sam Jones by Black Nick. Her dam was by Jim Ned by Pancho. She was the dam of Harmon Baker, Jr., in 1920 and of One-Eyed Billy in 1919.

SARAZAN. Sarazan was sired by Billy Sunday, and she was out of Lurianca by Little Joe. She was owned by Ott Adams, of Alfred, Texas. She was the dam of Sleepy Sam by Billy Sunday.

SAUCY SUE. Saucy Sue was sired by Toni Chief (TB), and she was out of Rainy Weather by Rainy Day. She was owned by Henry Wiescamp, of Alamosa, Colorado. She was the dam of Scooter W by Plaudit in 1945.

SCHUHART. Schuhart was sired by Magician by Rainy Day and out of a Quarter mare. She was bred by a man named Mangold, of Lacoste, Texas and later owned by L. B. Wardlaw, of Del Rio, Texas. She was the dam of Cuter by Big Nigger in 1935.

SCOOTER'S SISTER. Scooter's Sister was sired by Lone Star by Gold Enamel (TB), and she was bred by Eugene Schott, of Riomedina, Texas. She was the dam of Medina Sport by Uncle Jimmy Gray.

*SELIMA. *Selima, a bay, was by the Godolphin Arabian and out of a mare by Hobgoblin. She was foaled in 1745 in England and died in 1776 in America. She had a small star blaze and white on a hind foot. She was bred by Lord Godolphin and sold to Benjamin Tasker, of Maryland, in 1750. She was a great race mare in America, and she had six foals for Tasker. When Tasker died, she was sold, and at the age of sixteen she was taken to Mount Airy, the Virginia plantation of John Tayloe II, where she had four foals. Her eighth colt was Spadille, the great Quarter Horse sire owned by Wyllie Jones, of Halifax County, North Carolina. Spadille was sired by *Janus. *Selima was also the dam of the famous Quarter mare Nancy Wake by Babram and Belair, Pardner, and Ariel, all by Morton's *Traveler.

SENATRESS. Senatress was sired by Senator by Leadville (TB). She was raised by C. F. Cusack, of Denver, Colorado. Senatress was the dam of Swiftly Home, a brown colt foaled in 1927 by Straight Home (TB).

SIDNEY. Sidney was sired by Captain Daugherty (TB), and she was out of Alice by Renfro's Cold Deck. She was bred by Matt Renfro, of Menard, Texas. Sidney was the dam of Red Buck by Everett (TB) in 1929.

SILENTINA. Silentina was sired by Silent Friend and out of Fleecie P by Bulletin (TB). She was bred by Tom King, of Belmont, Texas. She was the dam of Fashion by Anthony in 1887 and of Lemonade by the same sire in 1888.

SILK STOCKINGS. Silk Stockings was sired by Billie Tom and bred by Monty Corder, of Sanderson, Texas. In 1925 she foaled Ring Master by Red Seal by Seal Skin.

SILKY. Silky was by Billie by *Janus. Bruce calls her "Smokey" Wilson's Celebrated Quarter Mare (1:641). She is not listed in Edgar. She was the dam of Hannibal by *Medley.

SILVER. Silver was foaled around 1928, sired by Blue Eyes by Possum. She was the dam of a racing family that includes Peggy C by Doc by Possum and Dutchess by the same sire. She was owned and raised by Chester Cooper, of Roosevelt, Arizona.

SILVER. Silver was sired by Chickasha Bob by Pid Hart (Rocky Mountain Tom?) and she was owned by Will Stead, of Tulia, Texas. About 1920 she foaled Spark Plug by Jack McCue. She also foaled Will Stead by Billy McCue by Jack McCue.

SILVER. Silver was by Dave Waldo. She was owned by D. Bryant Turner, of Colorado Springs, Colorado. In 1923 she foaled La Plata by Booger Red.

SILVER FINN. Silver Finn was sired by Senator. She was owned by A. E. Peterson, of Elbert, Colorado. She was the dam of Spiegel by Mont Megellon by Gold Coin by Senator.

SILVER HEEL. Silver Heel was by Rex Squirrel, and she was owned by William Shelts, of Spearman, Texas. She was the dam of Teddy, a bay colt foaled in 1931, sired by Brave Bob.

SILVER HEELS. Silver Heels was sired by Old Liberty by *Janus. She was owned by Lipscomb Ragland, of Halifax County, Virginia. She was the dam of Ragland's Diomed.

SILVER HEELS. Silver Heels was the dam of Priest Bob by Anthony foaled in 1886. Little more is known about her.

SILVER QUEEN. Silver Queen was sired by Warrior by Captain Sykes, and she was owned by Ott Adams, of Alfred, Texas. She was the dam of Del Monte by Little Joe.

SILVER TAIL. Silver Tail was sired by Jim Ned, and she was owned by Si Dawson and Coke Roberds, of Hayden, Colorado. She was the dam of Old Nick by Old Fred.

SIR HOPKINS. In spite of the name Sir Hopkins was a mare sired by Suffragist (TB). She was bred and named by E. E. Wisdom, of San Antonio, Texas. She was the dam of Jiggs by Uncle Jimmy Gray in 1924.

SIS. Sis, a bay, was foaled in 1886 (?). She was sired by Joe Collins and out of Gray Alice by Steel Dust. She was bred by Jim Brown, of Giddings, Texas. Later she was owned by Clay McGonigal, of Midland, Texas, and by Bill Moore, of San Angelo, Texas. She had the following foals of record: Blue Skinny, a gray colt by Alex, in 1890; Katy Bell, a black filly, by Buck Shot in 1908; and Myrt, a filly, by Little Traveler in 1909.

SIS. Sis was by Doc Horn (TB) and out of Queenie by Dedier (D. J.). She was owned by Sheriff Pechou, of Ville Platte, Louisiana. She was the dam of Dee Dee, a bay colt foaled in 1939 by Flying Bob.

SISTER. Sister was sired by Uncle Bob by Luke Blackburn (TB). Luke Blackburn was by *Bonnie Scotland and out of a Lexington mare—ideal Thoroughbred blood for a Quarter

Horse. She foaled Dewey by *Sain in 1899. Dewey was probably the Thoroughbred who went to Louisiana and cleaned up the Cajun country. He was never allowed to leave but was bought by the Stemmonses and the Broussards and began breeding Louisiana short horses. Dewey held sway until Dedier arrived, and then Dedier was crossed on Dewey mares.

SISTER, LITTLE. Little Sister was by Jim Ned and out of Old Bonnie, a Thoroughbred owned by Sam Harkey, of Sheffield, Texas. In 1905, at Christoval, Texas, she ran a 220-yard match race against King Cole in 12 seconds. She lived for twenty years and had fourteen fillies and one colt, Old Jim. Two of her better-known fillies were Tempest by Libyan (TB) and Ada Chenney by Alex Mitchell. The colt, Old Jim, was foaled in 1922, sired by Little Texas Chief.

SISTER, LITTLE. Little Sister, a sorrel, was foaled in 1887, owned and bred by J. R. Nasworthy, of Bridgeview Farm, San Angelo, Texas. She was sired by Buck Walton and was out of Lizzie Parks by General Hood. Her second dam was by Shiloh. She was the dam of Old Steve by Stranger in 1895 and Dena by Caliph in 1897.

SISTER, LITTLE. Little Sister was sired by Little Joe by Traveler and out of Jeanette by Billy by Big Jim. She was bred and owned by Ott Adams, of Alice, Texas. She was the dam of Filipe (Felipe Angeles) by Paul El in 1932 and of Cotton Eyed Joe, a bay stallion foaled in 1936 by Joe Abb.

SISTER IDA (TB). Sister Ida, a Thoroughbred, was owned by John Wilkins, of San Antonio. Wilkins bred her to Peter McCue, and she foaled Charley Howell in 1910.

SISTER OF JUNE BUG, see ALICE.

SMILING POLL. Smiling Poll, a red sorrel, was foaled in 1775. She was sired by *Janus, and her dam was by *Jolly Roger. She was bred by John Goode, Sr., of Mecklenburg County, Virginia. She was exceedingly well formed. She and her half sister Poll Smiling were probably lookalikes. It is certain that both could run. Edgar lists Smiling Poll as a famous American running mare. She was bought by that astute racehorse man Henry Delony when she was three years old, and she was later owned by William Davis.

SNIP. Snip was sired by Si Ding by Ding Bob and was owned by Leonard Horn, of Walcott, Colorado. She was the dam of Young Peekaboo by Bob H.

SOPHIE. Sophie was sired by Billy Tom, and she was bred by Monty Corder, of Sanderson, Texas. She was the dam of Rambling Sam by Red Seal by Sealskin in 1923.

SORREL, LITTLE. Little Sorrel was sired by Kingwood (TB) and was owned by George McGonigal, of Midland, Texas. She was the dam of Old Tom by Big Apple by Joe Collins.

SORREL ALICE. Sorrel Alice was foaled around 1915. She was sired by Chickasha Bob, and she was bred by E. Shelby Stanfield, of Thorp Springs, Texas. Later she was owned by S. B. Barnes, of Tulia, Texas. In 1917 she foaled Billy McCue by Peter McCue.

SORREL NELL. Little is known about this grand old mare. She may have been raised by Mike Finley, of Sylvan Grove, Kansas, or by John Day, of Aswata, Kansas. Both had excellent Quarter mares. She was the dam of John Reed by Little Pete in 1884, Honest John by Sleepy Jim in 1886, and Sorrel John by Sleepy Jim. All three were crack Quarter racers, as good as their Kansas origins.

SPANISH DUNN, see HUNTSINGER MARE.

SPECKLEBACK (YOUNG SPECKLEBACK). This excellent bay mare was foaled about 1800. She was sired by Randolph's Aber, and her dam was Speckleback by Mead's Aber. She was bred and owned by John Patrick, of Charlotte County, Virginia. In 1805 she was bred to the imported stallion *Whip, and in 1805 she foaled Kentucky Whip, one of the all-time great Quarter Horse sires.

SPRINTER. Sprinter was owned by C. Ward, of Nebraska. In 1880 she foaled Long John by Black Nick by Stewart's Telegraph.

SQUAW. Squaw was by Peter McCue and out of an Old Fred mare. She was bred by Coke T. Roberds, of Hayden, Colorado. She could run, and when she was bred, she produced Big Enough, a brown mare foaled in 1931 by A. D. Reed, and Little Squaw, a bay mare foaled in 1936 by Dundee (TB).

SQUAW. Squaw was sired by Possum (King), and she was out of a Gardner mare. She was bred by Claude Gardner, of Wilcox, Arizona. She was the dam of Mose by Old Mose by Traveler in 1914.

SQUAW LADY (SQUAW). Squaw was sired by Cockle Burr by Rex and out of Minnie Ortag by Rex. She was bred and owned by Dutch and Roy Mouse, of Canute, Oklahoma.

STELLA. Stella was sired by Booger Red by Rancocas (TB), and she was bred by Ernest Myers, of Hochne (?), New Mexico. She was the dam of Pacific by Plaudit.

STING LILLY. Sting Lilly was foaled shortly before 1780. She was sired by *Janus, and her dam was by Old Peacock. She was probably bred by General Nathaniel Cargill, of Virginia. Edgar lists her as a Celebrated American Quarter Running Mare.

STOCKINGS. Stockings was foaled in 1917 (?). She was by Old Fred, and she was bred and owned by Coke T. Roberds, of Hayden, Colorado. She was the dam of Buck Thomas by Peter McCue, Coke T (Prince) by Brown Dick, Goldie by Fred S, and the Brown Dick Mare by *Deering Doe (TB).

STOCKINGS. Stockings was bred by C. B. Campbell, of Minco, Oklahoma, and she was later owned by Dan Armstrong, of Doxey, Oklahoma. She was the dam of Speedy Ball and of Fear Me (1914), both sired by Tom Campbell. Fear Me was raced by Dan's brother, Reed Armstrong.

STOCKINGS. Stockings was sired by Sheik and out of Squaw by Dutch Martin. She was bred and owned by Earl Moye, of Arvada, Wyoming.

SUE, LITTLE. Little Sue, a sorrel, was foaled in 1929. She was sired by Sam Watkins by Hickory Bill and out of Sorrel Perez by Chaquiz. She was 14-3 hands high and weighed 1,130 pounds. She was bred by George Clegg, of Alice, Texas, and later owned by Bert Benear, of Tulsa, Oklahoma. Dick Truitt used Little Sue as a rodeo horse. Jim Nesbit bulldogged on her and matched her for short races. She was the dam of Black Hawk, a black stallion foaled in 1937 by San Simeon. Black Hawk was owned by King Merrit.

SUN DIAL. Sun Dial, a bay, was foaled in 1910. Her breeding is unknown. She may have been bred by Jack Saski, of Cuero, Texas. Two days after a match race in which she ran a 24-second quarter, she foaled Ace of Diamonds by Johnny.

SUNDOWN. Sundown was sired by Billie Tom. She was bred by Monty Corder, of Sanderson, Texas. She was the dam of Red Seal II by Sealskin in 1927.

SUSIE (SUZIE), see SUZIE McQUIRTER.

SUZIE, LITTLE. Little Suzie was a Trammell mare bred by Walter Trammell, of Sweetwater, Texas. She was the dam of Si by Joe Lucas.

SUZIE McQUIRTER. Suzie McQuirter's name is sometimes spelled Susie (or Suzie) McWhorter; under either spelling it is pronounced the same. She was by Little Ben Burton or by Old Ben Burton by Barney by Steel Dust. She was out of

Aury by Dutchman by Rondo. Her second dam was by Little Brown Dick. She was bred by Webb Christian, of Big Spring, Texas, and later owned by Dick Baker, of Weatherford, Texas. She was the dam of Old Joe Bailey by Eureka in 1907 and of Bobbie Lowe by Eureka in 1909.

SUZIE McWHORTER, see SUZIE McQUIRTER.

SWEEPINGTAIL. Sweepingtail, foaled in the late 1770s or early 1780s, was a full sister of Broomtail, sired by *Janus and out of the great mare Poll Pitcher. Like Broomtail, she was a Celebrated American Quarter Running Mare. She was bred by Joseph John Alston, of Halifax, North Carolina.

SWEET, see SWEETHEART.

SWEETHEART. Sweetheart was by Johnny Corbett by Little Steve and out of Fly by Little Steve. She was bred by R. W. McDonald, of Glenwood Springs, Colorado, and later owned by Dan D. Casement, of Whitewater, Colorado. She was the dam of Yampah by Desperate in 1929 and of Interrogate by Concho Colonel in 1927.

SWEET LIP. Sweet Lip was foaled in 1872. She was by Old Billy and out of Paisana. She was bred and owned by William Fleming, of Belmont, Texas. She foaled Pink Reed, Shiloh Fleming, and Fashion, all by Anthony.

SWEET MARY. Sweet Mary, a gray, was foaled in 1766, sired by *Jolly Roger and out of *Shock. She was a Celebrated American Quarter Running Mare. She was bred by Henry Davis, of Mecklenburg County, Virginia. She stood 14-3 hands, rather large for a short horse of that era. When she ended her racing career, she was sold to John Goode, Sr. Mackay Smith says that she may have been the dam of Paddy Whack.

SWING CORNERS (TB). Swing Corners, a Thoroughbred, was owned by Dan Armstrong, of Doxey, Oklahoma. When bred to Peter McCue in 1913, she foaled Red Fish.

SWITCH, HUNT'S. Hunt's Switch, a bay, was foaled in 1804. She was by Twigg and out of a mare by Federalist. She was bred by Colonel William Hunt, of Granville County, North Carolina.

SWITCH, PUCKETT'S. Puckett's Switch, foaled in the 1760s, was a Famous American Quarter Running Mare. She was a very well formed chestnut and stood barely 14 hands high. She was sired by *Janus, and so were her dam and her dam's dam. She was bred by Shippey Allen Puckett, of North Carolina. In 1766 she was purchased by John Goode, Sr. Goode bred her to *Janus and got Old Twigg. Later Jacob Bugg bought Switch, and he in turn sold her to Henry Delony, of Virginia. She was also the dam of Holman's Babraham and of a fleet filly by Mead's Celer. She is listed in Edgar and in Bruce.

SYLVIA. Sylvia was sired by Bob H by Old Fred and was bred by Marshall Peavy, of Clark, Colorado. She was the dam of Nick S by Sheik by Peter McCue.

T

TEETER. Teeter was sired by Concho Colonel and was owned by R. R. Lamont, Jr., of Larkspur, Colorado. She was the dam of Surprise by Tad H (TB).

TERN (TB). Tern, a Thoroughbred, was owned by Sam Watkins, of Petersburg, Illinois. She was the dam of Bay Billy Sunday by Peter McCue in 1908 and of Tern's Trick by the same stallion.

TEXAS CHIEF MARE. The Texas Chief Mare was sired by Traveler and out of the Hallettsville Mare by a son of Rondo. She was bred by Dow and Will Shely, of Alfred, Texas, and later bought by George Clegg, of Alice, Texas. She was the dam of San Antonio by Hickory Bill and of Sutherland by the same stallion.

TEXAS LASSIE. Texas Lassie was sired by Suffragist (TB) and out of Emma Hill by Peter McCue. She was owned by W. H. Askey, of Sisterdale, Texas. She was the dam of Star Lad by High Star (TB) in 1934, Star Tex by the same stallion, and Red Eagle by Lion D'Or (TB).

THIRD PARTY, see MARY KEITH.

THOMPSON FILLY, see KATE.

THREE o'CLOCK. Three o'Clock was sired by Cameron by Texas Chief, and she was owned by C. Manuel Benevides Volpe, of Laredo, Texas. She was the dam of Buddy by Charley by Zantanon in 1930.

TIMOLEON MARE. The Timoleon Mare was sired by (who else?) Timoleon. She was the dam of Long Measure by Bertrand and Bill Austin by the same sire in 1831.

TOPSY. Topsy was by Fox by Young Dr. Mack, and she was owned by the Reynolds Cattle Company, of Fort Worth, Texas. She was the dam of Rooster by Daedalus (TB).

TOUCH ME NOT. Touch Me Not was sired by Traveler and owned by J. M. (Monty) Corder, of Sanderson, Texas. She was the dam of Muy Pronto by Esquire (TB) in 1926.

TRAVELER GAL. Traveler Gal was by Red Seal by Sealskin (TB) and out of a Traveler mare. She was owned by J. M. (Monty) Corder, of Sanderson, Texas. She was the dam of Skipper's Delight by Red Seal in 1925.

TRILBY. Trilby was by Bill Punch by Whalebone and out of Lightfoot by a Morris Ranch (Texas) Thoroughbred. She was owned by Santana Cruz, of Driftwood, Texas.

TRIXIE. Trixie was by Delmor (TB), and she was owned by James Ashcroft, of Ramah, New Mexico. She was the dam of Shalako by Crippled Dick.

TRIXIE. Trixie was sired by Oklahoma Shy by A. D. Reed, and she was out of Gray Kate by Star Shoot (TB). She was bred and owned by Curtis Sears, of Logan, New Mexico.

TRIXIE. Trixie was sired by Press, an Arab stallion, and she was owned by Keller Cooper, of Elk City, Oklahoma. She was the dam of Tom (Scooter) by Midnight by Badger.

TRIXIE. Trixie was sired by Midnight by Badger and out of a Norfleet mare. Norfleet was by *Brettenham (TB). She was owned by the JA Ranch, of Palo Duro, Texas. She was the dam of Young Midnight by Midnight by Badger.

TRIXIE W. Trixie W was by Fib (TB), and her dam was Lynn Lady by Traveler. She was bred by James Owen, of Berlin, Illinois, and later owned by Fred Attaberry, of Oakford, Illinois. She produced Belle of Oakford in 1899 after being bred to Bowling Queen (TB). Belle of Oakford's name on the short track was Carrie Nation.

TULLOS. Tullos was sired by Pancho Villa, and her dam was a running mare of unknown parentage. She was owned by Emory Tullos, of Charlotte, Texas. She was the dam of Drowsy Henry (Tullos Stud) by Uncle Jimmy Gray.

TWO BITS. Two Bits was sired by Little Dan, and she was owned by Charles Logan, of Tucson, Arizona. She was the dam of Riley by Jack McCue.

TWO STEP. Two Step was by Red Bird by Buck Thomas, and her dam was Dainty Dancer by Young Fred by Old Nick. She was bred and owned by Earl Moye, of Arvada, Wyoming.

U

UCHENO. Ucheno was reportedly by Billy. She was owned by J. W. Bond, of Ramah, New Mexico. She was the dam of Windingo by H. T. Waters (TB) in 1927.

USEEIT. Useeit, a brown, was foaled in 1907. She was sired by Bonnie Joe (TB) and registered in the Jockey Club as out of Effie M by Bowling Green (TB). Helen Michaelis and Quentin Reynolds both wrote that she was a Quarter mare. She was bred by Charles B. Campbell, of Minco, Oklahoma, and later owned by Mrs. R. M. Hoots, of Tulsa, Oklahoma. Useeit foaled Black Gold by Black Tony in 1921, Catch Me by Jenkins Bob Wade in 1920 (?), and U Tell 'Em by the same sire in 1923 (?).

U TELL 'EM. U Tell 'Em was foaled in 1923 (?), sired by Jenkins Bob Wade and out of Useeit by Bonnie Joe (TB).

V

VELMA. Velma was sired by Fib (TB) and bred by James Owen, of Berlin, Illinois, or possibly by Samuel Watkins, of Petersburg, Illinois, who owned her most of her life. She was the dam of Walter P by Peter McCue.

VERGIE. Vergie, a brown, was foaled in 1886. She was by Cold Deck by Steel Dust, and her dam was the Quarter mare Cherokee Belle by Cherokee. She was undoubtedly bred by Joe Lewis, of Hunnewell, Kansas, and later purchased by Mrs. H. A. Trowbridge, of Wellington, Kansas. *The American Stud Book* (8:1053) shows her as "retired" by the American Breeders' Protective Association. Few Quarter Horses entered in the Thoroughbred studbook were expelled. Vergie was the dam of Waynoka by Don Jose in 1893, Little Danger by Okema in 1894, and Our Breezy by the same stallion in 1895.

VETO GIRL. Veto Girl was by Lexington, and she was owned by Eli Dillingham, of Gallatin, Missouri. She was the dam of Jim Bell, a sorrel colt foaled in 1883 by Orphan Boy.

VOLOGNE. Vologne, a bay, was foaled in 1886. She was bred and owned by James Owen, of Berlin, Illinois. She was sired by Voltigeur (TB), and her dam was sired by Marion by Lexington. Her second dam was Nannie Reap by Dr. Cash, and her third dam was June Bug by Harry Bluff. She was the dam of four racing fillies by the Thoroughbred Fib: Marchee A, Gertrude W, Anna H, and Bertha Nell.

W

WAMPUS CAT. Wampus Cat was sired by Reclus (TB), and her dam was Queen by West by Rex. She was bred by Ronald Mason, of Nowata, Oklahoma. She was the dam of Sailor Boy by Field Marshal, a Man o' War colt.

WASH, BIG. Big Wash, a sorrel, was foaled in 1840. She was sired by Ben Dudley by Bertrand, and her dam was Pocahontas by Sumpter. She was bred by G. P. Theobald, of McKinney, Texas.

WESTERN BEAUTY. Western Beauty was sired by Bobby Lowe by Eureka, and she was out of Christine C by Palm Reader (TB). She was bred by Webb Christian, of Big Spring,

Texas, and was owned by Louis Sands, of Glendale, Arizona. She was the dam of Ten File by Filemaker (TB).

WHITEY. Whitey was by Little Earl by Little Earl (Old Earl) and out of Pet Dawson by Jeff. She was the dam of Oklahoma Squaw, a gray mare foaled in 1936, sired by Oklahoma Star.

WILD GOOSE. Wild Goose, a dark gray, was sired by *Fearnought (Dandridge's), and her dam was a *Janus mare. She was probably bred by John Dickinson, of Granville County, North Carolina. Edgar says that she was an excellent racer and that she won a great deal of money and property.

WILLIE GROW. Willie Grow was by Traveler's Boy by Traveler, and she was bred by J.M. (Monty) Corder, of Sanderson, Texas. She was the dam of Pedro Rico by Red Seal by Sealskin (TB).

WINDSOME MAY. Windsome May was sired by Gaylord, Jr., and was owned and bred by Henry Pfefferling, of San Antonio, Texas. She foaled Day Book by Uncle Jimmy Gray in 1929.

WISE MAN, see BELLONA.

WOLF. Wolf was sired by Albert by Hickory Bill, and she was out of Brown Mule, a mare bred by Crawford Sykes, of Nixon, Texas. She was the dam of Country Girl (O'Brien's), a bay mare foaled in 1937 by Morange (TB).

WOOLEY. Wooley, a bay, was foaled in 1890 (?). She was sired by Little Steve and bred by Mike Smiley, of Sylvan Grove, Kansas. Later she was owned by Ben Owens, of Colorado, and still later by Casimiro Barela, of Trinidad, Colorado. She was the dam of Sadie M, Senator, and Miss Bell, all by Leadville (TB).

WYLIE. Wylie was sired by Texas Chief and owned by Will Wylie, of Palo Duro, Texas. She was the dam of Miller Boy by Hobart.

Z

ZORA B. Zora B, a bay, was foaled in 1897. She was sired by Shannon, and her dam was Lou B by Jim Douglas. Her second dam was Ita by Brick. She was bred by John Adams, of Woodland, California.

IX

Source Materials

With a few happy exceptions, information on the older short-horse mares is extremely difficult to obtain. After a long trial-and-error search, any information uncovered makes the work seem worthwhile.

One source of information from the past is no longer available. That is the personal recollections of the early breeders. I was fortunate in the 1930s and the early 1940s to know personally a few of the breeders who began their work right after the Civil War. From them I obtained some of the best and most accurate information. They were getting old then, but men like Ott Adams, Coke Roberds, George Clegg, Coke Blake, and Dan Casement had sharp memories. Another source that was available to me (and is also available to the reader) is the records that were gathered and kept by Helen Michaelis. They are now in the possession of the American Quarter Horse Association, along with my records.

Still other good sources that are still available are the old records kept by the better breeders. They are not in print, and most of them were written in a poor, hurried handwriting in some kind of notebook. Each breeder had his own abbreviations and style. Such records are found by going to the area where a prominent stallion stood or a productive breeder kept his mares. Then one attempts to run down a surviving member of the family who may still have the records. Many years ago I visited William Anson's old Head of the River Ranch, near Christoval, Texas. Anson had died some years before. Mrs. Anson had graciously invited me to look through his records. When we went down to the basement of the ranch house where the records were stored, we found that a flood of the Concho River a couple of years earlier, while Mrs. Anson was in England, had left the trunk water-damaged and the records unreadable. You don't win them all.

One method, which requires a lot of reading for just a bit of useful information, is searching old printed materials—newspaper, periodicals, and books. In the *Kentucky Farmer* of 1835, John Harris listed many of his mares and their produce. Many match races were written up in sporting journals, and biographies, like *The Spell of the Turf,* by Sam Hildreth, can be rewarding. Studbooks, such as Edgar's and Bruce's, are also invaluable. Edgar called a Quarter Horse a Quarter Horse and gave pedigrees for the early ones. The appendix in Bruce is good for the nineteenth-century sprinters. Magazines like *Western Horseman,* the *Quarter Horse Journal,* and *Speedhorse* have many historical articles. Turf records, such as *Goodwin's Turf Guide,* are also useful. One has to expect errors in the printed word and should not accept any record as accurate unless it can be corroborated in some other source. Unfortunately that is not always possible. Likely as not, the second source will differ from the first.

State-fair associations, especially those in older states that have been operating for well over a hundred years, are excellent sources. Pedigrees, owners, and breeders can often be identified for horses shown or raced. All that is necessary is to be certain of the identity of the horse.

Once the researcher reaches the 1890s, information concerning the best mares is generally available in magazines, newspapers, and other records. If the record is incomplete, the recollections of old-timers may help fill in the vacant spaces.

It is worth repeating here that pedigree research is not an exact science and mistakes will occur. For example, the spoken word coming out of a tape recorder may make Hunnewell, Kansas, sound like Honeywell. When two authorities disagree and the researcher has no way of telling which was right, he may find different pedigrees for closely related animals, particularly with full or half brothers and sisters. The result is that sometimes information on the same horse differs from section to section of a book. For this book, when no corroborating evidence for either version was found, I have left the records as given in or by the source.

Index

NOTE: The registry is omitted from the Index.